International
Encyclopaedia of
Winter Sports

International Encyclopaedia of Winter Sports

HOWARD BASS

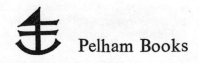

Pelham Books

First published in Great Britain by
PELHAM BOOKS LTD
52 Bedford Square
London, W.C.1
1971

7207 0458 8

Set and printed in Great Britain by
Tonbridge Printers Ltd, Peach Hall Works,
Tonbridge, Kent, in Times ten on twelve
point, on paper supplied by P. F.
Bingham Ltd, and bound by James Burn
at Esher, Surrey

Contents

CONTENTS

Illustrations

ILLUSTRATIONS

Introduction

Skiers, skaters and other active winter sportsters blend colourfully with mountain scenery. They afford endless amusement and look marvellous from a comfortable deck chair on the sun terrace.

Their cries of joy mingle well with the clink of ice in a frosted glass. They have gargantuan appetites, so everyone else benefits from the enormous helpings the hotels have to serve. They are too tired to do full justice to the nightly rave-up called *apres-ski*. They set the pace before going to bed at midnight, leaving the rest of the revels for those who conserved energy earlier.

If one is worried about feeling lively in the crisp air of an invigorating winter's day, one can always wait, like G. K. Chesterton, for the mood to pass away. But the probability is that the resolved non-participant will become bemused by the sheer elegance of skiing or the smooth grace of skating sufficiently to succumb and learn after all. Once at the resort, it takes mis-spent willpower to remain on the sidelines. So one happily falls victim of the booking agent's subtle psychology.

Wooing the first-timer is his major headache. He has to combat complete ignorance of what winter sports are really like, what health-giving pleasures and wonderful company one has been missing and, above all, how utterly different is the moisture-free climate and texture of mountain snow to that damp, mist-ridden spludge which many townsfolk erroneously believe to be similar.

But satisfied customers are the best publicity of all and that is why snow and ice sports are booming in a way undreamed of even a decade ago.

Winter sports are pastimes which, for most, entail lengthier travel. Although urban areas now have their own indoor ice rinks and pre-ski schools, recreations on a naturally frozen surface are holiday

9

attractions which, in recent years, have inspired a revolution in vacation habits.

The very term winter sports has become a misnomer with the development of snow-making machines, electrically refrigerated ice, plastic ski slopes and a bewildering variety of mechanical mountain ascents. Modern engineering can provide suitable ice all the year round and access to snow for a large part of it, while easier communications enable the professional skiing adherent to follow the snow continuously, just as his counterpart in so-called summer sports keeps up with the sun.

Londoners and New Yorkers eventually will become as accustomed to reports of world skiing championships in August – which first happened in 1966 – as they are to Davis Cup tennis at Christmas.

One cannot expect to achieve championship status in sport today without learning as a youngster and undergoing arduous schedules of concentrated training. But the vast majority can start very late and participate for healthful pleasure at whatever standard suits.

Doubts about the physical limits of one's ability to derive such enjoyment may be dispelled by mention here of some commendably inspiring, yet surprisingly little known, examples of participants who surely merit wider acclaim.

There are innumerable octogenarians who ski or skate at appropriate tempo and in greater safety than when trying to cross a main road. Lady Astor skated at St Moritz, Switzerland, when in her eighties. At a similar age, Sir Arnold Lunn has preferred skiing to walking around the car-less Swiss streets of Mürren. Lord Dowding, the chief of R.A.F. Fighter Command during the Battle of Britain, said that skating for him was the perfect exercise when he was seventy-five.

At the younger end of the scale, polio sufferers, children with rickets and various muscular weaknesses have successfully improved their physical well-being by taking up skating on medical advice. Despite fantastic handicaps, there are some in this world whose undaunted, courageous exploits on skis command the utmost respect and admiration.

There are quite a number of one-legged skiers who have learned to *schuss* down the snow slopes as capably as the rest. Every year at Innsbruck, Austria, as many as 20 one-legged skiers compete against others with various physical handicaps, several with only one arm.

Harry Whitton, a Londoner in his fifties, has skied and skated for years without any feet. Despite below-knee amputations, he passed preliminary proficiency tests, both in figure skating and skiing, wearing two artificial limbs.

Perhaps even more remarkable is the annual *Ridderenn*, the Race of Knights, at Beitostolen in the Norwegian Valdres mountains. In this 15 kilometres cross-country skiing event along specially prepared tracks, half the 400 participants have been totally or partially blind, each partnered by eminent, sighted volunteers who have included King Olav himself, Crown Prince Harald and Norwegian government ministers.

With interest mushrooming on every continent, knowledge of sports on snow and ice is more widely sought nowadays, creating a demand for authentic information which this book seeks to satisfy. Its aims are to tickle the palate still further while recording within a single volume a substantial amount of facts, descriptions, histories and major records of winter sports.

The coverage embraces alpine and nordic ski racing, ski jumping and biathlon; figure, dance and speed skating; luge and skeleton tobogganing; bobsledding, curling and ice hockey. Even bandy, barrel jumping and ice yachting are included. There is deliberate consideration for the recreative pursuits of holiday skiers and pleasure skaters, while the second section specially caters for the worldwide public interest in Olympic events.

This inter-related field is broader than that embraced by any previous winter sports book but, as a dividing line had to be drawn somewhere, snow touring and mountaineering were considered to be beyond the fringe and, in any case, of too wide and general a nature to be suitably annexed.

An encyclopaedia need not be dull nor lack a lively style. Masses of detail must be uniformly assembled, but the goal has been to achieve this and, at the same time, fan the flames of enthusiasm.

'For when the One Great Scorer comes
To write against your name,
He marks—not that you won or lost—
But how you played the game.'

GRANTLAND RICE

All-Time Top Twenty?

Singling out individuals for biographical classification is an embarrassing responsibility. Hence the question mark above. Whoever is included, attention inevitably will be drawn to others conspicuous through absence. Suffice to emphasise, therefore, that the following are just an *élite* few of the outstanding exponents of winter sports, past or present, whose achievements have been truly exceptional in their respective sports.

The number has been limited to 20 and comprises three alpine ski racers, a cross-country skier, a ski jumper, two figure skaters, a skating pair, an ice-dance couple, two speed skaters, a bobsledder, a luge tobogganist, a skeleton tobogganist, a curler and three ice hockey players.

Given the chance of substituting without simply adding anyone else, who could be fairly omitted to make way for another? It is surely a fascinating poser for any would-be selector reasonably considerate to claims from every sport on snow and ice.

BALLANGRUD, Ivar   Born March 7, 1904
Probably the greatest all-round master in speed skating history. This Norwegian's long world championships career spanned 16 seasons, 1924–39, and in three Winter Olympics his medals tally comprised four gold, two silver and a bronze. International successes in all four major events underlined his ability as a sprinter as well as a middle-distance racer. Ballangrud's best event was the 5,000 metres His stylish action and economic stride drew fascinated admirers to tracks wherever he raced.

Olympic titles – 500 metres, 1936; 5,000 metres, 1928, 1932, 1936; 10,000 metres, 1936. **World titles** – overall, 1926, 1932, 1936, 1938; 1,500 metres, 1926, 1932, 1935, 1936; 5,000 metres, 1926, 1928, 1929, 1932, 1933, 1936, 1938; 10,000 metres, 1926, 1930, 1932, 1938.

European titles – overall, 1929, 1930, 1933, 1936; 500 metres, 1930; 1,500 metres, 1930, 1933, 1936; 3,000 metres, 1936; 5,000 metres, 1929, 1930, 1933; 10,000 metres, 1928, 1929, 1930, 1933. **World record holder** – 3,000 metres, 1935; 5,000 metres, 1929, 1930, 1936; 10,000 metres, 1938.

BIBBIA, Nino   Born September 9, 1924
The Italian star performer in skeleton tobogganing, Bibbia has mastered the hazardous Cresta Run course at St Moritz, Switzerland, more consistently than any rival. Olympic gold medallist in 1948, Bibbia set the two main Cresta Run speed records from Top and from Junction, both in 1965.

He won the Grand National from Top an unprecedented seven times, 1960–61–62–63–64, 1966 and 1968, and was also first to win the Curzon Cup from Junction eight times, 1950, 1957–58, 1960, 1962–64, 1969. Throughout his successes, Bibbia owned a sports shop at St Moritz and so enjoyed as much home course advantage as the Swiss.

BUTTON, Dick   Born July 18, 1929
The United States figure skater who had the unique distinction of holding five major titles simultaneously in 1948, Dick Button was world champion five consecutive times, 1948 to 1952, twice Olympic champion, 1948 and 1952; thrice North American champion, 1947, 1949, 1951; seven times United States champion, 1946 to 1952, and once European champion, 1948, the last occasion when the latter was open to Americans.

He began skating at the age of 12, won the U.S. junior championship when 15 and, at 16, became the youngest man to hold the U.S. senior title. The first skater to perform a triple jump, three mid-air revolutions before landing, Button achieved the triple loop jump in time for the 1952 Winter Olympics in Oslo and spearheaded a new era of athleticism in jumping on skates.

FORD, Bernard   Born September 27, 1947
TOWLER, Diane   Born December 16, 1946
The record books show that Bernard Ford and Diane Towler were ice dance skating champions of the world, of Europe and of Great Britain for four consecutive years, 1966–69. What those statistics do not convey is that this stylishly immaculate couple

14

attained a technique ahead of that of any contemporaries or predecessors.

Nobody else displayed such elegant posture as that which Miss Towler maintained throughout her most difficult body sways. Moving with complete understanding and meticulous timing, Ford guided her always in masterly, even-flowing style.

They acquired a rare ability to retain graceful movement even while leaning at acute backward angles. Their free, non-skating legs were exceptionally well synchronised, while their versatile footwork and slick changing of tempo were prime characteristics. It is no exaggeration simply to describe them as the greatest ice dance couple of all time.

GOITSCHEL, Marielle   Born September 28, 1945
At Chamonix, France, in 1962, Marielle Goitschel, a member of the French national team for two years, became world alpine ski combined champion at 16. A double Goitschel triumph stole the public's heart at Innsbruck, Austria, two years later, when two sisters won a gold medal apiece in the same Olympic Games – and each also won a silver medal as runner-up to the other.

Marielle won the giant slalom, and her elder sister, Christine, reversed the order in the slalom. A tall, powerfully built girl, Marielle took the 1964 world combined title and outshone all other women skiers during subsequent seasons. In 1966 at Portillo, Chile, she won her third consecutive world combined championship and also the giant slalom. She became the first woman to gain three combination victories in the international Arlberg-Kandahar, winning in 1964, 1965 and 1967.

Runner-up to the Canadian, Nancy Greene, in the first World Alpine Ski Cup contest, in 1967, Marielle Goitschel ended a great career with a world and Olympic slalom victory at Chamrousse in 1968.

HENIE, Sonja   Born April 8, 1912 – Died October 12, 1969
If the present popularity of ice skating is due more to one person than any other, that one must be Sonja Henie. The first Winter Olympics, at Chamonix in 1924, was the scene of her international debut, as a diminutive Norwegian champion at the remarkable age of 11.

She finished last of eight in the women's figure skating, but was

15

gold medallist at each of the next three Winter Olympics, 1928, 1932, 1936, and won ten consecutive world championships, 1927–36. She also gained six successive European titles, 1931–36.

With an instinctive flair for showmanship, Miss Henie caught on early to the idea of ending a spin with a distinctive jerk or toss of the head, which she found not only dramatically effective but substantially helpful to recharging the whirling mind.

She introduced the shorter skirt and also set a new fashion with a more theatrical style of performance. Her wide repertoire of fast spins and spectacular jumps combined with a personality appeal which amassed a fortune after she turned professional in 1936. That May, Miss Henie greatly accelerated the public awareness of her sport in the first full-length skating film, *One in A Million*.

She subsequently starred in nine others – *Sun Valley Serenade, Lovely to Look At, Thin Ice, Happy Landing, My Lucky Star, Second Fiddle, Everything Happens at Night, The Countess of Monte Cristo* and *Hullo London*. She toured the world with lavish, lucrative ice revues, insuring her legs for £1,000 a week.

Howe, Gordie   Born March 31, 1928
The Canadian ice hockey player for Detroit Red Wings from 1946, Gordie Howe has been often described as the best all-round exponent the sport has seen. This outstanding, six-feet-tall right winger achieved the National Hockey League record for the most goals scored, most assists, most points and most games played. By 1967, he had played 21 seasons in the N.H.L. – longer than anyone else; more remarkable when considering that the average N.H.L. career was less than seven seasons.

By 1968, he had scored 743 goals, 678 in N.H.L. matches and 65 in Stanley Cup play-offs. Winner of the Art Ross Trophy a record six times, 1951–4, 1957 and 1963, the Hart Trophy a record six times, 1952–3, 1957, 1958, 1960 and 1963, also the Kester Patrick Trophy in 1967 'for outstanding service to hockey in the United States.'

Hull, Bobby   Born January 3, 1939
The Canadian ice hockey player for Chicago Black Hawks from 1956, this muscular, fast-moving winger probably possessed the hardest shot in the sport – one was timed at 116.3 m.p.h. – and could skate at remarkable speed while retaining full control of the puck. He was once recorded at 29.4 m.p.h. Hull became the first National

Hockey League player to score 50 goals in a season more than once – 50 in 1961–2, 54 in 1965–6 and 52 in 1966–7.

He achieved the N.H.L. point-scoring record of 97 in a season (54 goals and 43 assists) in 1965–6. Three times winner of the Art Ross Trophy, 1960, 1962, 1966, twice winner of the Hart Trophy, 1965 and 1966, and recipient of the Lady Byng Memorial Trophy in 1965.

JERNBERG, Sixten   Born February 6, 1929
The Swedish cross-country ski racer who has been most successful in major international events, Sixten Jernberg had an ideal preparation for this rigorous sport, starting his working life as a blacksmith, then – as a lumberjack – felling trees for hours a day before and after ski-training.

Specialising in the longer distances, Jernberg was four times world champion of the energy-sapping 50 kilometres marathon (1956, 1958, 1962, 1964). He also held the 30 kilometres world title in 1960 and was in three world championship-winning Swedish relay teams (1958, 1962, 1964).

Possessing stamina as noteworthy as his skilful technique, in 1964 Jernberg, at the age of 35, gained his last two Olympic gold medals, making an Olympic tally of four gold (30 kilometres, 1960; 50 kilometres 1956 and 1964; relay, 1964), three silver and two bronze.

KILLY, Jean-Claude   Born August 30, 1943
When this French ski racer clocked the fastest time in the first heat of a slalom, anyone who believed that he might play safe and take fewer chances in the second descent just did not know Jean-Claude Killy. Caution was never a word in Killy's dictionary and that is why he became a household name in winter sport the world over.

In 1964, he took fifth place in the Innsbruck Olympic giant slalom. The following year, his championship-winning potential became obvious and, in August 1966, Killy led a dominant French team in the world championships at Portillo, Chile. His fifth place in the giant slalom and eighth in the slalom were good enough to secure the combined title after a downhill win. He returned to France to receive the National Order of Merit from President de Gaulle.

Convincing winner of the first two World Alpine Ski Cup contests during the winters of 1967 and 1968, Killy went down in history as king of the 1968 Winter Olympics, with victories in all three alpine ski events.

KÖHLER, Thomas   Born June 25, 1940

The East German luge toboggan rider who won five world and two Olympic titles, Köhler was the first man to win the world men's singles for a third time, in 1967. He was also successful in 1962 and 1964.

Olympic solo victor in 1964, he added another Olympic gold medal in the 1968 two-seater event, partnered by Klaus Bonsack, with whom he achieved such a high degree of co-ordination that they gave the impression of there being only one man in the sled.

MONTI, Eugenio   Born January 23, 1928

The most successful bobsleigh driver the sport has known, Italian Eugenio Monti won 11 world titles, eight of them in two-man sleds (consecutive wins from 1957–61 and again in 1963, 1966, 1968) and three in four-man sleds (1960, 1961 and 1968). He retired after winning both gold medals in the 1968 Winter Olympics at Alpe d'Huez, France, and subsequently became Italian team manager.

An incident which characterised Monti's reputation for good sportsmanship occurred in 1964 during the two-man world and Olympic championships at Igls, Austria. With brakeman Sergio Siorpaes, Monti was defending world champion. The British pair, Tony Nash and Robin Dixon, were among his most dangerous challengers.

When Nash clocked the second fastest time during the first of the four runs, his axle cracked and withdrawal seemed inevitable. But after Monti completed his second and last descent of the day, he worked like a beaver to remove his own axle and transfer it to the British sled just in time for Nash's second run.

Nash was thus again able to set the second fastest time in the second heat – and next day went on to beat Monti and win the Olympic gold medal. Monti's noble gesture deprived himself of the sport's most coveted honour, until his final and only victorious Olympic year in 1968.

BELOUSOVA, Ludmila   Born November 22, 1935
PROTOPOPOV, Oleg   Born July 16, 1932

Winners of four world and two Olympic pair skating titles, Russian husband and wife Oleg Protopopov and Ludmila Belousova – she always used her maiden name for skating – were probably the most classical ice skating partnership the world has seen.

In 1968 at Grenoble, France, they successfully defended the Olympic title first gained four years previously at Innsbruck, Austria. In 1968 they also won the world and European titles, both for a fourth consecutive time, at Geneva, Switzerland, and Västerås, Sweden, respectively.

These final successes were achieved at the remarkable ages of 35 and 32; both had taken up the sport at the unusually late age of 16. Their smooth, ballet-style movements were particularly notable for cleverly timed lifts and characteristic one-handed death spirals, during which the back of Miss Belousova's hair usually brushed the ice – a feat which other skaters strove to emulate.

RICHARDSON, Ernie   Born August 4, 1931
This outstanding Canadian curler from Regina, Saskatchewan, in 1959 first took his national championship four to Scotland, where he won the first international tournament for the Scotch Cup, emblematic of the world curling championship until replaced by the Silver Broom in 1968. Richardson's sound victory over the home team led by Willie Young, then doyen of the Scottish game, stressed the supremacy of Canadian curling, which Richardson largely dominated for the next six years.

Whether sliding out with his nose over the stone for the first 30 feet of travel following delivery, or shrewdly and imperiously directing proceedings from the 'house' target area, Richardson always set an impressive example which others followed. In his first three Scotch Cup successes, Richardson and his family team – brother Garnet and cousins Arnold and Wes – won 16 straight games.

RUUD, Birger   Born August 23, 1911
In a career spanning nearly 20 years, the victories of this outstanding Norwegian ski jumper almost certainly would have been more numerous but for the intervening war years. Five times world champion, 1931–32, 1935–37, and twice Olympic gold medallist, 1932 and 1936, he emphasised the duration of his greatness by adding an Olympic silver medal in 1948 when 36.

He set a world record jump of 92 metres at Planica, Poland, in

1934, but his excellent style and posture, more than sheer distance, were the keynotes of his performances. Ruud's rare versatility was underlined by his feat as an alpine skier in the 1936 Winter Olympics, when he finished fourth in the alpine combination after winning the downhill race. Unfortunately, separate medals were not then awarded for the downhill, thus depriving Ruud of becoming the only Olympic gold medallist in both nordic and alpine skiing.

SAILER, Toni   Born November 17, 1935
The Austrian plumber from Kitzbühel who became alpine ski racing hero of the 1956 Winter Olympics at Cortina, Italy, Toni Sailer was the first to win all three men's races, each by impressive margins, and was hailed as the most brilliant and daring performer the sport had yet seen. Concurrently, he became world champion in the three events and took the combined title too.

Twelve years later, Jean-Claude Killy of France equalled the achievement. Sailer turned professional while still at his peak but not before again winning the world downhill, giant slalom and combined titles in 1958 on his native snow at Bad Gastein.

SAWCHUCK, Terry   Born December 28, 1929
The Canadian ice hockey player who joined Detroit Red Wings in 1950, after playing as a junior in Ontario for Gault Red Wings, and thence for Omaha and Indianapolis. Sawchuck was transferred to Boston Bruins in 1955 but returned to Detroit two years later, moving to Toronto Maple Leafs in 1964 and to Los Angeles Kings in 1967. Widely regarded as the greatest goalminder the game has seen, Sawchuck won the Calder Trophy in 1951, with 11 shut-outs – his speciality – in his first National Hockey League season. He achieved a record 100th for the N.H.L. in 1967.

He inspired the now normal crouching stance, goalies before him having usually stood straight. In a career of nearly two decades, he won the Vezina Trophy four times, 1952–3, and 1955, and was joint holder in 1965.

SKOBLIKOVA, Lydia   Born March 8, 1939
The Soviet speed skater who seemed as capable in sprints as over the longer distances, Lydia Skoblikova became the first to win four gold medals at one Winter Olympics. In 1964 at Innsbruck, she came first in all four women's events, 500, 1,000, 1,500 and 3,000

20

metres, settling three record times in the process, and all in the space of four days.

She also won four gold medals in the previous Winter Olympics, for the 1,500 and 3,000 metres in 1960 at Squaw Valley, U.S.A. She was twice world overall champion, 1963–4.

Alpine Ski Racing

Now practised in more than 40 countries, alpine ski racing originated on, and derived its name from, terrain of the European Alps, generally more suitable than the more gently undulating snow fields of Scandinavia, where the longer established competitions in nordic ski racing developed.

Alpine ski racing comprises downhill and slalom events and a major championship meeting normally recognises four titles – downhill, slalom, giant slalom and combined. The latter is academic, being calculated on a points basis to decide the best all-round performance.

The originators were British skiers, notably Sir Arnold Lunn, who instigated the world's first downhill race in 1911 at Montana, Switzerland, for a challenge cup presented by Lord Roberts of Kandahar. Early competitors started together in literal races down wide courses, but this 'first past the flag' principle was soon abolished in favour of the obviously safer method of timing contestants starting at one-minute intervals.

The first modern-style slalom race was held in 1922 at Mürren, Switzerland, which was also the venue in 1931 of the first world championships in alpine ski racing. The sport gained Olympic status in 1936 at Garmisch, Germany. World titles are now contested every two years – concurrently with, and two seasons after, each quadrennial Winter Olympics.

World Alpine Ski Cup awards, inaugurated in 1967, are based on each racer's highest score in fifteen of twenty-one selected top international events at different venues during the season. The first ten skiers in each of these events score 25–20–15–11–8–6–4–3–2–1.

A special category of races classed 'Citadin', established in 1937, is restricted to competitors not resident in mountain resorts. The most important annual international meeting of this kind is the Martini Kandahar Citadin, which has attracted entries from as many as 18 nations. This joint promotion stemmed from co-operation between the Kandahar Ski Club, experienced since 1924 in organising international races, and the Martini International Club, formed in 1960 to sponsor and support the best kind of sporting and cultural events.

The equipment used by racers has undergone such revolutionary changes in recent years that a first visit to a sports store by a new enthusiast can be quite bewildering. Confronting him may be glistening forests of skis in every colour of the rainbow and every permutation of wood, metal and plastic.

There is a staggering choice of safety toe-release and heel-release gadgets, boots with laces or clips, sticks to aid balance and an astonishing array of accessories ranging from ski wax in aerosol cans to goggles with adjustable ventilation. A protective helmet is a compulsory part of the racer's kit.

Aided by highly scientific research and the finest high-precision instruments, keen rivalry among manufacturers has ensured ever-improving equipment for the present-day racer, and this in turn has proportionately advanced what is available for the ordinary holiday skier.

While the latter normally uses one all-purpose pair of skis, the senior racer now requires a different, highly specialised type of blade for each of the downhill, slalom and giant slalom events. Similarly, the choice of wax for the racer has developed into a very fine art compared to the needs of the pleasure skier. To suit the prevailing snow conditions and temperature, the correct choice and amount of wax applied to the underneath of the skis can make a vital difference to a racer's time.

Downhill courses are set with length, steepness and degree of difficulty appropriate to the standard of competitors. The average senior championship course has a vertical descent of something between 2,500 and 3,000 feet (around 750 to 900 metres) and a length varying from $1\frac{1}{2}$ to 3 miles (2.4 to 4.8 kilometres), according to the nature of terrain.

A winner's average speed is usually between 40 and 50 m.p.h. (65 and 80 k.p.h.). The 1968 Olympic downhill champion achieved an average of 53.93 m.p.h. (86.79 k.p.h.) but skiers have exceeded

100 m.p.h. (160 k.p.h.) on extra steep, specially prepared courses, usually to test or publicise a particular piece of equipment.

The aim is to cover the course from top to bottom in the quickest possible time, with freedom to select whatever route is considered most suitable. Competitors are allowed to practise on a downhill course and acquaint themselves with its characteristics before a race is due to take place.

Slalom courses are considerably shorter than downhill and comprise a series of pairs of poles with flags, known as gates, carefully positioned at different angles to test the judgment, fluency of movement, power of control and skill in turning and pace-checking, rather than the sheer speed of the skier.

Officials watch at each gate and a racer who misses one is disqualified unless he climbs back to pass through it. Men's world championship courses have 50 to 75 gates and a vertical drop between 650 and 975 feet (200 and 300 metres). Women's courses are shorter and less difficult.

A slalom event normally consists of two runs, either over the same course or two different tracks, the winner being the person with the fastest aggregate time.

In contrast to downhill races, slalom competitors are not permitted to try the course beforehand. They have to memorise the gate positions while ascending to the starting point. The distance between the two flags of each gate should be not less than 10 feet (3 metres) and the distance between gates must be at least 2 feet 6 inches (75 centimetres). The flags are 6 feet (1.8 metres) above the snow and each pair is distinguished by red, yellow or blue colours.

The slalom aids improvement in technique and has become essentially a test of turning and checking skill, whereas downhill places a higher demand on courage and fitness. Many racers, according to their temperament, excel noticeably more in one than the other and many distinguished slalomers lack some of the extra daring which top-class downhill racers need.

Giant slalom courses blend characteristics of the downhill and slalom in one event. The trail is longer than the slalom and the gates are set wider and farther apart.

Should a racer lose a ski in any alpine event he is not disqualified if able to finish the course on the remaining ski. One is not permitted to descend any part of the course while ski-less. 'Stick-riding', holding both hands on the same stick, is not allowed, nor is 'tobogganing' on skis or deliberately slithering down on part of the body.

In 1952, 21 years after the first world championships, a title was won for the first time by someone not representing an Alpine nation. Stein Eriksen's giant slalom triumph for Norway that year was followed by his slalom, giant slalom and combined victories in 1954, from which time Alpine racing events achieved wider following than the nordic cross-country racing which previously had been dominant.

Toni Sailer in 1956 won all three Olympic alpine events by impressive margins and was then hailed as the most brilliant and daring exponent yet seen. His feat was not equalled until 1968 when, at Chamrousse, Jean-Claude Killy ended on the highest note a career which for three years spearheaded a French take-over from Austria in world supremacy. Marielle Goitschel, before and during the same period, led an outstanding group of French women racers.

The longest career of distinction has been that of the Austrian, Karl Schranz, whose remarkable series of world, Olympic, Arlberg-Kandahar and World Cup successes spanned 14 seasons from 1957. A German girl, Christel Cranz, holds the greatest number of world titles. She won 12 in all – 4 slalom, 3 downhill and 5 combined – between 1934 and 1939. Sailer holds most men's world titles – 7 in only 2 seasons, 1956 and 1958.

As with so many sports, British pioneers were initially prominent. Esmé Mackinnon was the first women's world champion in both downhill and slalom, in 1931. Her compatriot, Evie Pinching, won the downhill and combined titles five years later but no Briton has since tasted victory, due mainly to the geographical handicaps which restrict the amount of snow time available for training.

Next in international importance to the world and Olympic championships has been the annual Arlberg-Kandahar competition, founded in 1928 by Lunn and the Austrian ski school coach, Hannes Schneider. Its name derived from the joint-sponsoring Arlberg (Austrian) and Kandahar (British) clubs.

Generally known as the A–K, it was the first senior open downhill-slalom competition, preceding the first world championships by three years, and its instant success accelerated official recognition of alpine ski racing as a sport in its own right.

Held for the first three years at St Anton, Austria, the A–K was then staged alternately at Mürren, Switzerland, and St Anton, where it was cancelled in 1938 in protest against the arrest of Schneider by the Nazis.

The French, Italians and Germans were subsequently invited to join the organising clubs, allowing three more venues, Chamonix, Sestrière and Garmisch, to come in on a rota basis.

The meeting can draw a stronger international entry than the Winter Olympics because, whereas each nation's Olympic team is limited to four competitors in any one race, there is no such restriction for the A–K, in which a prominent country like Austria or France could well enter more than 20 skiers, all of whom may be better than some of the Olympic entrants from the weaker skiing countries.

With unusual emphasis on the rivalry of individuals rather than nations, the A–K has maintained a reputation for its friendly atmosphere during some of the most keenly contested competitions by the world's foremost exponents.

An outstandingly consistent competitor has been Schranz, who in 1969 won the combined title for a fifth time, having first gained it 12 years previously. Nobody else has been combined winner on more than three occasions, a distinction shared by Otto Fürrer (Switzerland), James Couttet (France) and Anderl Molterer (Austria). Schranz has won the downhill six times, thrice more than any other skier. The greatest number of women's combined victories has been three, by Marielle Goitschel, of France, 1964–5 and 1967.

Early racing technique developed and advanced mainly in Switzerland, Austria and France, but modern styles are based on an international blend of the best and the days have passed when the tourist promoters from a leading nation in racing could attract more holiday skiers in the belief that its national ski schools were the best.

The French tendency to dominate in the 1960s was a triumph for a modern technique advocated by team manager Honoré Bonnet. The style he pursued was not entirely inherited from that handed down by such fellow countrymen as Emile Allais, Henri Oreiller and Jean Vuarnet. For eight years Bonnet meticulously studied technique in Austria and much of what he learned there was incorporated in a revised system which most countries have adopted to varying degrees. Characteristics are a pronounced forward lean from the waist, coupled with a hip-swinging *wedeln* style.

There are ideal courses for senior alpine racing in Austria (notably Bad Gastein, Innsbruck, St Anton), Canada (Garibaldi), Chile (Portillo), Czechoslovakia (Vysoké Tatry), France (Chamonix,

Chamrousse, Val d'Isère), Italy (Cortina, Sestrière, Val Gardena), Japan (Sapporo), Norway (Oslo), Poland (Zakopane), Sweden (Åre), Switzerland (Davos, Mürren, St Moritz), West Germany (Garmisch) and U.S.A. (Aspen, Jackson Hole, Squaw Valley).

The sport is governed by the International Ski Federation, best known by its French initials, FIS. It had 47 members in 1970. The 1968 world and Olympic championships were watched by 102,000 spectators at Chamrousse, France, and were contested by 248 competitors from 33 countries.

These included entrants from Australia and New Zealand, where racing facilities have progressed quickly in recent years and now attract a number of European and American coaches who, by 'following the snow', thus instruct nearly all the year round, a trend among leading skiers which, as in tennis, looks likely to create an almost continuous international circuit for the stars of the future.

GLOSSARY

Christie (or **Christiania**): a medium-to-fast swing turn with skis parallel.
Edging: tilting the skis so that the metal edges dig into the snow to gain a firm grip.
Egg position: a crouching, compact stance for downhill, with elbows and hands tucked well in to lower wind resistance.
Fall-line: direction of steepest descent.
Gate: two poles with flags in matching colours between which slalom and giant slalom competitors must pass.
Herringboning: method of climbing with tips of skis turned outwards, leaving a fishbone pattern in the snow.
Piste: a prepared downhill trail made firm by pressure of many feet or by machines.
Pre-jumping: technique used to clear bumps or sudden changes in gradient.
Safety bindings: accident-prevention devices which automatically release the foot from the ski when falling.
Schuss: a straight downhill run at speed without turning.
Seelos: a special series of three slalom gates, with the middle gate at right angles to the other two.

Sideslipping: method of controlled sideways or diagonal sliding by raising the ski edges.

Sidestepping: climbing sideways with skis parallel.

Stemming: pushing out the heel of one or both skis to achieve an angle to the direction of movement.

Stem-christie: turn initiated by stemming and ended by a christie.

Traversing: moving directly or diagonally across a slope.

Vorlage: a pronounced forward lean with weight of the body well over the balls of the feet.

Wedeln (or **godille**): technique involving a rhythmic succession of linked, hip-swinging turns.

WORLD ALPINE SKI CUP WINNERS

MEN

1967	Jean-Claude Killy	(France)
1968	Jean-Claude Killy	(France)
1969	Karl Schranz	(Austria)
1970	Karl Schranz	(Austria)
1971	Gustavo Thoeni	(Italy)

WOMEN

	Nancy Greene	(Canada)
	Nancy Greene	(Canada)
	Gertrud Gabl	(Austria)
	Michele Jacot	(France)
	Annemarie Proell	(Austria)

Bandy

Blending some of the basic characteristics of association football, field hockey and ice hockey, bandy is a team game played on ice with a small hard ball. Curved sticks, known as bandies, are used. There are 11 skaters on each side and the rules are largely similar to those used for soccer.

The playing area should be between 295 and 360 feet (90 and 110 metres) long and between 145 and 195 feet (45 and 60 metres) wide. The goals are 11 feet 6 inches (3.5 metres) wide and 7 feet (2.1 metres) high. A form of this game was played in England during the late 19th century and slight variations of it have been known as shinty in Scotland and ice hurling in Ireland.

Although now widely superseded by ice hockey, bandy has maintained popularity particularly in Scandinavia and Poland. The first recorded match in Norway was played in Oslo in 1905. National championships have been held annually in Norway and Sweden, where the game has remained a leading winter recreation.

An exhibition international tournament between Sweden, Norway and Finland was included in the 1952 Winter Olympic programme in Oslo. Each country played two games and won once, Sweden gaining overall victory on goal average, with Norway runners-up.

Barrel Jumping

This sport on skates demands considerable courage because an error of judgment or fatigue could result in serious injury. It involves leaping over a series of cylinders placed in a row on the ice, the winner of a competition being the skater who clears the greatest number.

It originated on the frozen lakes and canals of Holland during the late 17th century, when skaters there became accustomed to hurdling obstacles that blocked their path. Deriving its name from the salt barrels frequently used, the sport has been mostly practised at United States and Canadian rinks but its pre-war following in England was revived in the 1960s.

It has been estimated that speeds of more than 40 m.p.h. (65 k.p.h.) can be achieved at the moment of take-off, increasing to as much as 50 m.p.h. (80 k.p.h.) while in the air. Each cylinder should measure 18 inches in diameter.

Prominent past exponents include Ed Lamy, Terry Browne, Leo Lebel, Kenneth Browne and Jimmy Waldo, all Americans. Richard Widmark, from Park Ridge, Illinois, became world champion on March 10, 1968, when he covered about 30 feet (9 metres) through the air to clear 16 barrels, defeating the Canadian, Jacques Favero, of Montreal, who needed an extra attempt to clear the same number.

Biathlon

Essentially a participant's sport, if only because watching it is somewhat difficult, biathlon combines cross-country ski racing and rifle shooting. Although practised for more than half a century, it was little known outside northern Europe until 1958, when the first world championships were contested at Saalfelden, Austria. Two years later, when it became an Olympic sport at Squaw Valley, U.S.A., many doubted whether it would survive another Winter Olympics but biathlon has since gained increasing world-wide support from new enthusiasts.

As a combined test of skiing and rifle marksmanship, its usefulness in military training first developed particularly in Scandinavian and Soviet territory. In more recent times, countries in warmer climates have appreciated the fact that training for the shooting at least is possible without snow. The experts are usually servicemen because they are ideally situated for the preparation.

Championships are normally decided over a 20 kilometres (nearly $12\frac{1}{2}$ miles) cross-country ski course. Competitors are required to carry their rifles throughout the event with 20 rounds of ammunition when they start skiing. Each participant fires at targets on four rifle ranges which are spaced at intervals along the course, at or near the 4, 8, 12 and 16 kilometres marks, (approximately every $2\frac{1}{2}$ miles). Five rounds are expended at each range.

The biathlete's overall time, both while skiing and on the ranges, is penalised by a two-minute addition for each shot which misses its target. Officials at each firing range ensure that due safety measures are enforced. A contestant is not permitted to load before he has been assigned a target and may not leave before showing that his breech is empty.

The art of unslinging one's rifle, falling to the prone firing position and getting up again with minimum delay and without disarranging

35

skis is an important factor to help keep down the time. On a 20 kilometres course, the skiing and shooting together can be accomplished by experts in less than an hour and a quarter.

The kind of rifle used need not be uniform but must be a single-shot type with normal sights. Automatic rifles or telescopic sights are taboo. The all-round skill of marksmanship is well tested. The distance of each range is different, normally 100, 150, 200 and 250 metres (approx. 328, 492, 656 and 820 feet).

An upright stance is compulsory at the 100 metres range but at each of the longer distances the shooter may choose a standing, kneeling or prone position. The added hazards of shooting while physically tired or during very windy conditions can add to a truly challenging trial and the exercise serves an obvious twofold role, as a sport and as an excellent form of military training.

The outstanding exponent has been a Russian, Vladimir Melanin, who won the world individual championship four times, first in 1959 and then three straight wins in 1962–4, also gaining the Olympic gold medal in 1964 at Seefeld, Austria. World titles are awarded to national teams of four as well as to individuals. For more than 20 years, the event has been monopolised by Russians, Norwegians, Swedes and Finns.

Bobsledding

Although various forms of sleigh-riding on ice have been popular for centuries, bobsledding – as a recognised sport distinct from tobogganing – originated in Switzerland in 1888, when an Englishman, Wilson Smith, connected two sleighs with a board to travel from St Moritz to Celerina. This relatively unsophisticated structure was quickly improved and the first organised competition was staged at St Moritz in 1898 on the Cresta Run, which had been built for one-man tobogganing and was not really suitable for the faster-moving bobsleds. A special, separate bob run, the world's first, was built at St Moritz in 1904.

The world administration, now called the International Bobsleigh Federation, was formed in 1923 and known as the International Federation of Bobsleigh and Tobogganing until 1957, when tobogganing became separately controlled. The federation organised the first world and Olympic four-man championships, decided concurrently, at Chamonix, France, in 1924. The first world title for two-man crews was not introduced until 1931 at Oberhof, Germany, and this category became an Olympic event the following year at Lake Placid, U.S.A. Only events for crews of two and four are now recognised. Crews of five have not raced since 1928, from which time all riders have been required to sit.

Originally of wooden construction, sleds are now precision-built machines of steel and aluminium. They have two axles, with two rounded runners mounted on each. The rear axle is fixed and the front one turns for steering. The sled may be steered either by ropes or a wheel. Americans tend to favour the steering wheel whereas most Europeans prefer the sensitivity of ropes.

The brake, a bar made of hardened steel located between the two rear runners, has a serrated edge which cuts into the ice. But because the ruts it makes can cause the course to become dangerous, hard braking is not encouraged during a competition except in emergency.

The first regular bobsleigh maker was a Swiss blacksmith, C. Mathis, of St Moritz. The majority of championship sleds during the early post-war years were Swiss Feierabends, made at Engelberg. From the early 1950s Italian Podars built at Cortina acquired a near monopoly until, in more recent years, mechanical improvements by the former Italian racer, Sergio Siorpaes, were frequently adopted and nations and crews tended more to make their own developments.

The length of a two-man sled, often called a boblet, must not exceed 8 feet 10 inches (2.7 metres). For four-man crews the length limit is 12 feet 5 inches (3.8 metres). The width of each must not be greater than 2 feet 2½ inches (67 centimetres). The crew seats are no more than 8 inches (20 centimetres) above the ice. The fronts of the sleds are fitted with streamlined cowlings which reduce wind resistance.

The maximum weight used to be 363 pounds (165 kilogrammes) for a two-man sled and 507 pounds (230 kilogrammes) for fours but revised championship rules stipulated a maximum weight of bobs with their teams, namely 375 kilogrammes (827 pounds) for twos and 630 kilogrammes (1,389 pounds) for fours. Within these limits additional weights may be bolted to the sled to assist light crews. All bobs with their team members are weighed before starting. Since 1951, this rule has eliminated the previous advantage which heavy riders had when only the weight of bobs and not their crews was taken into account.

Championship bobsleigh courses are designed with permanent concrete or stone foundations on which wet snow and water freezes under suitable natural conditions. Consistently ideal ice at vital points of some courses is now maintained by electrical refrigeration.

To comply with international championship regulations, a course must be at least a mile or 1,500 metres long and contain a minimum of 15 banked turns. The walled banking at some turns rises to 20 feet (6 metres), with an overturning lip of ice to help keep the sleds on the track.

The world's major championship courses are at Alpe d'Huez, France; Cervinia and Cortina d'Ampezzo, Italy; Garmisch-Partenkirchen, West Germany; Igls, Austria; Lake Placid, U.S.A., and St Moritz, Switzerland. All these except Cervinia have been Winter

Olympic venues. The first track to be artificially frozen throughout opened in 1970 at Königsee, West Germany.

A championship event normally comprises four heats or runs, two on each of two consecutive days if conditions permit, the lowest aggregate of times for the four runs determining the winner. Runs are timed electrically – nowadays a vital factor, with hundredths of a second frequently deciding the issue. All important points on the course are linked by telephone, to ensure that the course is clear and safe and making it possible for spectators at all points to be kept informed of progress elsewhere by public address loudspeakers. Each nation in a world championship event can be represented by a maximum of two teams.

In this thrill-packed sport there are fewer serious accidents than one might expect – fortunately, because a spill at the speeds achieved on a hard and slithery surface is not a pleasant prospect. Peak speeds sometimes exceed 90 m.p.h. (145 k.p.h.). Four-man bobs are slightly faster than twos. Goggles, crash helmets, knee and elbow pads are equipment essentials.

Although bobsledding calls for considerable skill and nerve, it is possible to reach world class after relatively little preparation – compared, that is, with the years of arduous training necessary to become a top-flight figure skater or slalomer.

An intimate knowledge and experience of the course are none the less of prior importance before participating in competitions. If one's sled ascends the steep, packed ice banking, one is likely at least to lose a vital split second. At the start, initial impetus is given by members of the crew other than the driver when they push, while holding rear and side handles, before jumping into their seats.

Arts of the driver's craft which help to reduce decimal time fractions include the trick of turning his head before moving into a bend, the pace being too quick to enable him otherwise to realign his sights for the new direction on exit. The skill of weight transference to the required degree to correct a skidding sled has also to be acquired by dint of trial and error.

The brakeman has to check skids and stop the sled at the end of the run. The official practice runs, which usually take place on four of the five days preceding a championship, are essential for learning the characteristics of the course.

The value of the two middle men in a crew of four is often underrated. They are much more than human ballast or 'sacks of potatoes,' as is sometimes suggested. Their synchronised timing of weight transference when cornering is a prime factor and efficiency of their team work in pushing at the start can well save more than half a second. Bobsledding bears certain similarities to rowing, teaching a corresponding kind of team cohesion, and to motor racing.

In motor racing there is a similar war of tension, particularly in the aspect of waiting. The suspense between runs can tax a man's nerves far more than the actual racing. Near the course in the buildings which house the sleds, there is a feverish atmosphere reminiscent of motor racing pits. With earnest dedication, mechanics toil tirelessly on the chassis, metal runners and cowlings, acutely conscious that any tiny adjustment may prove decisive.

Large and usually knowledgeable crowds pack each steeply banked corner to admire the daring technique of strong-nerved riders as they hurtle down a terrifying, zig-zagging chute of solid ice. To do that takes real courage, especially for the drivers who hold other men's lives in their hands. To many schoolboys these men are fearless idols, a short step from astronauts, with a similarly intriguing attraction of helmeted protection.

The outstanding bobsledder in world championships has been the Italian driver, Eugenio Monti, who took 11 titles, eight of them in two-man sleds, retiring in 1968 when he gained both Olympic gold medals. The most notable British racer has been Tony Nash, who, with Robin Dixon as his brakeman, won the Olympic and world boblet titles in 1964. They retained their world crowns the following year.

William Fiske, of U.S.A., has been the only pilot to win two Olympic gold medals in the four-man event. Another American, Fred Fortune, who took part in the 1948 Winter Olympics and was still piloting one of the U.S. sleds in 1969, has had an international career spanning 22 years. Among the sport's other most successful drivers have been Fritz Feierabend, Franz Kapus and Frederich Enrich (Switzerland), Hans Kilian and Andreas Ostler (Germany), Stan Benham (U.S.A.) and Vic Emery (Canada). The most consistent nation since the war has been Italy, largely due to the Cortina track being more available than most for practice and also to the country's considerable mechanical success in sled-building.

One of the most dramatic happenings occurred during training for the 1969 world championships meeting at Lake Placid, when an

American four led by Lester Fenner crashed, throwing and badly bruising the riders. In a storybook comeback only an hour later, they recovered enough to roar down in 1 minute 4 seconds, easily the best time ever recorded on the course, representing an average speed of about 60 m.p.h. (96 k.p.h.) along the snaking mile-long track.

Entries in the 1971 world championships at Cervinia, Italy, were whittled by enough different reasons to tax the imagination of Agatha Christie. There were more than a score of accidents. A Spanish brakeman, Luis Lopez Solanes, flew over the banking and died after crashing into a tree, and among others injured were the British driver, Prince Michael of Kent, cousin of the Queen.

The course at Cervinia was not then considered by the experts to be unduly dangerous. The crashes were attributed mainly to attempting speeds beyond some drivers' capabilities and, in some cases, because of insufficient practice on the track. The latter factor is one which can and should be rectified.

Solanes was the second bobsledder to be killed that season. Josef Schnellrider, the Austrian brakeman, died after an earlier accident at Königsee, West Germany. An Italian rider, Leopoldo Gaspari, was killed at Cervinia in 1967. There were also two bobsleigh deaths in 1966, when the West German driver, Toni Pensberger, crashed during the world championships at Cortina, Italy, and the Italian driver, Sergio Zardini, died at Lake Placid, U.S.A.

Clearly, bobsledding is not for the timid.

Cresta Run Tobogganing

As the whizzing sled gathers more and more momentum on its daredevil, zig-zag dash down the steeply banked, winding track of treacherous ice, the Cresta Run rider in action is an exciting spectacle to be seen only at one place in the world – St Moritz, glamour winter resort of the Swiss Alps.

In this thrill-packed sport a fall at the hair-raising speeds achieved on the hard and slippery surface could easily prove fatal, but there are far fewer accidents than one might imagine. Goggles, crash helmets, knee and elbow pads are equipment essentials.

The course has a long and proud history. British and American enthusiasts visiting Switzerland are known to have constructed a run down the Klosters road, near Davos, as early as 1882. Two years later, Major W. H. Bulpetts built a track down the Cresta Valley at St Moritz. It was then a snow run with ice patches and rudimentary banks, but the first toboggan Grand National took place on it in 1885, attracting 20 contestants.

All rode in those days in a sitting position. The present technique of riding prone and head first seems to have been generally adopted some ten years later.

The sport's administrative body, the St Moritz Tobogganing Club, was founded in 1887 and the skeleton type of toboggan now used was introduced by Bulpetts in 1892. An improved, snub-nosed version appeared in 1903 and it is believed that the run by then consisted of solid ice, with no snow to ride through. The early riders pulled themselves forwards and pushed themselves backwards by means of a polished leather platform until a leading rider, John Bott, introduced the sliding seat in 1901.

It is impractical to make valid comparisons between riders past and present because times of one year do not necessarily bear relation with those of another owing to the variations in annual course rebuilding.

In the 1890s Captain B. Dwyer was outstanding, his only serious rival being the Hon. H. Gibson. Then came the duel that lasted for about ten years between Bott and E. Thoma-Badrutt. Of the pioneering women riders, Miss Wheble was particularly prominent, winning the women's Grand National seven times. Her time of 61 seconds in 1911, only 1.4 seconds slower than the fastest descent that year by a man, 59.6 seconds, shows clearly that she must have been a formidable rider. The event for women has not been held since 1921, which is hardly in keeping with modern feminine trends in other sports.

Improvements in the design of skeleton toboggans through the years may have contributed to increased speeds, but very fast times are still being recorded by riders using toboggans over 20 years old.

Used exclusively for one-man toboggans, the Cresta Run – which is entirely separate from the St Moritz bobsleigh course – is now fitted with the most modern electrical timing devices. With steeply banked bends, including the notorious Stream Corner, the course from Top is 1,213 metres long – approximately three-quarters of a mile – with an elevation of 514 feet (156.7 metres). The record – 54.67 seconds by the Italian ace, Nino Bibbia, in 1965 – was set with an average speed around 50 m.p.h. (80 k.p.h.).

From Junction a shortened course measures 971 yards (887.9 metres), with a drop of 332 feet (101.2 metres). An average speed of about 45 m.p.h. (72 k.p.h.) was achieved by Bibbia when setting the record of 43.59 seconds for the shorter distance, also in 1965.

The two annual classic races on the Cresta Run are the Grand National from Top and the Curzon Cup from Junction. The average gradients are, respectively, 1 in 7.7 and 1 in 8.6 To be the winner of one or other of these two events is the ambition of every Cresta rider. Veteran Bibbia has been the star performer, winning the Grand National seven times and the Curzon Cup eight times. He became a St Moritz sports shop owner, living on the doorstep of the course. The British rider, Colin Mitchell, has won each event twice, including the double in 1959.

The normal Cresta season occupies most of January and February, but because the upper portion of the run can only be opened during the latter part of the season, the competition for the Curzon Cup tends to have a larger entry than that for the Grand National. Other coveted prizes include the speed cups which are awarded to the riders who record the lowest times from Junction and Top during the season. There is always a much-sought glory in being the fastest man of the year.

Skeleton tobogganing has been on the Olympic programme twice, in the 1928 and 1948 Games, both at St Moritz, when the American, Jennison Heaton, and Bibbia were the respective gold medallists.

The sport was superseded in the 1964 Winter Olympics by luge tobogganing, in which the rider adopts a sitting position. Because there is only one Cresta Run, the sport cannot hope to be as internationally representative as lugeing and further Olympic recognition seems only possible if the Winter Games are held at St Moritz for a third time.

Every season sees some new idea being tried and tested on this unique run, whether it be a new toboggan design or a novel riding technique, but perhaps one of the Cresta's greatest charms is that the answer is seldom certain. Mysteriously and challengingly, the Cresta somehow retains its secrets.

CRESTA RACING RULES SUMMARY

No restriction of toboggan weight, size or design.

No mechanical steering-gear or brake permitted.

Preliminary runs not allowed on race day.

Races normally to comprise three heats, aggregate times determining results.

Ties decided by aggregate of two extra runs.

Starting order decided by draw.

For start, rider must stand beside toboggan up to ten feet behind timing line. Freedom of choice in starting technique.

A rider falling in the run, but not out of it, may remount and continue provided nobody touches his toboggan.

GRAND NATIONAL WINNERS

(Cresta Run race from Top)

Year	Winner	Year	Winner	Year	Winner
1885	C. Austin	1909	G. Slater	1938	W. Fiske
1886	P. Minsch	1910	G. Slater	1939	Baron Gevers
1887	G. Guthrie	1911	C. Webb-Bowen	1940–46	No competition
1888	E. Cohen	1912	E. Quicke	1947	W. Hirogoyen
1889	J. Vansittart	1913	No competition	1948–54	No competition
1890	R. Towle	1914	V. Gibbs	1955	D. Connor
1891	J. Patterson	1915–20	No competition	1956	No competition
1892	H. Topham	1921	H. Giles	1957	D. Connor
1893	H. Gibson	1922	W. Bodmer	1958	No competition
1894	H. Topham	1923	L. Smithers	1959	C. Mitchell
1895	H. Topham	1924	H. Goodrich	1960	N. Bibbia
1896	H. Gibson	1925	No competition	1961	N. Bibbia
1897	B. Dwyer	1926	Lord Northesk	1962	N. Bibbia
1898	R. Bird	1927	J. Heaton	1963	N. Bibbia
1899	B. Dwyer	1928	Lord Northesk	1964	N. Bibbia
1900	P. Spence	1929	J. Heaton	1965	C. Mitchell
1901	J. Bott	1930	R. Capadrutt	1966	N. Bibbia
1902	J. Bott	1931	J. Coats	1967	H. Küderli
1903	E. Thoma-Badrutt	1932	No competition	1968	N. Bibbia
1904	C. Martin	1933	J. Coats	1969	B. Bischofberger
1905	J. Bott	1934	J. Coats	1970	H. Küderli
1906	J. Bott	1935	J. Coats	1971	B. Bischofberger
1907	J. Bott	1936	W. Fiske		
1908	G. Slater	1937	J. Coats		

Curzon Cup Winners

(Cresta Run race from Junction)

1910	G. Slater		1931	A. Lanfranchi
1911	C. Bacon		1932	Lord Grimthorpe
1912	E. Thoma-Badrutt		1933	J. Heaton
1913	V. Gibbs		1934	C. Holland-Moritz
1914	V. Gibbs		1935	W. Fiske
1915–19	No competition		1936	B. Bathurst
1920	J. Moore-Brabazon		1937	W. Fiske
1921	H. Giles		1938	J. Crammond
1922	J. Moore-Brabazon		1939	W. Keddie
1923	W. Bodmer		1940–46	No competition
1924	N. Marsden		1947	R. Bott
1925	N. Marsden		1948–49	No competition
1926	Lord Northesk		1950	N. Bibbia
1927	J. Moore-Brabazon		1951	C. Holland
1928	Lord Northesk		1952	P. Arnold
1929	R. Hawkes		1953	P. Arnold
1930	J. Heaton		1954	C. Mitchell

1955	D. Connor
1956	D. Connor
1957	N. Bibbia
1958	N. Bibbia
1959	C. Mitchell
1960	N. Bibbia
1961	H. Küderli
1962	N. Bibbia
1963	N. Bibbia
1964	N. Bibbia
1965	L. Ciparisso
1966	L. Ciparisso
1967	L. Ciparisso
1968	J. Glattfelder
1969	N. Bibbia
1970	J. Glattfelder
1971	P. Gallian

47

Curling

When the Canadians succeed with their persistent bids to stage the Winter Olympics, they are likely to insist on the inclusion of curling, exercising the host nation's traditional right to introduce a new sport to the official schedule.

There are more than half a million curlers in Canada, compared to 25,000 in Scotland, the game's early pacemaker. Other countries where curling noticeably flourishes include France, Italy, New Zealand, Norway, Sweden, Switzerland, West Germany and U.S.A.

Although curling is reputed to have originated in the Netherlands more than four centuries ago, the sport owes its development to Scotland, where it has progressed and prospered since the early 16th century. The first club was formed in 1510 at Kilsyth, near Glasgow. Curling was introduced by the Scots to Canada in 1807 and the first United States club, Orchard Lakes, was formed at Pontiac, Michigan, in 1820.

The international administrative body, the Royal Caledonian Curling Club, has permanent headquarters in Edinburgh. It was inaugurated in July, 1838, as the Grand Caledonian Curling Club. Four years later, the royal prefix was granted following a special exhibition of the game before Queen Victoria and Prince Albert – on the polished floor of the Palace of Scone's spacious drawing-room. The Prince Consort was at the time presented with a pair of curling stones. He consented to become a patron of the club and has been succeeded in this office by subsequent monarchs.

The first of an irregular series of large-scale 'Grand Match' outdoor tournaments (*bonspiels*) in Scotland took place in 1847. In 1849, the Glaciarium at Southport, England, became the first indoor ice rink to stage curling. The first match in Switzerland was played in 1881 at St Moritz. Annual Gordon Medal international matches between Canada and the United States began in 1884.

In 1903, the first in a series of Strathcona Cup matches was played between Scotland and Canada. Exhibition tournaments during the Winter Olympics were held at Chamonix, France, in 1924, won by a Canadian team from Manitoba led by J. Bowman, and at Lake Placid, U.S.A., in 1932, won by a British team skippered by T. Aikman.

The world championship, contested originally for the Scotch Cup and from 1968 for the Silver Broom, was inaugurated in 1959 and won six times by Canada before American and Scottish teams were successful. Among the most prominent teams have been the Canadian quartet skipped by Ron Northcott and the Scottish four led by Chuck Hay.

Curling schools have opened up in Switzerland on almost as large a scale as the country's well organised ski-teaching system. The game attracts more than 2,000 women curlers in Scotland, where perhaps the most successful woman player has been Jessie Young of Falkirk.

South of the Anglo-Scottish border, the sport's expansion has been severely limited because of the great hold which skating maintains at England's indoor ice rinks. Even an ardent infiltration at Richmond, Surrey, has been restricted to a few hours' playing time per week. The converse situation has existed at most of Scotland's rinks, where few managements could afford to take much appreciable time from curling to satisfy the skaters' demands.

Curling is often dubbed the 'roaring game' because of the humming sound made by the stones as they speed and veer towards the tee. No particular clothing is required except that the footwear, usually rubber soled and of material suitable to give sufficient warmth, must not have spikes or other contrivances which could break or damage the ice surface.

Some characteristic appendages associated with the sport include a multitude of badges adorning lapels and breast pockets, colourful bobbles attached to the stone handles to denote which side they represent, and in Scotland the Balmoral or Kilmarnock bonnet with a gay toorie.

In many respects curling resembles bowls, the fundamental difference being that, instead of rolling woods on grass, polished disc-shaped granite stones are propelled across a sheet of ice 14 feet

(4.25 metres) wide and 138 feet (42 metres) long. The stones, which have smoothly curved edges, do not need to be picked up from the ice during the course of a game, which is just as well because they are heavy to lift and many in fact weigh up to the maximum 44 pounds (20 kilogrammes). They are limited to 36 inches (91 centimetres) in circumference and the minimum height permissible is one-eighth of that circumference.

One 'sole' of the stone is usually designed for use on hard ice and the other for a softer surface, the metal handle by which it is set in motion being detachable and interchangeable according to which sole is used. Stones are often named after the regions in which they have been quarried, hence such colourful nomenclatures as Ailsa Craigs, Carsphairn Reds, Crawfordjohns or Burnocks.

Many curling terms are similar to those in bowls. The playing area is called a rink, it has a tee (a jack in bowls) at each end, the distance between the two tees being 114 feet (34.75 metres). A circle of six feet (1.83 metres) radius is marked round each tee.

A curling team – also, somewhat confusingly, termed a rink – consists of four players, who each use two stones, playing them alternately with those of an opponent. Thus, with eight players – four on each side – 16 stones are delivered in each end or 'head.' Matches comprise either an agreed number of heads or period of time, with important games under the jurisdiction of an umpire.

Each stone is played from a point called the 'hack' or 'crampit' in a line known as the 'foot-score,' situated 12 feet (3.65 metres) behind each tee. Any stone not passing the 'hog-score', a line 21 feet (6.4 metres) from the tee, is termed a 'hog' and removed, as is any stone which rolls over or comes to rest on its side or top. When an end of 16 stones has been played, a point is scored for each stone lying nearer the tee than an opposing stone.

The equivalent of 'bias' in bowls is achieved by the degree of twist to right or left given to the handle at the moment of delivery. The stone thereby rotates during its journey and accordingly curls to the right or left as it finally slows to a halt.

One of the major differences from bowls is the way in which the course and speed of a curling-stone may be influenced *after* it has left the player's hand. Because particles of ice-dust and, if outdoors,

51

snow-flakes can retard or otherwise affect the stone's progress, two players are authorised by their team captain (the all-important 'skip,' whose orders in this game are absolute law) to sweep rapidly and skilfully with special brooms just ahead of the moving stone – but without touching it – in order to adjust its pace and direction as required.

This is known as 'sooping,' and to the uninitiated it is perhaps the most curious spectacle of curling, inevitably accompanied by that deep-throated, reverberating roar which comes not only from the gliding stones but also from the 'Soop! Soop!' shouts of the skip. In certain conditions sooping can add three yards or more to a stone's distance, as the skip directs operations from the seven-foot circle. Another player in the team temporarily takes over the skip's duties when he plays his own stones.

The skill and subtlety attached to the method and moment of delivering the stone and the very technique of sooping, together with the varying tactics and strategy, provide a constant fascination which never wanes for the player and has attracted as many as 25,000 spectators to a Canadian national championship final.

Another form of curling, less widely practised, is known as German curling, Bavarian curling or *Eisschiessen*. It dates from the late 19th century and is played primarily in Germany and Austria, also much less extensively in Czechoslovakia, Yugoslavia, the South Tyrol region of Italy and the canton of Engadine, Switzerland. This version also has been demonstrated during the Winter Olympics, in 1936 at Garmisch, and in 1964 at Innsbruck. The fact that two distinct kinds of curling have been drawn to the International Olympic Committee's attention may well have hampered the prospects of Olympic inclusion. If the Germans and Austrians transferred greater interest to the more widely played game, the fuller participation of these two countries could well sway the Olympic balance of favour.

Eisschiessen is played with a wooden, iron-ringed disc weighing between 11 and 13 pounds (5 and 6 kilogrammes), having an upright wooden handle not longer than 14.5 inches (37 centimetres). The idea is to propel the disc either over a specified distance or at a target. Points are scored by individual players or by teams of four, headed by the 'moar,' whose role corresponds to that of the skip in ordinary curling.

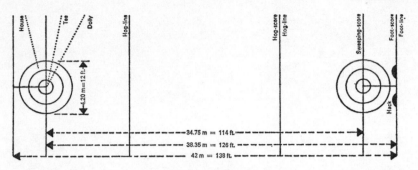

DIAGRAM OF A CURLING RINK

GLOSSARY

Bonspiel: Scottish word for tournament.
Burnt stone: one touched by a broom during sweeping and conse-
quently removed from the game.
Crampit: a narrow sheet of metal, about 4 feet (1.2 metres) long,
fixed to the ice on the foot-score line, marking the point from which
each player delivers his stones.
End: the period during which all 16 stones are delivered from one end.
Foot-score: a line 12 feet (3.65 metres) behind each tee.
Hack: a variation of the crampit, a metal ridge on which a player
places the sole of his foot when delivering the stone.
Head: another word for end.
Hog: a stone which fails to cross the hog-score and is removed.
Hog-Score: a line 21 feet (6.4 metres) from the tee.
House: the circles forming the curling target, in the centre of which
is the tee.
Rink: the playing area; also the curling team of four players.
Skip: the captain of a team.
Sole: the top and bottom surfaces of a stone.
Soop: the shouted instruction by the skip to his sweepers.
Tee: the target for the stones.

Dance Skating

A relatively modern offshoot of figure skating, ice dance skating – despite its name – is a sport in its own right, with movements based largely on those learned in figures. There is a much greater difference between ice dancing and pair skating than the layman may readily discern.

In ice dancing, for example, no skater should ever have both feet off the ice at the same time. Lifts are not permissible and free-dancing, more specific in its requirements, should ideally consist of a non-repetitive performance of novel movements and variations of known dances, or parts thereof, combined into a programme with originality of design and arrangement.

Certain free-skating movements are allowed which are in keeping with the character of the dances, but feats of strength and skating skill which do not form part of the dance sequence, but which, to quote the rule book, 'are inserted to show physical prowess', are counted against the competitors using them.

Free-skating movements, such as some spins, brief arabesques or pivots, and separations to accomplish changes of position, are only suitable for ice dancing when used with the following limitations: separations of partners must not exceed the time necessary to change position. Arabesques or pivots must not exceed in duration the longer movements of the compulsory dances. Spins must not exceed one and a half revolutions. The maintenance of any position should not be prolonged.

To the non-skater the differences in some respects can be very subtle, but the rule-makers are constantly vigilant to curb any infiltration of irrelevant movements that are more suitable in pair skating. Synchronisation with the music is naturally more vital and, for the masses, participation at public rink sessions has a social appeal which much accelerated popularity since 1950. Since then in

Britain, at least one in every five who set out to learn to skate has done so primarily with ambitions to take part in rink ice dancing. Preliminary skating instruction has been regarded by many impatient beginners merely as a means to this end.

It is recorded that Samuel Pepys danced on the ice with Nell Gwynn during the Great Frost of 1683, but ice dancing in any form resembling that which is recognised today did not become apparent for another two hundred years, when early inspiration came from the waltz-struck, Strauss-minded Vienna Skating Club in the 1880s. There is evidence of the waltz being skated on ice at Halifax, Nova Scotia, as early as 1885 and of an exhibition waltz demonstrated at the Palais de Glace, Paris, in 1894, which may well have incited its early popularity in London.

The first organised set-pattern dance specially for skaters was the ten-step, now more generally called the 14-step because the original *chassé* is repeated. It was originated in 1889 by a Viennese, Franz Schöller, and was sometimes called the Schöller march. The European waltz, of unknown origin, followed soon afterwards. The kilian, invented by Karl Schreiter, also emerged from Vienna in 1909. The tango, jointly created by Paul Kreckow and Trudi Harris in 1931, was the first in a string of London developments during the 1930s.

A foxtrot was invented in 1933 by Erik Van der Weyden and Eva Keats. The blues was originated the following year by Robert Dench and Lesley Turner. Two other major dances were conceived in 1934 by Van der Weyden and Miss Keats. These were the rocker foxtrot and the Viennese waltz. The same couple introduced the Westminster waltz in 1938, when three more dances were added by Reg Wilkie and Daphne Wallis, the British champions from 1937–46. Their important contribution comprised the Argentine tango, the quickstep and the paso doble.

Yet another dance invented in London in 1938 was the somewhat unorthodox but impressive rhumba, devised by Walter Gregory. Another important dance is the American waltz, of uncertain origin. Later dances to gain prominence were the starlight waltz and the silver samba, both devised in 1963 by Courtney Jones and Peri Horne.

Graduated proficiency tests, for which certificates and medals are awarded, are organised in many countries on a national basis, with dances suitably divided into levels of difficulty. All dances progress in a counter-clockwise direction round the rink.

As with so many sports, the British pioneered ice dancing, some of its development evolving from techniques earlier acquired in roller dance skating. The first British championship, at Richmond in 1937, was won by Reg Wilkie and Daphne Wallis, an appropriate success because Wilkie contributed much to the sport's progress. The first United States national champions were Walter Bainbridge and Lois Waring, at Washington in 1948.

In 1952, Paris staged the first world championship, one of four straight wins by Britain's Lawrence Demmy and Jean Westwood. This run was twice equalled – by the Czechs, Pavel Roman and Eva Romanova, and by another British couple, Bernard Ford and Diane Towler, the most accomplished performers ice dancing has known.

The first European title also went to Demmy and Miss Westwood, at Bolzano, Italy, in 1954. Ford and Miss Towler were the first couple to win this event four times, but Courtney Jones had five successes, three of them partnered by Doreen Denny and two by June Markham.

Until 1970, all world and European champions were British except the four world and two European successes of the Czechs, Roman and Miss Romanova, and one European win by the French couple, Jean-Paul and Christiane Guhel. But Russian strength grew ominously until the world title was captured in 1970 by the Soviet couple, Aleksandre Gorshkov and Ludmila Pakhomova. American and German challenges also became persistently strong. Olympic inclusion has been seriously considered by the I.O.C. but the go-ahead has yet to be given.

Championships are divided into two halves, compulsory dances and freestyle, each worth fifty per cent of the total marks, assessed by a panel of judges as in figure skating. For the compulsory section, three specific dances are drawn from an international schedule. Each couple also skates an original set dance in their own style. The judges give one set of marks for each of the four compulsory dances and two sets of marks for the free-dancing. In the latter, they separately assess technical merit (difficulty, variety, clearness, sureness and originality) and artistic impression (harmonious composition, conformity to music, utilisation of space, flow of movement and deportment).

If any individual merits singling out for technical know-how, that one is Gladys Hogg, of London, unquestionably the world's foremost ice dance coach and holder of five gold skating proficiency medals. Her roll of distinguished ice dance pupils includes Bernard Ford with Diane Towler, Lawrence Demmy with Jean Westwood, John Slater with Joan Dewhirst and Courtney Jones with both June Markham and Doreen Denny.

The need for lessons is just about parallel to the requirements in ballroom dancing. Just as one who has never danced before can hardly expect to cope seriously at the local ballroom, so a skater requires elementary tuition before participating in rink dances. But, as in ordinary skating, provided the learner possesses the basic essentials of sense of rhythm and ear for the beat, few lessons are required to enable enjoyable participation as distinct from polished performance.

The most popular of all is the European waltz, the earliest standardised ice dance and the easiest to learn fundamentally; the most graceful and rhythmical, yet it is no mean achievement to perform the waltz really well. The initial hazard seems to be the tendency to hurry, through anticipating the beat. Smooth, clean turns should be essayed, with threes (half turns from one edge to the opposite edge on the same foot) turned between the partner's feet.

If possible, as in ballroom dancing, it is advisable to learn with a reasonably experienced partner. The instructions for executing all the steps of every ice dance are fully set out and illustrated by diagrams in a standard International Skating Union approved booklet, obtainable from national skating associations.

In the accepted waltz hold, the man's right hand should hold his partner firmly between the shoulder blades. The lady's left hand should rest equally firmly a little below her partner's right shoulder, her left elbow resting on his right elbow. The man's left arm and the lady's right arm should be extended and held sufficiently firmly to enable synchronised movement.

A couple should skate the waltz as closely together as possible in order to retain proper control. It is a common error, when learning, to hold one's partner at too much distance. The back should be arched and the chest thrown out. The body should be carried erect and over the employed skate, checking any inclination to bend forward at the waist.

The fourteen-step dance is also among the most popular, with a lively, military-style tempo. Common errors to counter in this dance occur in the execution of mohawks (half turns from an edge of one foot to the same edge of the other foot), the man's tendency to double track (skate on both feet simultaneously) in backward movements and the lady's inclination to lean forward on backward *chassés*.

In addition to the waltz and 14-step, 14 other standard ice dances have been recognised internationally. After the lively kilian, the tango came as a welcome variation and is most attractive when well performed. With partners close together, the foxtrot is seen at its best when executed with strong, well-curved edges. It expresses the syncopation of modern foxtrot music, skated not in the facing waltz position, but side-by-side, comparable to the 'conversation' position in the ballroom. Thus, with the man's right hip touching the lady's right, the man's right hand goes on his partner's right shoulder blade and the lady's left hand is placed on his shoulder. The man's left hand holds his partner's right hand, extended in front.

The popular blues to slow music is skated with bold edges. Important in this is mastery of the choctaw (a half turn from an edge on one foot to the opposite edge on the other foot). The Argentine tango is a difficult set-pattern dance performed at accelerated speed. The quickstep is comparatively simple. The paso doble, speedy and circular, is less easy to skate well.

In the American waltz, a series of half-circles or lobes are skated along each side of the rink and joined at the ends by six-beat outside edges. Although the sequence of steps is the simplest form of any ice dance, it is among the most difficult to skate correctly, owing to the control needed in an excessive amount of rotation.

The rocker foxtrot allows an attractive flowing movement. The high-spirited Viennese waltz is danced at a good pace with strongly curved edges. The Westminster waltz is partly skated in kilian position, using the thumb pivot grip for the hands to facilitate the changes of sides by the partners. The lady's hands are held above the man's, with the thumbs extended downwards into the man's fists.

Ice dances also internationally practised are the somewhat unorthodox but impressive rhumba, the more modern silver samba and the starlight waltz, which is particularly pleasing to the eye and relatively easy to perform.

Figure Skating

In how many sports do the majority of supporters only watch half of a championship? This is a novel aspect of figure skating. The spectacular appeal of freestyle jumps and spins magnetises capacity stadium crowds and millions of fascinated televiewers, but the compulsory figures which precede all this usually take place at a comparatively deserted rink, in a hushed atmosphere of almost cathedral-like dignity, when a sudden burst of laughter would seem quite out of place.

Many a past champion, notably American Dick Button and Parisian Jacqueline du Bief, have expressed the belief that figures – which must be learned as the solid basis of technique – should comprise no part of a championship at all and that free-skating should be the sole criterion for the judges. The controversy continues but the fact remains that figure skating championships are divided into two distinct sections, each worth fifty per cent of the maximum possible marks. (Only 40% for figures from September 1, 1972).

The first section, compulsory skating, requires solo competitors to trace with their skates on the ice up to six specific figures drawn from an internationally recognised schedule, and requires pair skaters to perform a series of prescribed movements. The second section, free-skating, provides up to five minutes for men and pairs (four minutes for solo women) to skate a freestyle performance of their own creation.

Each compulsory figure is started from a stationary 'rest' position and is composed of a prescribed pattern in the form of either a two-lobe or three-lobe 'eight'. The figures vary greatly in degree of difficulty and are drawn to suit the standard of the event. Each figure is skated three times, each tracing an indentation on the ice.

The judges are concerned not only with the merits of the tracings but also with the skater's control, posture and balance. The positions of hands, fingers and non-skating foot are taken into consideration, also a smooth, steady speed; a change from one foot to the other by a single stroke from the skate edge and not from the toe.

When the skater completes a figure, the judges converge on the tracing. They stoop and sometimes even get down on their hands and knees to examine the pattern left by the sharp edges of the skate. The print on the ice is of prime concern, followed closely by carriage and flow of movement.

A bulge in a circle, a 'flatting' of the skate or an improper change from one blade edge to the other will cost tenths of points. Points up to a maximum of six are awarded by each judge for each figure and these marks are subsequently multiplied by a factor, according to the recognised standard of the figure.

The free-skating is the climax of the competition, in which the precise edges and turns learned in figures are combined to create intricate footwork embellished with jumps and spins. The performer is in no way restricted in what is attempted, how he performs or in what sequence. This, by far the more theatrical part of the contest, is naturally what most onlookers more readily appreciate.

One's permitted freedom in free-skating is influenced by the need to incorporate as many difficult movements as possible within the time allotted, in order to gain the highest possible marks. These are awarded in two sets, separately assessing technical merit and artistic impression. Scoring is again graded up to a maximum six for each and the totals are multiplied by a factor to ensure an aggregate parity with the marks awarded for figures.

The judges have to assess the variation of contents, degree of difficulty and manner of performance. They must decide, for example, whether speed was gathered without visible effort, whether the skater mixed in original footwork on toes and edges, and whether the transitions and changes in tempo were smooth. Then, too, the skater must always be in proper position, with toes pointed and back straight, and make intelligent use of the entire ice area. His performance should give the feeling of being planned and skated to the music, rather than of being a set show where the music is only incidental.

When devising a free-skating programme, jumps and spins should be varied and spaced between spirals and linking steps. Spirals simulate moving statues – one-foot glides in forward or backward direction, performed while holding various body postures. Holding the position unwaveringly is the hallmark of a good spiral and the ability to control them provides a sound basis for a freestyle repertoire.

Each figure skating blade, being hollow-ground, has two edges, inner and outer, and nearly all movements in this sport should be performed on an edge. Skating on an edge entails a lean of the body over the appropriate edge to cause a forward or backward movement in a curve. The sense of balance is comparable to that of a cyclist's lean as he turns a corner. The lean is proportionately greater according to the speed and angle of the turn, and just as the cyclist leans over with the cycle, so a skater leans over with the edge of the blade he is using.

The art of jumping depends very much on the strength of spring as well as timing of the take-off. The **three jump** comprises a half-turn in mid-air, taking off from the forward outside edge of one skate and landing on the back outside edge of the other.

The **loop jump,** requiring a full revolution in the air, is important as the basis of several more advanced jumps. The take-off is from a back outside edge, landing on the same edge of the same foot.

Starting from the spreadeagle position – with feet well apart and toes turned outwards – the **spreadeagle jump** is executed on either the inner or outer edges and is effected by holding the original position until the last moment, when the heels are pulled closer together and a half turn or full turn is made in mid-air while retaining the spread position.

The **split jump,** adopting the split position, begins with a back edge take-off (inner or outer), landing on a forward edge.

Most jumps entail counter-clockwise rotation in the air, a notable exception being the difficult **lutz jump** with reverse, clockwise rotation. The lutz take-off is from a back outer edge, landing on the outside back edge of the opposite foot to that used in the take-off.

An almost full turn in the air is accomplished in the advanced **salchow jump,** starting from a back inside edge and landing on the back outside edge of the other skate.

The **axel jump** requires extra rotation in the air – one and a half turns – starting from a forward outer edge and terminating on the back outer edge of the other skate. It is in fact a three jump combined with, and continued into, a loop jump.

There are other variants of the foregoing jumps and such further advanced jumps as the double or triple salchow, loop and lutz, their names indicating the number of mid-air rotations involved, the doubles and triples calling for greater height to give time in which to complete such turns.

A good spin is executed on one spot without any 'travel'. The single **flat-foot spin** is performed on the flat of the skate, with balance centred over the ball of the foot. A single **toe-spin** is similarly performed, except that the weight is on the toe-point.

The **sit-spin** starts as a standing spin, the skater then sinking on his skating knee in a sitting posture, with the free leg extended forward. The **camel spin** is performed with the torso and free leg parallel to the skating surface and with the back arched. More advanced are change-foot spins, which lead to jumping from one spin to another.

Perhaps most impressive of all is the **cross-foot spin,** performed on the flat of both skate blades, with the legs in crossed position, toes together and heels apart. This is often used to conclude a performance because of its dramatic effect with speedy rotation.

An advanced freestyle repertoire is enhanced by combining jumps and spins, and so have been evolved, for example, the flying sit-spin and the flying camel.

Ice pair skating competitions are also divided into compulsory and freestyle sections. For the former, pairs are required to skate specified movements, their skill in performing them being worth a quarter of the contest's total marks.

In the freestyle, competitors are unrestricted within the limits of regulations which state that the two partners must perform movements giving a homogeneous impression and, although both partners need not always perform the same movements as each other, and may separate from time to time, they must give an overall impression of unison and harmonious composition. 'Shadow skating' is the term generally applied to those parts of the pairs programme where both skaters perform with unity of movements but while separated – that is, not touching.

Pair skating essentially requires teamwork in every sense. Ideally, the man should be slightly taller and the couple should match in ability and appearance to pleasing effect. Each partner must learn to understand the other so that they can anticipate and match each other's every step.

Skiers getting a lift out of life. *Above:*
A moment of happy anticipation on
a Norwegian chair lift above Voss

Left: A blend of ancient and modern
as an airborne cabin-load of skiers
passes a 15th century church at
Davos, Switzerland

1968 Olympic joy is shared at Grenoble, France, by figure skating champion Peggy Fleming (U.S.A.), flanked by runner-up Gaby Seyfert (East Germany) and, *right*, bronze medallist Hana Maskova (Czechoslovakia)

Left: Karol and Peter Kennedy (U.S.A.), 1950 world pair skating champions

Among the favourite specialised pair skating highlights, as distinct from synchronised solo shadow movements, are the death spiral, the lasso lift, the overhead axel lift, the split lutz lift and the catch-waist camel spin.

The **death spiral** is the popular name given to a movement whereby the man swings his partner round at very great speed while retaining virtually the same pose, the girl apparently risking 'death' by her repetitive proximity to the surface while revolving round her partner and, in the process, sometimes allowing her hair to touch the ice. The styles can be varied with one- or two-handed holds in various grips.

In the single **lasso lift,** from a side-by-side, hand-to-hand position, the lady is lifted overhead in an outside forward take-off, turning one and a half rotations with the man's arms stretched (lasso pose) and the lady's legs in split position. The man remains forward to complete a backward landing on the right outside edge.

In the spectacular **axel lift,** the girl is turned one and a half times completely over her partner's head and the man rotates beneath the girl throughout the movement.

After a competition has ended, a complicated majority placings system frequently causes delay in calculating the result, but such delays are greatly reduced in major events through the use of advanced computerised methods.

Ambitious figure and pair skaters improve their technical standards in an absorbing way by taking graduated proficiency tests, very simple ones at first, progressively winning bronze, silver and gold medals. The highest test one has passed determines for what class of competition he is qualified to enter.

The administrative pioneer in figure skating was an Englishman, H. E. Vandervell, who invented the bracket, counter and rocker figures. What is now the National Skating Association of Great Britain's figure skating committee was founded under his chairmanship in 1880 and he is the man credited for instigating the whole idea of proficiency tests. It was his original conception of a graduated system of figure tests which was subsequently improved upon and universally adopted by the International Skating Union.

Freestyle technique in Vandervell's time was completely subordinated by enthusiasm for figures, a restrained and dignified science in an era of unwieldy Victorian dress. In the late 19th century, the English and freer Viennese styles became separately recognised until the latter eventually dominated and became established as the international style adopted for all major championships.

The first world championship in ice figure skating was won at St Petersburg (now Leningrad) in 1896 by Dr Gilbert Fuchs (Germany). The third championship, in 1898 in London, was held at the then National Skating Palace in Argyll Street, on the site where now stands the Palladium Theatre.

The first separate women's world championship, in 1906 at Davos, Switzerland, was won by Madge Syers (Great Britain). European championships date from 1891, when Oskar Uhlig (Germany) was successful in Hamburg. Fritzi Burger (Austria) won the first women's European title in Vienna in 1930.

The first world ice pair skating championship was won in 1908 at St Petersburg by the German, Heinrich Burger and Anna Hübler. The first European title was contested in Vienna in 1930 and won by the Hungarians, Sandor Szalay and Olga Orgonista.

Ice figure skating for men, women and pairs became Olympic events when the summer Games were held in London in 1908, 16 years before the first separate Winter Olympics.

The most dominant men figure skaters through the years have been two Swedes – Ulrich Salchow, ten times world champion and the first Olympic gold medallist, and Gillis Grafström, winner of three Olympic and three world titles. Norway's Sonja Henje, with three Olympic and ten consecutive world victories, has been the outstanding woman. The most successful pair were the Russians, Oleg Protopopov and Ludmila Belousova, twice Olympic and four times world champions.

The ice figure skate is easily distinguished from speed or hockey skates by its 'teeth' – the 'toe-rake' used for spinning – at the front of the blade. The blade is very slightly curved from heel to toe. The underneath 'business' part of the blade is about an eighth of an inch wide and is not flat but has a hollow ridge right along the centre. The sides of this hollow ridge are called the edges, constantly referred to as the outside edge and the inside edge – abbreviated in skating parlance simply to 'o' and 'i'.

The figure skating boot, made mainly of black leather for men and white suède or nubuck for women, has a strong arched support reinforced with steel, and a stiffening material around the heel and under the arch.

DIAGRAMS OF THE FORTY-ONE INTERNATIONALLY
RECOGNISED COMPULSORY ICE SKATING FIGURES

Abbreviations:

R = right	o = outside	B = Bracket
L = left	i = inside	RK = Rocker
f = forwards	T = Three	C = Counter
b = backwards	LP = Loop	

Figure	No.	Description	Factors of Value
		Curve Eight	
	1.	Rfo—Lfo	1
	2.	Rfi—Lfi	1
	3.	Rbo—Lbo	2
	4.	Rbi—Lbi	2
		Change	
	5a.	Rfoi—Lfio	1
	b.	Lfoi—Rfio	1
	6a.	Rboi—Lbio	3
	b.	Lboi—Rbio	3
		Three	
	7.	RfoTbi—LfoTbi	2
	8a.	RfoTbi—LbiTfo	2
	b.	LfoTbi—RbiTfo	2
	9a.	RfiTbo—LboTfi	2
	b.	LfiTbo—RboTfi	2

67

Figure	No.	Description	Factors of Value
10		**Double-Three**	
	10.	RfoTbiTfo—LfoTbiTfo	2
	11.	RfiTboTfi—LfiTboTfi	2
	12.	RboTfiTbo—LboTfiTbo	3
	13.	RbiTfoTbi—LbiTfoTbi	3
14		**Loop**	
	14.	RfoLPfo—LfoLPfo	3
	15.	RfiLPfi—LfiLPfi	3
	16.	RboLPbo—LboLPbo	4
	17.	RbiLPbi—LbiLPbi	4
19a		**Bracket**	
	18a.	RfoBbi—LbiBfo	4
	b.	LfoBbi—RbiBfo	4
	19a.	RfiBbo—LboBfi	4
	b	LfiBbo—RboBfi	4
20a		**Rocker**	
	20a.	RfoRKbo—LboRKfo	5
	b.	LfoRKbo—RboRKfo	5
	21a.	RfiRKbi—LbiRKfi	5
	b.	LfiRKbi—RbiRKfi	5

Figure	No.	Description	Factors of Value
 22a		**Counter**	
	22a.	RfoCbo—LboCfo	4
	b.	LfoCbo—RboCfo	4
	23a.	RfiCbi—LbiCfi	4
	b.	LfiCbi—RbiCfi	4
 24a		**One-Foot Eight**	
	24a.	Rfoi—Lfio	3
	b.	Lfoi—Rfio	3
	25a.	Rboi—Lbio	4
	b.	Lboi—Rbio	4
 26a		**Change—Three**	
	26a.	RfoiTbo—LboiTfo	3
	b.	LfoiTbo—RboiTfo	3
	27a.	RfioTbi—LbioTfi	3
	b.	LfioTbi—RbioTfi	3
 28a		**Change—Double-Three**	
	28a.	RfoiTboTfi—LfioTbiTfo	3
	b.	LfoiTboTfi—RfioTbiTfo	3
	29a.	RboiTfoTbi—LbioTfiTbo	4
	b.	LboiTfoTbi—RbioTfiTbo	4

69

Figure	No.	Description	Factors of Value
30a	30a. b. 31a. b.	**Change—Loop** RfoiLPfi—LfioLPfo LfoiLPfi—RfioLPfo RboiLPbi—LbioLPbo LboiLPbi—RbioLPbo	 4 4 6 6
32a	32a. b. 33a. b.	**Change—Bracket** RfoiBbo—LboiBfo LfoiBbo—RboiBfo RfioBbi—LbioBfi LfioBbi—RbioBfi	 5 5 5 5
34a	34a. b. 35a. b.	**Paragraph Three** **(Three—Change—Three)** RfoTbioTfi—LfiTboiTfo LfoTbioTfi—RfiTboiTfo RboTfioTbi—LbiTfoiTbo LboTfioTbi—RbiTfoiTbo	 4 4 4 4
36a	36a. b. 37a. b.	**Paragraph Double-Three** **(Double-Three—Change—Double-Three)** RfoTbiTfoiTboTfi—LfiTboTfioTbiTfo LfoTbiTfoiTboTfi—RfiTboTfioTbiTfo RboTfiTboiTfoTbi—LbiTfoTbioTfiTbo LboTfiTboiTfoTbi—RbiTfoTbioTfiTbo	 5 5 6 6

Figure	No.	Description	Factors of Value
38a		**Paragraph Loop** (Loop—Change—Loop)	
	38a.	RfoLPfoiLPfi—LfiLPfioLPfo	6
	b.	LfoLPfoiLPfi—RfiLPfioLPfo	6
	39a.	RboLPboiLPbi—LbiLPbioLPbo	6
	b.	LboLPboiLPbi—RbiLPbioLPbo	6
40a		**Paragraph Bracket** (Bracket—Change—Bracket)	
	40a.	RfoBbioBfi—LfiBboiBfo	6
	b.	LfoBbioBfi—RfiBboiBfo	6
	41a.	RboBfioBbi—LbiBfoiBbo	6
	b.	LboBfioBbi—RbiBfoiBbo	6

Holiday Skiing

The post-war expansion of holiday skiing is one of the modern wonders of sporting development. The rate of progress has been almost as startling as that in aviation. Perhaps because of this, many today still regard both flying and skiing with awe as uncertain quantities.

It is not easy for the layman to grasp that skiing is possible, and progressively popular, in warm-sounding latitudes at suitable altitudes. The snow sport thrives in the mountains of Lebanon, the Spanish Pyrenees and even in Cyprus, Greece, India, Iran, Iraq and Turkey. And eight South American countries are now actively concerned with skiing.

A European ski instructor who alternates between coaching in the Alps and in Australia has said that he has not seen a summer for more than 20 years. New roads concerned with the big Snowy River hydro-electric scheme in the 1960s opened vast new areas of suitable Australian terrain. In New Zealand, skiers flock every year to Mount Cook and Mount Coronet in the South Island, and to Mount Ruapehu and Mount Egmont in the North Island.

On the African continent, Oukaimedan is a thriving ski resort in Morocco, with lifts at 8,650 feet (2,636 metres). There is limited skiing in Kenya above 15,000 feet (4,572 metres) and on the snow of the Drakensberg mountains, some 9,000 feet (2,743 metres) up near the border of Natal and Basutoland, only 150 miles (242 kilogrammes) from Durban.

In Japan, literally millions of people ski, notably at Akakura and Goshiki, the leading resorts north of Tokyo, and in the northern island of Hokkaido, where the sport's growth increased from the moment Sapporo became the chosen site of the 1972 Winter Olympics.

But the main concentration of holiday skiing takes place in the

73

European Alps, Scandinavia and the North American Rocky Mountains, Appalachians, Sierra Nevada and Laurentians. The numbers of once-a-year holiday skiers have become legion throughout the world. The commercial inducements are highly geared, locking nations in earnest competition.

The vastly improved amenities at resorts (fast-multiplying mechanical ascents, specialised hotels and mass instruction classes) plus the exploitation by travel organisations of reduced-rate 'package' party systems, have all helped to make skiing far more familiar to the masses than seemed at all possible in the early 1950s.

Aviemore, Scotland, is a typical example of a modern self-contained resort in which millions of pounds were invested to provide skiers' hotels, chair lifts, ice rinks, cinemas and a host of indoor entertainments as well as much better skiing facilities. The growth here was more rapid than usual and the development transformed the lives of people in the area.

Any unexpected lack of snow at a popular resort can cause not only frustration to the skiers but considerable financial losses to local commercial concerns. Such is the scale of the lucrative industry which holiday skiing has created. 'There's no business like snow business,' is a meaningful parody of the song title. Obviously, the business will be still bigger tomorrow and to its aid already have come scientific answers to problems of unseasonable weather.

Where snow becomes sparse, areas are sprayed with ammonium nitrate so that the snow, which subsequently falls, hardens to form a crisper surface for skiing. Ski centres can sometimes extend their normal season and suitable areas with insufficient snowfalls can also be transformed at will into ideal terrain through snow-making machines.

Through a special process of combining water and compressed air, this advanced system can produce good snow, varying from powder to granular to suit requirements, whenever and wherever the temperature falls to freezing point. This man-made snow in fact packs better and may last three times as long as that which falls naturally.

In snow-less lowland areas, science also aids the sport with plastic ski slopes, appreciably augmenting the amenities of 'dry' ski schools, now numerous in cities and towns. The courses at these schools are carefully devised to tone up the right muscles and to enable beginners to familiarise themselves with skis and master such basic movements as the kick-turn, thereby saving precious snow time later. The exercises also provide valued pre-season conditioning for the more advanced skiers.

It all started about 5,000 years ago. The most ancient ski in existence was found well preserved in a peat bog at Höting, Sweden, is claimed to be at least 4,500 years old, and may be seen at the Djugarden Museum in Stockholm, Sweden. A rock carving of two men on skis hunting elks was discovered at Rödey, Norway, and attributed to the Stone Age, around 2,000 B.C. This is on view among a fascinating collection of skiing relics at the Holmenkollen Ski Museum near Oslo, Norway.

Procopius mentioned 'gliding Finns' in literature of the sixth century. Mythology of the early ninth century Scandinavian sagas named Ullr (or Skade) the god and Undurrdis the goddess of skiing. King Sverre of Norway used ski scouts in 1200 before the battle of Ilsen, near Oslo.

Skiing, like skating and sled sports, evolved from primitive transport and hunting needs. The ski is assumed to have existed before the skate, both originating in Scandinavia, but because the ancient Norwegians used the same word, *ondur*, for both ski and skate, some confusion arose in translating. The first skis were made from bones of large animals and strapped to the feet with leather thongs. Wooden skis apparently originated in northern Asia several thousand years ago. A single wooden staff, sometimes as much as 8 feet (2.4 metres) long, served for balance and braking. Shorter twin ski poles are relatively new.

Modern skiing dates from the invention of ski bindings in the 1880s by Sondre Nordheim, of Morgedal, Norway. Early Norwegian emigrants from Nordheim's Telemark area became pioneers of skiing all over the world in the late 19th century. In the United States, they skied in Wisconsin in 1841. A pioneer in California from 1856 was John 'Snowshoe' Thompson, who was born in Telemark and used to carry mail by skis across the Sierra Nevada.

Other Norwegians are reputed to have introduced skiing to Australia in 1855, to New Zealand two years later and to South Africa in 1904. They are known to have used skis in Canada in 1879 and in South America in 1890. Norwegian gold diggers went to Alaska on skis in 1896, a Norwegian missionary skied in China in 1899 and a Norwegian consul in Kobe, Petter Ottesen, skied in Japan in 1902. In Europe, they demonstrated this useful mode of travel in northern Germany as early as 1854, in Hungary in 1888, in

75

Austria, Czechoslovakia and France around 1890 and in Spain at the turn of the century. So far as can be ascertained, the first ski club was the Trysil, Norway, in 1861. The Kiandra, Australia, was formed in 1870, and America's first, the Nansen at Berlin, New Hampshire, in 1872.

The holiday downhill-type sport, as practised so extensively today, evolved largely via an Austrian, Mathias Zdarsky, who in 1896 published the first methodical analysis on how to turn on skis and developed the first skis and bindings specifically designed to assist turning.

An Englishman, E. C. Richardson, was the first to devise a systematic form of skiing proficiency tests. In 1903, he helped to found the Ski Club of Great Britain, which astonishingly goes on record as the world's first national skiing administrative body (superseded in that capacity by the National Ski Federation of Great Britain in 1964). The National Ski Association of America (now called the United States Ski Association) was inaugurated in 1908 and the International Ski Federation, the sport's world administration, in 1924.

Though a good workman is best with his own tools, the purchase of skis for the beginner is neither necessary nor an attractive proposition when considering the price and bother of transporting them. A wide variety from which to choose – according to one's height, weight and personal preference – is always available for hire at recognised ski centres and until some of these have been tried one can hardly be in a position to judge exactly what kind of new pair would suit best. Whether hiring or buying, materials, camber, weight, length, breadth and flexibility are factors to be taken into account.

Skis are not perfectly straight, but slightly arched. This enables the whole length of the skis to share evenly the skier's weight, which should be sufficient to depress the full length of the running surface. Thus, if the running surfaces of each ski are placed flat against each other, while touching simultaneously at the tail and upturn, this camber should cause a gap of about three inches between the two skis at the middle.

It is generally considered that the most suitable length of skis should equal, approximately, the height from the ground of one's palm or the base of the fingers when the hand is stretched directly above the head, but it really depends on one's weight and build. The width of a ski is greatest at the upturn and narrowest at the centre, the width at the tail being somewhere between these two.

Average width at the tip is usually a little less than 3½ inches or 9 centimetres; at the centre, 2⅜ inches or 6 centimetres; and at the tail, 3¼ inches or 8 centimetres. A shorter ski is advocated for easier turning, particularly for the novice, and many of the more enterprising ski schools provide a set of graduated lengths to accelerate early progress.

Wood is still the basic material in all types of ski. Full hickory skis are now seldom made, nearly all having an inner core of ash. But the greater the proportion of hickory, the stronger the ski. During the early 1960s, the metal ski usurped the wooden one in the higher price range, but the plastics development of epoxy-fibreglass materials later stimulated new thinking.

Like metal skis, these plastic models are built around an inner core of wood. The strength and shock-absorbing qualities of the plastics mean that a ski can be produced which is lighter and more easily skiable than metal.

All skis, whether of wood, metal or plastic, must be covered with a waterproof top surface and finished with steel edges and a running surface. Most top surfaces nowadays are of plastic.

Ski poles are used to aid balance and to assist in turning, stopping and climbing. The shafts are made of steel, bamboo, aluminium, tonkin or fibreglass. The small disc-shaped 'baskets', some three inches from the pointed ends, prevent their sinking into the snow. The leather thong, attached to the tip, should be strong and should fit snugly round the wrist.

Poles should be strong, yet light, and reach just about the height of the armpit. A pole can be best measured indoors by holding it upside down, gripping immediately under the basket. With the top of the pole touching the ground, the arm will be horizontal with the right length of pole – giving the true length as it will be when placed upright in the snow. Ski poles are easy to hire.

Good boots and average skis are better than average boots and good skis. This observation puts the relative importance of the most essential equipment in true perspective, as the need for painstaking consideration in selecting good, well-fitting boots can hardly be over-emphasised. A ski boot should possess a strong, rigid sole and uppers of thick, stiff waterproof leather unless of the newer plastic type. The toes are almost square shaped to enable the

77

toe-irons to grip securely. The boots are normally soled with rubber, to prevent snow from clinging as well as for warmth.

Lacing has been largely outmoded by the clip boot, which truly 'arrived' in 1965, although invented eleven years earlier by Hans Martin of Austria. As there are fewer adjustments with clips than with lacing, it is more important that the boots should fit perfectly in the first place. They should be fitted over a thin pair of socks only and, if possible, worn for a while at home before skiing.

A still newer development is the revolutionary foam-filled ski boot, using an aerated urethane foam that expands when injected into the boot to conform to the skier's foot. Fitting procedure involves injecting the foam mixture into the boot while the skier sits and waits for the chemistry to happen.

That very important part of equipment known as binding, which clamps the boot tightly to the ski by means of clips and strong cables, makes skis and skier more rigidly united as one than in the earlier days of looser bindings, which allowed a certain degree of 'play' both at the heel and toe.

There are a large variety of modern release bindings from which to choose, and usually the latest, simplest and least complicated are preferable. These bindings, which efficiently release the boot in an emergency twist, are a blessing to the present-day skier and anyone skiing without them who has an accident should not condemn the sport any more than the injured motorist should blame his car if it has faulty brakes.

The emergency release adjustment must be set correctly to be fully effective, but this is a matter requiring but a little worth-while patience. Retaining straps should be fitted in association with release bindings, so that when the foot is released the ski does not run away. In the early 1950s, release bindings were still rare enough to be objects of curiosity. Today, the skier not wearing them would be the odd one out at any resort.

Aided by highly scientific research and the finest high-precision instruments, there are doubtless rich rewards still to be won in the equipment makers' keen battle to cash in on the skiing boom. The modern holiday skier may pay for his equipment 20 or 30 times what it cost his grandfather, but he is taking far fewer risks. Accident-free skiing indeed is the common goal of skilled backroom 'boffins' throughout this highly competitive trade.

The essential clothing items for holiday skiing are a pair of elasticated ski trousers, a waterproof anorak or otherwise suitable ski jacket, a pair of gauntlet-style mittens or ski gloves, two or three pairs of thick woollen ski socks and a similar number of thin under-socks, a cap or ear muffs, blouses or shirts and long sleeved pullovers, not forgetting a change of clothing for *après-ski* wear. All these are available from sportswear shops and careful selection can ensure that most garments are suitable for use after the holiday.

The need to take sun spectacles cannot be over-stressed, the snow-reflected sunshine often being too strong for the naked eye. One hopes too that anti-sunburn cream will, with any luck, become necessary.

Accessories are not complete without ski wax, which is applied to the soles of the skis for smoother, speedier running. There are very many specialised types of scientifically prepared wax on the market and the most suitable kind varies according to the prevailing circumstances. It is best to select some after arrival at the chosen resort and after seeking local expert advice. Broadly speaking, in warm snow or slush a soft wax is used and hard, colder snow requires a harder wax. Correct judgment of the right type for the right occasion is something which personal experience can teach best, particularly as local conditions at the time have to be taken into account.

Unless skiing in a country where free health service arrangements are operative, insurance is strongly advised as a sound investment for peace of mind. For a modest premium, loss of or damage to skis or baggage can be usually included as well as cover for accidents sustained or caused. Statistically, the chances of a skiing accident are small, but the thought of costs that could be involved in any of the other contingencies seems to make this a worthwhile extra.

When a snowball is rolled down a slope it follows the direct line of descent which, in skiing parlance, is known as the fall-line. This quickest way down forms the natural course for a straight downhill run or *schuss*.

In downhill running, ideally the nose, knees and toe tips of the boots should remain in a vertical line, however far one crouches forward, and early consciousness of this will assist in maintaining a good stance and balance, with the weight on the balls of the feet.

The knees should be kept together, with one – either one – slightly in front of the other, so that the rear knee just tucks into the side of the front one. If the knees are kept close, the feet will automatically keep reasonably together or very slightly apart.

With elbows consciously a little backwards, the hands should be held forwards and low, about a foot from the side, and the poles, used as stabilisers, should point naturally backwards and never forwards. Knees and ankles serve as shock absorbers. If the muscles are completely relaxed, the knees and ankles, on being bent in a dip and slightly straightened on the brow of a bump, will minimise the jarring effects on uneven terrain.

The faster the speed and steeper the gradient, the more weight has to be put forward. Even when crouching low to gain speed or counteract wind resistance, the poles should be held behind and not tucked under the arms.

After learning the rudiments of simple, straight downhill *schussing*, thoughts will turn naturally to **traversing** across a slope. The action is basically similar to that of the direct descent except that the highermost ski should be a few inches forward of the lower one with rather more of the weight on the lower ski. With skis pointing diagonally across the slope, pressure is applied on the higher edges of both skis through pushing the knees forwards over the toes into the slope in a semi-kneeling position, with the body from the waist up leaning outwards. The amount of **edging** necessary is proportionate to the steepness of the slope. One has to counteract a natural instinct to lean in and instead lean out away from the slope. Early practice in elementary traversing helps appreciably to teach a better sense of edges and general control of one's skis.

There is need for caution in skiing at excessive speed before one masters the art of braking. The skier's most elementary method of controlling speed is by the **snow-plow,** which should be practised in the first instance during a direct gentle descent down the fall-line. The plow 'brake' is effected by swinging out the tails of the skis while keeping the tips together to form an arrowhead shape. One starts the move with the ski tips level and about a foot apart; then, using the ankles, the tails of the skis are pushed outwards, bringing the tips in together. The weight must be centralised, distributed equally on both skis. The knees are bent forwards and inwards, applying just a little pressure on the inside edges.

Learning the fundamentals of the snow-plow serves as a prelude to practising controlled turns, but before doing so an understanding of the power of body torsion or rotation is invaluable. The sense of body rotation can be felt when standing in the stationary symmetrical snow-plow position and, with eyes fixed on a central point in front, keeping the head still while rotating the body first to one side, then to the other. The feel of knee and ankle movement in this exercise helps later when consciously using counter-rotation in making turns.

A series of turns in alternate directions during a downhill descent is the second big thrill of skiing, the first having been the straight *schuss*. During this first turning experience, one becomes more conscious of the part played by the poles. They should be held loosely between the thumb and forefinger and be supported, when out of the snow, by the third and little fingers.

Used to change direction while traversing, the **stem turn** enables anyone to enjoy the sport really well. It is practical to execute on most types of snow and at varying speeds. In the stem turn, when the two skis are held at an angle the outer ski is weighted, effecting a brake as it is pressed against the snow, causing the inner ski to skid round. Once the technique is understood, the logical sequel is to practise a series of alternate stem turns in each direction, but there should be a reasonably long traverse between each turn.

Sideslipping is a particularly useful movement when one wishes to lose height while traversing without changing direction or to descend a steep, icy slope too narrow for normal traversing. As the name implies, the method entails sliding sideways, obliquely, but with both skis parallel and close together.

Sideslipping is an excellent introduction to learning the first of the speedier turns, the **christiania.** Altogether less tiring and more practical than the stem turn, the 'christie' is achieved by counter rotation of the body, keeping the skis parallel throughout this swing turn. Before attempting the full downhill christiania turn, however, the stop christiania and the stem-christiania should first be learned thoroughly.

The **stop christiania** into the hill from a traverse constitutes, in fact, the last part of a full christiania turn. To start the stop christie movement, while running in a traverse across the slope, one should first slowly 'wind' the body away from the slope in preparation for the counter-rotation, then – 'unwinding' – while applying increasing weight on the inner ski, swing the outside shoulder well forward and down, with the outside hand low in front of the knees. This body torsion initiates a controlled sliding turn into the slope to a stop.

During the turn, the ski tips will tend to point away from each other at a slight angle, with the outer, unweighted, ski trailing a little. Smooth, rhythmical rotation of the body without jerking will make the movement more graceful and efficient, making sure that the outside shoulder is well forward and down at the conclusion. In deep snow the stop can be satisfyingly spectacular in a shower of white spray, but bumpy terrain should be avoided when executing this turn.

The **stem christiania** or 'stem christie' turn is speedier than the stem turn and differs from it mainly in that there is less emphasis on stemming and more in keeping the skis parallel, which is why it is faster. While traversing down a slope at speed, with the higher ski leading a little and with weight on the lower ski, the movement is started by stemming out with the upper ski into a 'half-plough' position. This is achieved by thrusting the outer ski and outer hip forward. The faster the speed, the less the angle of the stem.

Thus, in turning left on a traverse one should at first have weight on the left ski, with body and hips leaning away from the slope and knees in towards it. The left hand should be low and forward.

Crouching low while flattening the left ski, with weight still on it and knees well forward, the right ski is thrust uphill into the stem position. Rising and transferring the weight from the heels to the balls of the feet, the weight of the whole body is then swung slowly over the right, outer ski just enough to start the skis moving downhill. The right shoulder and hand are brought well forward and low as the left hand moves back to waist level. The left ski is pulled on its outer edge to lead slightly as the right ski skids round and the body resumes the crouching position with knees well forward, right shoulder forward and down and right hand just in front of the knees.

Increased edging on the left ski will check the sideslipping and, with turn accomplished, the body rises to adopt once more the normal traverse position. This most useful and widely used turn is completed with skis in parallel position, a main difference between this and the stem turn.

Only the really experienced skier will be wise to attempt the more difficult and further advanced movements like the full **downhill christiania**, the **jump turn** and the now less commonly performed **telemark** turn. Only full practical experience of the technique already referred to can properly prepare one for the additional intricacy of control necessary. Broadly speaking, the principles of christiania down the fall-line are similar to those already described, but starting with both skis flat on the snow. The jump turn is used in conditions when the normal turns are not practicable, in narrow areas or on snow covered by a light, icy surface – known as breakable crust.

The hitherto recognised orthodox method of learning to ski, known as the classical Arlberg technique, codified in the 1920s by Hannes Schneider, has been largely superseded by the somewhat revolutionary style known in German as *wedeln* ('wagging the tail') or, in French, *godille*. It puts more emphasis on rhumba-like hip and leg swinging and less on shoulder movements. It is a technique almost universally adopted by leading championship competitors and is being taught at most ski schools.

One's advancement and sense of achievement can be more satisfying by participating in the various proficiency tests or competitions – some of them very elementary – which are arranged at many resorts, and also the official graduated tests and races organised by the national ski associations.

In most European countries and in North America, the skiing techniques taught today are probably much the same. The best elements of the Austrian and French schools of techniques in recent years have tended to be merged everywhere in varying degrees, but most nations still retain recognisable characteristics of style in their ski schools and this applies particularly to the Austrian and French.

Most snow resorts have ski schools for all grades of performer. The graduated school standards are shrewdly supervised to help one progress always on level terms with fellow class members. This way, nobody seems embarrassed and there is always extra help for the slower learner. The fact that class members tend voluntarily to stay together for social *après-ski* evenings contributes much to the overall holiday pleasure.

During the early or late season, it is prudent to select a high altitude resort – or a centre with mechanical access to high snows – to increase the likelihood of ideal skiing conditions. Although the base (i.e. residential) altitudes of selected resorts are listed in this book, it should be stressed that most have easy access to skiing at much higher levels, details of which are usually clarified on each resort's skiing brochure.

A Selection Of The World's Holiday Ski Resorts

Base Altitudes in Feet
(1 foot=0.3 metres)

ALGERIA
Chrea, Djurdjura, 5,080
Tikjda, Djurdjura, 5,400

ARGENTINA
Bariloche, Rio Negro, 3,000

AUSTRALIA
Ben Lomond, Tasmania, 5,160
Charlotte's Pass, N.S.W., 5,740
Falls Creek, Victoria, 6,000
Hotham Heights, Victoria, 6,100
Mt Buffalo, Victoria, 4,000
Mt Buller, Victoria, 5,250
Mt Field, Tasmania, 4,000
Perisher Valley, N.S.W., 5,650
Thredbo, New South Wales, 4,480

AUSTRIA
Bad Gastein, Tyrol, 3,552
Berwang, Tyrol, 4,382
Ehrwald, Tyrol, 3,267
Fieberbrunn, Tyrol, 2,591
Gargellen, Vorarlberg, 4,667
Gaschurn, Vorarlberg, 3,211
Igls, Tyrol, 2,949
Innsbruck, Tyrol, 1,883
Ischgl, Tyrol, 4,516
Kitzbühel, Tyrol, 2,499
Kühtai, Tyrol, 6,448
Lech, Vorarlberg, 4,736
Lermoos, Tyrol, 3,264
Lienz, Tyrol, 2,224
Mayrhofen, Tyrol, 2,066
Obergurgl, Tyrol, 6,320
Obertauern, Salzburg, 5,704

Reutte, Tyrol, 2,801
Saalbach, Salzburg, 3,290
St Anton, Tyrol, 4,221
St Christoph, Tyrol, 5,799
St Johann, Salzburg, 2,165
Schruns, Vorarlberg, 2,263
Seefeld, Tyrol, 3,870
Semmering, Lower Austria, 3,280
Sölden, Tyrol, 6,790
Steinach, Tyrol, 3,437
Thiersee, Tyrol, 2,581
Vent, Tyrol, 6,209
Westendorf, Tyrol, 2,572
Zell Am See, Salzburg, 2,483
Zürs, Vorarlberg, 5,632

BULGARIA
Pamporovo, Rhodope, 5,400
Vitosha, Rhodope, 5,950

CANADA
Banff, Alberta, 4,538
Garibaldi Whistler Mt, B.C.
Hidden Valley, Ontario, 935
Kamloops, British Columbia
Lake Louise, Alberta
Mt Echo, Quebec, 1,000
Mt Norquay, Alberta˙
Mt Orford, Quebec, 1,250
Mt Sutton, Quebec, 1,450
Mont Tremblant, Quebec, 870
Sunshine, Alberta

CHILE
Farrellones, Andes, 7,550
Portillo, Andes, 9,500

CZECHOSLOVAKIA
Jasna, Tatras, 3,100
Stary Smokovec, Tatras, 3,000
Tatranska Lomnica, Tatras, 2,875
Vratna Dolina, Tatras, 1,900

FINLAND
Kilpisjärvi, Lapland, 1,525
Koli, Central, 1,148
Kuopio, Central, 770
Lahti, South, 390
Pallastunturi, Lapland, 2,692
Rovaniemi, Lapland, 350
Rukatunturi, Lapland

FRANCE
Alpe d'Huez, Isère, 6,102
Auron, Alpes Maritimes, 5,249
Autrans, Isère, 3,445
Avoriaz, Haute Savoie, 5,900
Chamonix, Haute Savoie, 3,445
Chamrousse, Isère, 5,348
Courchevel, Savoie, 6,070
Flaine, Haute Savoie, 5,200
La Clusaz, Haute Savoie, 3,412
La Plagne, Savoie, 6,400
Les Contamines, Haute Savoie, 3,819
Les Deux Alpes, Isère, 5,446
Les Gets, Haute Savoie, 3,845
Les Houches, Haute Savoie, 3,307
Les Rousses, Jura, 3,773
Megève, Haute Savoie, 3,652
Méribel, Savoie, 5,249
Mont Dore, Puy-de-Dôme, 3,455
Montgenèvre, Hautes Alpes, 6,102
Morzine, Haute Savoie, 3,281
St Gervais, Haute Savoie, 2,953
Samoëns, Haute Savoie, 2,690
Serre Chevalier, Haute Alpes, 4,429
Superbagnères, Haute Garonne, 5,905
Tignes, Savoie, 6,900
Valberg, Alpes Maritimes, 5,577
Val d'Isère, Savoie, 6,070
Valloire, Savoie, 4,692
Villard de Lans, Isère, 3,445
Vissavona, Corsica, 3,000

GREAT BRITAIN
Aviemore, Cairngorms, 2,150
Blairgowrie, Glenshee, 2,470
Meall A'Bhuiridh, Glencoe, 2,386

INDIA
Gulmarg, Jammu & Kashmir, 8,890

IRAN
Abe-Ali, Alborz, 7,500

ITALY
Abetone, Pistoia, 4,554
Alpe di Siusi, Bolzano, 6,135
Bardonecchia, Turin, 4,304
Bormio, Sondrio, 4,016
Breuil-Cervinia, Aosta, 6,580
Canazei, Pesara, 4,805
Cortina d'Ampezzo, Belluno, 3,969
Cesana Torinese, Turin, 4,408
Claviere, Turin, 5,774
Courmayeur, Aosta, 4,029
Dobbiaco, Bolzano, 4,012
Limone-Piemonte, Cuneo, 3,314
Macugnaga, Novara, 4,353
Madesimo, Sondrio, 5,032
Madonna di Campiglio, Trento, 4,992
Ortisei, Bolzano, 4,079
San Martino, Trento, 4,718
Sauze d'Oulz-Sportina, Turin, 4,950
Sestrière, Turin, 6,678
Val Gardena, Bolzano, 5,158

JAPAN
Akakura, Honshu, 3,250
Iwappara, Honshu, 3,650
Sapporo, Hokkaido,
Shiga Kogan, Honshu, 4,900

LEBANON
Cedars, North, 6,000

LIECHTENSTEIN
Malbun, Triesenberg, 5,250

MOROCCO
Oukaimeden, High Atlas, 8,700

NEW ZEALAND
Chateau Tongariro, North Is., 3,700
Coronet Peak, South Island, 3,880

NORWAY
Finse, Hallingdal, 4,010
Geilo, Hallingdal, 2,625
Gol, Hallingdal, 800
Hamar, Osterdalene, 1,650
Lillehammer, Gudbrandsdalen, 2,750
Mjolfjell, Kvamskogen, 2,060
Nordseter, Gudbrandsdalen, 2,780
Norefjell, Oslo, 2,730
Oppdal, Trondelag, 1,790
Tretten, Gudbrandsdalen, 2,050
Voss, Hordaland, 885

POLAND
Zakopane, High Tatras

ROMANIA
Poina Brasov, Transylvania, 3,483
Sinaia, Wallachia, 2,700

SPAIN
La Molina, Pyrenees, 4,800
Nuria, Pyrenees, 6,350

SWEDEN
Åre Jämtland, 1,480
Rättvik, Dalecarlia, 558
Sälen, Dalecarlia, 2,090
Storlien, Jämtland, 1,945

SWITZERLAND
Adelboden, Bernese Oberland, 4,452
Andermatt, Central, 4,869

Anzère, Valais, 4,921
Arosa, Grisons, 5,955
Celerina, Grisons, 5,656
Champéry, Valais, 3,452
Château d'Oex, Lake Geneva, 3,281
Crans, Valais, 4,987
Davos, Grisons, 5,118
Engelberg, Central, 3,445
Flims, Grisons, 3,773
Grindelwald, B. Oberland, 3,468
Gstaad, B. Oberland, 3,445
Kandersteg, B. Oberland, 3,835
Klosters, Grisons, 3,967
Lenk, Bernese Oberland, 3,514
Lenzerheide, Grisons, 4,856
Les Diablerets, L. Geneva, 3,789
Leysin, L. Geneva, 4,265
Montana, Valais, 4,825
Mürren, Bernese Oberland, 5,413
Pontresina, Grisons, 5,916
Saas-Fee, Valais, 5,899
St Moritz, Grisons, 6,008
Verbier, Valais, 4,922
Villars, Lake Geneva, 3,970
Wengen, Bernese Oberland, 4,183
Zermatt, Valais, 5,315

TURKEY
Uludag, Mt Olympus, 6,500

U.S.A.
Alpine Meadows, California, 5,940
Alta, Utah, 8,600
Aspen, Colorado, 8,000
Belleayre, New York, 2,541
Big Bromley, Vermont, 1,960
Boyne Mt, Michigan, 1,400
Buck Hill, Minnesota, 1,200
Cannon Mt, New Hampshire, 2,000
Crystal Mt, Washington, 4,400
Heavenly Valley, California, 6,600

Jackson Hole, Wyoming, 6,300
Jay Peak, Vermont, 1,900
Killington, Vermont, 550
Laurel Mt, Pennsylvania, 2,553
Loveland, Colorado, 10,500
Mad River Glen, Vermont, 1,600
Madonna Mt, Vermont, 1,100
Magic Mt, Vermont, 1,400
Mammoth Mt, California, 6,500
Mt Aleyska, Alaska, 250
Mt Baker, Washington, 4,200
Mt Hood, Oregon, 5,400
Mt Snow, Vermont, 1,700
Mt Werner, Colorado, 7,000
Squaw Valley, California, 6,200
Stowe, Vermont, 1,550
Sugarbush Valley, Vermont, 1,625
Sugarloaf, Maine, 1,600
Sun Valley, Idaho, 5,760
Taos Ski Valley, New Mexico, 9,300
Vail, Colorado, 8,200
Waterville Valley, New Hampshire, 1,850
Whiteface Mt, New York
Wildcat Mt, New Hampshire, 1,900
Winter Park, Colorado

U.S.S.R.
Bakuriani, Caucasus, 5,500

WEST GERMANY
Bad Reichenhall, Berchtesgaden, 1,542
Bayrischzell, Schliersee, 2,630
Berchtesgaden, Berchtesgaden, 1,730
Braunlage, Harz, 2,562
Feldberg, Black Forest, 4,085
Garmisch-Partenkirchen, Werdenfels, 2,364
Hindelang, Allgäu, 3,774
Mittenwald, Werdenfels, 3,018
Oberammergau, Werdenfels, 2,787
Oberstdorf, Allgäu, 2,757
Reit im Winkl, Chiemgau, 3,939

Ruhpolding, Chiemgau, 3,609
Schliersee, Schliersee, 3,609

YUGOSLAVIA
Bled, Slovenia, 1,425
Kranjska Gora, Slovenia, 2,430
Planica, Slovenia, 2,700

Ice Hockey

Twelve heavily padded men outwitting and outstriding each other in the world's fastest team game. Some of the speediest self-propelled humans deftly scoring goals with shots sometimes too rapid for the eye to follow. Robust clashing of bodies, flashy stickhandling skill and the skating ability to turn on a sixpence. All at an exciting, temper-testing pace demanding frantic inter-changing with substitutes every few minutes. This is thrill-a-second ice hockey, with every moment of actual play electrically timed – a tough, uncompromising man's game which repeatedly pulls spectators forward in their seats.

The sport's historical roots are deeply embedded in Canadian ice, stemming from a game played by Englishmen on the frozen expanse of Kingston Harbour, Ontario, in 1860. This, the first time a puck was used instead of a ball, clearly separated the game's identity from field hockey. The pioneer players were mainly Crimean War veterans in a Royal Canadian Rifles regiment. Montreal subsequently became the central point of the game's early progress.

In 1879, two Montreal students at McGill University, W. F. Robertson and R. F. Smith, devised the first rules by adding a few original ideas to what was basically a combination of field hockey and rugby regulations. A square puck was used, with nine players on each side, and this led to the formation of the first recognised team, McGill University Hockey Club, in 1880.

Leagues of all grades thrived throughout Canada, with nearly 100 clubs in Montreal alone, before the game was first played in U.S.A. in 1893 – by Yale University in New Haven and John Hopkins University in Baltimore. That same year, Lord Stanley of Preston, then Governor-General of Canada, donated the Stanley Cup as a permanent senior trophy which was destined to become the sport's most famous prize. It was first won in 1894 on natural ice by a team representing Montreal Amateur Athletic Association.

The U.S. Amateur Hockey League was founded in New York City in 1896 and the sport began to grow in Europe at the turn of the century. The International Ice Hockey Federation was formed in 1908, with Belgium, Bohemia, France, Great Britain and Switzerland its founder members.

Canadian demonstration popularised the game in Great Britain sufficiently to inspire a five-team league competition in 1903. The first game in Scotland took place at Crossmyloof, Glasgow, in 1908. The first European championship was won by Great Britain in 1910 at Les Avants, in the Swiss Alps. The British Ice Hockey Federation was not inaugurated until 1914, the five founder clubs being Cambridge, Manchester, Oxford Canadians, Royal Engineers and Princes.

The first Olympic title and, concurrently, the first amateur world championship, were won by Canada at Antwerp, Belgium, in 1920. Ice hockey mushroomed as more electrically frozen rinks came into being and progress in Britain was accelerated by the opening of London's Westminster rink in 1926. The nation's best years dated from 1934, when the Empire Pool, Wembley, came into being. Brighton Sports Stadium and London's Empress Hall and Harringay Arena followed Wembley's lead to promote a British pre-war big-rink era bolstered by Canadian talent. An international club tournament comprised four London sides, Wembley Lions, Richmond Hawks, Streatham and Wembley Canadians, and six European teams, Berlin, Français Volants, Milan, Munich, Prague and Stade Français.

One of the sport's peak years in Britain, 1936, coincided with the Winter Olympic Games at Garmisch, Germany, when Carl Erhardt led Britain in an historic defeat of Canada, the masters who, until then, had won every Olympic tournament held. The war rudely curtailed this promising forward surge, and teams and talent in Britain, afterwards faced with an acute shortage of large ice arenas with worthwhile spectator accommodation, faded considerably while ice hockey began to expand wherever else it was played.

There are now thousands of teams throughout North America taking part in league competitions comparable in diversity to those of soccer in Britain. The Allan Cup in Canada, first contested in 1908, is widely regarded as the most coveted amateur club trophy.

By 1970 the approximate number of players registered in the Soviet Union was 300,000; Canada 230,000; Sweden 140,000; Czechoslovakia 77,000; U.S.A. 48,000 and Finland 40,000.

In post-war years more than 20 nations have contested the quadrennial Olympic and annual world and European amateur championships, decided concurrently and organised primarily by the I.I.H.F. president, Londoner J. F. Ahearne, whose astute negotiation of television rights has provided much of the teams' travelling expenses. Outside Europe and North America, the sport has grown in proportion to the limited ice acreage available in such warmer-climate countries as Australia, Japan and South Africa.

The Canadians' general supremacy among the amateurs was never seriously questioned until U.S.S.R. won the Olympic tournament at Cortina in 1956 and afterwards dominated the world championships with teams noted for great skating skill which gave them quick manoeuvrability, coupled with a well drilled technique of keeping possession until the right scoring chance came. In 1968, nine of their players became the first in the sport to win second Olympic gold medals.

World championship tournaments in latter years have been divided into three groups of six or more teams which play each other in their group on a league points basis. The top team in Group A takes the world title and the highest placed European team takes the European title. Interest in the other groups is boosted by the annual promotion and relegation of top and bottom teams.

Ice hockey is a six-a-side game played with sticks and a rubber puck on an ice rink measuring, ideally, 200 feet (61 metres) long and 85 feet (26 metres) wide. Barrier boards which surround the rink are curved at each of the four corners and must be between 4 feet (1.22 metres) and 3 feet 4 inches (1 metre) high.

Red goal lines are 10 feet (3.5 metres) from each end of the rink. In the centre of these are the goals, 4 feet (1.22 metres) high and 6 feet (1.83 metres) wide, with nets not less than 2 feet (60 centimetres) deep at the base.

Two blue lines divide the rink equally into three zones, and a centre red line is equi-distant between them. The centre of the rink is marked by a blue spot surrounded by a blue circle of 15 feet (4.5 metres) radius. Four red spots in similar sized red circles, two in each half, are marked 15 feet (4.5 metres) out from the goal lines, midway between each goal post and barrier. Each side of these four face-off spots are red lines 2 feet (60 centimetres) long, parallel to the goal lines. Other red lines, 3 feet (90 centimetres) long, extend from each outer edge of the four red circles. There are two red spots

95

in the centre zone, 5 feet (1.5 metres) from each blue line and midway between the side barriers. Creases in front of each goal are indicated by 6 feet (1.8 metres) radius semi-circles (I.I.H.F. rules) or 8 × 4 feet (2.5 metres × 1.25 metres) rectangles (N.H.L. rules).

Amateur matches are controlled by two referees, one for each half of the playing area, but in professional N.H.L. matches one referee is in complete charge, assisted by two linesmen whose main duty is to whistle off-sides.

A game is divided into three periods, each of 20 minutes' actual playing time, measured by stopwatch only while the puck is in play. Although only six players from each team are allowed on the ice at the same time – the normal line-up being the goalminder, two defencemen and three forwards – substitutes are considered essential because of the fast, energy-sapping speed at which the game is played. A team usually carries between 11 and 18 players. Substitutes may be introduced at any time.

Play is commenced at the beginning of each period, and after a goal has been scored, by a face-off. The puck is dropped by the referee in the centre of the rink between the sticks of the opposing centremen. Play is restarted at other times of the game by a face-off on the nearest of the other marked spots to the point at which a misplay occurred. The puck becomes dead only when hit over the barrier or when the whistle blows for an infringement.

Goal judges signify a score by switching on a red light behind the goal concerned. A goal can be scored only by propelling the puck from the stick, not by kicking or throwing, nor when an attacking player is in the goal crease.

The two blue lines divide the playing area into three zones – defence, neutral (centre) and attacking zones. Only three players may be in their own defence zone when the puck is outside it. A player may only enter the attacking zone in line with or behind the puck or puck-possessor. He may not take a pass from a team-mate who is, at the moment of passing, in another zone. To stay on-side, a player can only pass to a colleague in the same zone (also to anyone in his own half if he is in his defence zone).

Because of the pace and frantic action involved, players are penalised for rough play by being sent off the ice for two or more minutes, according to the severity of the offence. The term of suspension is served in a penalty box, colloquially known as the 'sin bin'. Minor penalties of two minutes are imposed for charging,

Dick Button (U.S.A.), winner of five world and two Olympic figure skating titles

Pair skaters Ronald and Cynthia Kauffman (U.S.A.), four times world bronze medallists

A competitor takes off in the 1968 Olympic 90 metres ski jump

Gina Hathorn praised by her British team mates after coming fourth in
the 1968 Olympic slalom

elbowing, tripping, body-checking, high sticks or deliberately shooting out of the rink. A goalminder's minor penalty is served by a team colleague. More severe penalties of five or ten minutes, or for the remainder of the game, are imposed according to the seriousness of the offence.

Sticks, made entirely of wood, are limited to 53 inches (135 centimetres) handle and $14\frac{1}{2}$ inches (37 centimetres) blade, except in the case of the goalminder, who may use a heavier and wider stick. The angle between the blade and handle varies and blades are shaped to a player's individual needs.

Boots have lower ankle supports than those used for figure skating, coming up only four to five inches (10 to 12 centimetres) above the sole. Important features are the reinforced caps at toe and heel, moulded arch supports and tendon protectors.

The ice hockey skate blade is shorter than the speed skate and only $\frac{1}{16}$ inch (1.5 millimetres) wide. The blade is reinforced with hollow tubing for greater strength and lighter weight. The goalminder's more specialised skate is wider and less high, affording easier balance. Extra stanchions are fitted to prevent the puck from passing underneath his boots.

The puck is circular, made of solid vulcanised rubber, 3 inches (7.6 centimetres) in diameter, 1 inch (2.5 centimetres) thick, and weighs about $5\frac{1}{2}$ ounces (156 grammes).

Apparel is highly specialised to cater for the sport's protective needs. All the players wear knee-pads, shin-guards, elbow-pads, shoulder-guards, thick gauntlet-type gloves, long stockings that fit over the knee-pads, and a special type of shorts with sweaters in team colours to complete the outfit.

Helmets, though optional, are a wise precaution to minimise possible head injuries. For special protection, the goalminder wears extra large leather leg-guards, a chest protector and extra-padded gloves (a different type for holding the stick to the one for the catching hand). Some goalies also wear a face-mask to avoid possible cuts from skates or sticks after falling on the ice.

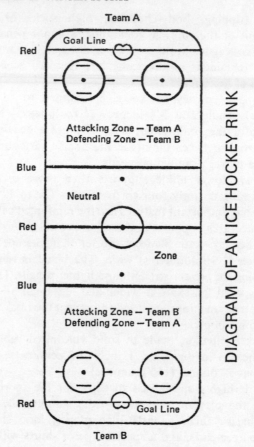

Team A

Goal Line

Red

Attacking Zone — Team A
Defending Zone — Team B

Blue

Neutral

Red

Zone

Blue

Attacking Zone — Team B
Defending Zone — Team A

Red

Goal Line

Team B

DIAGRAM OF AN ICE HOCKEY RINK

GLOSSARY

Assist: individual point-scoring credit to the player who makes the final pass to a goalscorer.
Board-checking: pushing a player deliberately on to the barrier boards.
Face-off: method of starting or re-starting play, when the referee drops the puck on the ice between two opposing players.
High-sticking: illegal carrying of the stick above shoulder level.
Hooking: illegally using the blade of a stick to hook an opponent from behind.
Offside: when an attacking player precedes the puck into the attack-

ing zone or when the puck travels untouched over more than one line.
Penalty shot: a clear shot at goal, awarded if an attacking player is
tripped or pulled down when in a scoring position in front of goal.
Only the goalkeeper is allowed to defend and no goal can be scored
from a rebound.
Power play: sustained attack by one team, particularly when the
opposition is numerically below strength.
Shut-out: goalkeeper's achievement of conceding no goal throughout
a match or period.
Stickhandling: retaining possession of the puck while in motion,
the equivalent of dribbling in soccer, achieved by flicking the puck
alternately with each side of the blade.

Ice Yachting

The fastest travelling humans during the last century were ice yachtsmen, exceeding 100 m.p.h. (160 k.p.h.). The sport of sailing on ice, obviously limited by climatic factors, has been practised principally in North America – near the coasts of New Jersey and New Hampshire and in the Great Lakes basin – and in Europe, along the Baltic coast. The technique corresponds very much to that of sailing on water.

The first recorded ice yachts were Dutch, dating from 1768. The greatest early progress was made during the late 19th century in the Hudson River valley, where the Poughkeepsie Ice Yacht Club was formed in 1865. The Hudson River I.Y.C., founded five years later, became the hub of the sport until the turn of the century, thanks largely to the active interest of Commodore John E. Roosevelt, uncle of President Franklin D. Roosevelt. The early Hudson River craft were heavy and cumbersome by later standards and Roosevelt's 1870 *Icicle* was the largest ever built – 69 feet (21 metres) long with 1,070 square feet (99 square metres) of sail.

A prototype of the present-day craft was the much sleeker *Robert Scott*, built by H. Relyea in 1879, and this Hudson River type remained dominant until 1930. *Debutante III*, built by Jacob and George Buckhout in 1915 with 680 square feet (63 square metres) of sail, is the largest ice yacht still in use.

An open competition for the Challenge Pennant of America dates from 1881. A long-standing world record, determined over 30 miles (48 kilometres) was set in 1907 by *Wolverine* at Kalamazoo, Michigan. Its time of 39 minutes 50 seconds remained unbeaten until 1953, when William Perrigo's *Thunderjet* took 29 minutes 4 seconds. A highest speed of 143 m.p.h. (230 k.p.h.) is credited to John D. Buckstaff, set in 1938 in a stern-steerer on Lake Winnebago, Wisconsin.

101

In 1928, the European Ice Yachting Union was inaugurated at Riga, Latvia, by founder members Austria, Estonia, Germany, Latvia, Lithuania and Sweden.

Built usually for only one or two occupants, ice yachts for competition purposes are classified simply by sail area. The most popular craft nowadays is the bow-steering Skeeter class, limited to 75 square feet (7 square metres) of sail. A 22 foot (6.7 metres) racing Skeeter, weighing about 300 pounds (136 kilogrammes), can be readily dismantled for easy transport on a car roof or light trailer. It has sharp-edged steel runners, normally 4½ inches (11.4 centimetres) high and 40 inches (101.6 centimetres) long.

Luge Tobogganing

Grim and spectacular crashes, one of them fatal, provoked controversy when luge tobogganing made its Olympic debut at Igls, Austria, in 1964. But, outside its Alpine development area, this daring ice sled sport had then been practised relatively little and it was soon realised that experienced riders on well designed tracks probably face no more danger than bobsledders.

One distinctive characteristic of lugeing is the rider's aerodynamic, backward-leaning sitting posture, as opposed to the forward prone position of a Cresta Run skeleton tobogganist. Another is the absence of any mechanical means of steering or braking, in contrast to bobsledding.

With an ancestry probably dating from primitive ice transport of several thousand years ago, tobogganing as a winter recreation was recorded in 16th century documents. In 1520, Hans Sachs described in a German manuscript the enjoyment he derived from it and in 1530 Conrad Schwarz wrote a treatise about it, using the word *rodel*, German for toboggan.

The development of lugeing as a racing sport is traceable to the middle of the 19th century, when British tourists started sled-racing on snowbound mountain roads in the European Alps. Out of this, three sports emerged – bobsleigh, Cresta Run skeleton tobogganing and luge tobogganing.

In 1879, two toboggan tracks were constructed at Davos, Switzerland. In 1881, a first national competition was staged on a course between Davos and Klosters. Its success prompted an international contest on the same track on March 12, 1883.

The course was more than 3,000 metres (9,850 feet) long. Twenty-one competitors represented Australia, Germany, Great Britain, Holland, Sweden and Switzerland. The result was a deadheat between Minch, a Swiss postman, and Robertson, an Australian

103

student of Oxford University. Davos has remained a popular centre for the sport, called *schlitteln* by the Swiss.

From Switzerland, lugeing soon spread to Germany and Austria. The first recorded competitions in the Austrian Tyrol were held in 1890 by the Innsbruck-based Academic Alpine Club. The first Bavarian course was built in 1894 at Brunnstein, near Oberaudorf, and the first Bavarian championships took place there in 1905. The Styrian Toboggan Club was founded in Austria in 1904. The South-West German Toboggan Club was formed with 1,600 members at Triberg, in the Black Forest, in 1911. The German Toboggan Association was inaugurated the same year and the first German national championships were held at Ilmenau in 1913. An International Tobogganing Association was also formed in 1913 by Austrian, German and Swiss racers. The first European championships were held in 1914 at Reichenfeld, Austria.

In the 1930s a big advance came when Martin Tietze, of Austria, invented the flexible sled. This was the beginning of the triumph of lugeing, making the possibilities as great as those of bobsleigh, but with everything done by the body, nothing mechanically.

After the curtailed activities during World War I, the potential predominance of lugeing over bobsleigh as a participant sport became obvious because of the ease with which tobogganing could be practised by the masses on natural courses down mountain paths and roads, as opposed to the inevitable bobsleigh restrictions to more elaborate, expensive courses and sleds.

Tens of thousands of active enthusiasts in the Austrian Tyrol alone provided early evidence of this trend. In 1945, Austria created its national federation and in 1952, when Bert Isatitsch became its president, an important era of his international influence began.

A major turning point and stimulus for the sport occurred in 1954, when the International Olympic Committee, meeting in Athens, officially acknowledged luge tobogganing as the future replacement of skeleton tobogganing as an Olympic sport.

In 1955, the first world championships were staged in Oslo. Lugeing gained a separate world administration in 1957, when the International Luge Federation was formed, with Isatitsch its first president. The sport previously had been controlled by the International Bobsleigh Federation (until then more commonly known by its full title, International Bobsleigh and Tobogganing Federation).

Because it was found impracticable to build a suitable run at Squaw Valley, U.S.A., in 1960, the luge toboggan's Olympic debut had to be deferred for a further four years. The 1964 events opened many hitherto uninitiated eyes and sparked a widening of interest and participation far beyond the central European area where, until then, the sport had thrived most.

It was appropriate that Austria, for long the world's leading tobogganing nation, should be the sport's first Olympic host. Igls, east of Innsbruck, was the selected venue and the course was planned meticulously, to the exact radius of every curve, on the drawing board before construction commenced.

Watched by crowds estimated in excess of 6,000, 38 men and 17 women participated, representing 12 nations whose names illustrated the growth of the sport – Argentina, Austria, Canada, Czechoslovakia, Germany, Great Britain, Italy, Liechtenstein, Norway, Poland, Switzerland and U.S.A.

The British rider, Skrzypecki, was killed in a crash during the week of training which immediately preceded the 1964 Winter Olympics. Despite this sad prelude and other accidents, it was not apparent that any part of the course became unreasonably dangerous for experienced contestants.

Treating the luge runners with suitable ski waxes has always been an accepted practice, but heating the runners to gain extra speed was a temporary phase in the years just prior to, and during, the keen competition for the 1964 Winter Olympics. The Austrians then had hollow runners which they filled with hot oil. A German heated his runners electrically on an immersion heater principle. Other Germans used blow lamps but, after the 1964 Igls event, the heating of runners was declared illegal by the I.L.F.

Three East German women were disqualified for contravening this rule during the sport's next big milestone, the 1968 Winter Olympic Games at Villard de Lans, France. This time, 58 men and 26 women competed, representing 14 nations, including separate East and West German teams and with France, Spain and Sweden participating for the first time.

Normally made of wood with twin metal runners, the luge is steered by the feet and a hand rope, aided by transference of body weight. The single-seater must not weigh more than 20 kilogrammes (44 pounds) nor be more than 1.5 metres (59 inches) long. The maximum width is 44 centimetres (17½ inches) and the height must be between 12 and 15 centimetres (4¾ and 6 inches). Only the sharp inside edges of the runners make contact with the ice. The double-seater, although longer, has the same weight limitation as the single-seater. The flexibility of the sled is possible because the front runners can be moved independently by leg pressure. Speeds of up to 80 m.p.h. (130 k.p.h.) have been achieved on some points of the Krynica run in Poland.

When turning, the luge tobogganer makes three basic movements: 1) the pulling-up of the runner on the side to which he intends to turn, which makes the runner's aft-tip brake a little; 2) the pushing-in of the fore-end of the runner on the opposite side to which he intends to turn; and 3) the placing of the weight on the outward runner, which makes it go faster than the inward runner. Each one of these three movements makes the sled turn a little. It is up to the rider to find the right combination of the three for every particular circumstance.

Equipment essentials are goggles, crash-helmets, knee-pads, elbow-pads, shoulder-pads and reinforced gloves. Spikes are fitted to the soles of the boots to assist pushing off and there are metal rakes on the toe-caps to help braking and steering with the feet.

Championships are held for single-seater and double-seater toboggans and the outcome is decided by the aggregate times of four runs, as in bobsleigh. Major courses are usually about 1,000 metres (3,280 feet) long, with a dozen or more bends. The banked luge runs are normally steeper than bobsleigh courses (maximum average gradient 11 degrees). The corners are narrower and a heavy competitor has hardly any advantage.

Austrians, Germans, Italians and Poles have dominated the annually contested world championships. The sport's outstanding male exponents have included Thomas Köhler (East Germany), Fritz Nachmann (West Germany) and Manfred Schmid and Josef Fiestmantl (Austria). Among the most successful women riders have been Erica Lechner (Italy), Marie Isser (Austria) and Ortrun Enderlein and Ilse Geisler (East Germany).

National Hockey League

The world's major professional ice hockey competition, the National Hockey League of North America, is contested between the foremost clubs in the United States and Canada and was inaugurated at Montreal in November 1917. The first season's championship was won in 1918 by Toronto Arenas, the original name of the club to become famous as Toronto Maple Leafs.

From 1943, the league settled to a regular contest between the big six teams – Boston Bruins, Chicago Black Hawks, Detroit Red Wings, Montreal Canadiens, New York Rangers and Toronto Maple Leafs – the champions winning the Prince of Wales Trophy and the four leading teams contesting the Stanley Cup.

Inevitably spiralling support demanded expansion and in the 1967–8 season the league was doubled in size to 12 clubs. The six new teams – Los Angeles Kings, Minnesota North Stars, Oakland Seals, Philadelphia Flyers, Pittsburgh Penguins and St Louis Blues – have since all competed in a West Division while the old ones have comprised an East Division. The expansion proved a quick success. In 1970–71, Buffalo and Vancouver were added to the East and Chicago moved to the West.

At the end of the N.H.L. matches, the top four in each division compete in two separate play-off series, the winners of each finally meeting in a best-of-seven-matches contest for the Stanley Cup.

The Stanley Cup is the oldest trophy competed for by professional athletes in North America. It was donated in 1893 by Lord Stanley of Preston when Governor General of Canada, originally for presentation to the amateur champions of Canada. Since 1910, it has been emblematic of North American ice hockey supremacy and, from 1926, has been competed for exclusively by N.H.L. teams. In 1971, Montreal Canadiens won it for the 17th time, six times more than

Toronto Maple Leafs, the next most successful side. The cup was originally purchased by Lord Stanley for £10, then less than $50. Subsequent alterations to its structure totalled $6,000 and the aggregate costs of annual engraving has exceeded $8,000. Accompanying the trophy is a monetary yearly award totalling $63,000, distributed to members of the winning team.

The average spectator accommodation at the 12 participating N.H.L. rinks is around 15,000 and many games draw capacity attendances. The rules of professional hockey, though controlled by a referee and two linesmen instead of two referees, are basically similar to those in the amateur sport, with only slight variations in interpretation.

The following annual awards are made to individual players:
Hart Trophy: player adjudged to be the most valuable to his team.
Vezina Trophy: goalminder of the team conceding fewest goals.
Art Ross Trophy: top points scorer at the end of a regular N.H.L. season.
Calder Trophy: most proficient player in his first season.
Lady Byng Trophy: player exhibiting best type of sportsmanship combined with high playing standard.
James Norris Trophy: defenceman demonstrating greatest all-round ability.
Conn Smythe Trophy: most valuable player for his team in Stanley Cup matches.
Lester Patrick Trophy: outstanding service to hockey in the United States.

The longest match on record, at Montreal on March 25, 1936, lasted 2 hours, 56 minutes and 30 seconds, when Detroit Red Wings beat Montreal Maroons 1–0 in the sixth period of overtime.

The possibility of N.H.L. players competing with amateurs in future world championships was approved by the I.I.H.F. when, in 1969, a maximum of nine professionals per team was agreed. This progress received a setback when Avery Brundage, president of the International Olympic Committee, warned that such mixing could jeopardise the acceptance of future Olympic entries. As a result, Canada refused to participate in the 1970 world championships and no nation included a registered professional in the tournament.

NATIONAL HOCKEY LEAGUE TEAMS

BOSTON BRUINS, Boston, Massachusetts, U.S.A. In 1924, became the first United States professional team in the N.H.L. First won the championship in 1929 and retained the title in 1930. The club's best years were 1939–41, when the championship was won three consecutive times. The Stanley Cup was won in 1929, 1939 and 1941. Home matches at Boston Garden. Capacity: 13,909. Ice dimensions: 83 by 191 feet. Players train in Canada at London, Ontario. Best players have included Frankie Brimsek, Dit Clapper, Bill Cowley, Johnny Crawford, Woody Dumart, Bill Hollett, Bobby Orr, Milt Schmidt, Eddie Shore and Nels Stewart. Colours: gold, black and white.

CHICAGO BLACK HAWKS, Chicago, Illinois, U.S.A. Joined the N.H.L. in 1926. Stanley Cup winners in 1934, 1938 and 1961, but did not become league champions until 1967. Players train and play home matches at the Chicago Stadium. Capacity: 16,666. Ice dimensions: 85 by 188 feet. Among the club's most successful players have been Max Bentley, Chuck Gardiner, Bobby Hull, Stan Mikita, Billy Mosienko and Earl Siebert. Colours: red, black and white.

DETROIT RED WINGS, Detroit, Michigan, U.S.A. First won the Stanley Cup in 1936, retaining it the following year and winning it again in 1943, 1950, 1952, 1954 and 1955. N.H.L. champions 13 times and the first club to win it seven times in a row, 1949–55. Home rink, Olympia Stadium, Detroit. Capacity: 15,692. Ice dimensions: 83 by 200 feet. Outstanding players have included Gordie Howe, Syd Howe, Red Kelly, Bill Quackenbush, Terry Sawchuck and Jack Stewart. Colours: red and white.

LOS ANGELES KINGS, Los Angeles, California, U.S.A. Formed in 1967 as one of six teams in the new West Division of the expanded league. Home rink: The Forum, Inglewood, California. Capacity: 15,651. Ice dimensions: 85 by 200 feet. Players train in Canada at the Memorial Gardens, Guelph, Ontario. Colours: royal blue and gold.

MINNESOTA NORTH STARS, Bloomington, Minnesota, U.S.A. Formed in 1967 as one of six teams in the new West Division. Home matches at the Metropolitan Sports Centre, Bloomington. Capacity: 14,400. Ice dimensions: 85 by 200 feet. Players train in Canada at Haliburton and Kingston, Ontario. Colours: green, white and yellow.

MONTREAL CANADIENS, Montreal, Quebec, Canada. One of the original four members which formed the N.H.L. in 1917. The most successful side in the league. Won the Prince of Wales Trophy for the 18th time in 1969 and, the same season, the Stanley Cup for the 16th time. In 1960, the club became the first to achieve a fifth successive Stanley Cup victory. Home rink: Montreal Forum. Capacity: 15,747. Ice dimensions: 85 by 200 feet. Prominent players have been Jean Beliveau, Toe Blake, Emile Bouchard, Bill Durnan, George Hainsworth, Doug Harvey, Aurel Joliat, Elmer Lach, Howie Morenz, Jacques Plante and Maurice Richard. Colours: red, white and royal blue.

NEW YORK RANGERS, New York City, U.S.A. Founded in 1926. Home games at the spacious Madison Square Garden. Capacity: 17,500. Ice dimensions: 85 by 200 feet. Players train in Canada at Kitchener, Ontario. N.H.L. champions in 1928, 1932 and 1942. Stanley Cup winners in 1928, 1933 and 1940. Outstanding players have included Bill Cook, Ott Heller, Ching Johnson, Lynn Patrick and Babe Pratt. Colours: blue, red and white.

OAKLAND SEALS, Oakland, California, U.S.A. Formed in 1967 as one of six teams in the new West Division of the expanded league. Home games at Oakland Colisium Arena. Capacity: 12,500. Ice dimensions: 85 by 200 feet. Players train in Canada at Port Huron, Michigan. Colours: kelly green, light green and blue.

PHILADELPHIA FLYERS, Philadelphia, Pennsylvania, U.S.A. Formed in 1967 to compete in the new West Division. Home games at the Spectrum, Philadelphia. Capacity: 14,700. Ice dimensions: 85 by 200 feet. Players train in Canada at Le Colisee, Quebec City. The first club to win the West Division championship, in 1968. Colours: orange and white.

PITTSBURGH PENGUINS, Pittsburgh, Pennsylvania, U.S.A. Formed in 1967 to enter the West Division. Home games at Pittsburgh's Civic Arena. Capacity: 12,580. Ice dimensions: 85 by 205 feet.

Players train in Canada at Brantford, Ontario. Colours: light blue, dark blue and white.

ST LOUIS BLUES, St Louis, Missouri, U.S.A. Formed in 1967 to join the West Division. Qualified for the Stanley Cup final in each of the club's first two seasons, losing both times to Montreal Canadiens. In seasons 1969 and 1970, the club topped the West Division. Players train and play home matches at St Louis Arena. Capacity: 16,100. Ice dimensions: 85 by 200 feet. Colours: blue, gold and white.

TORONTO MAPLE LEAFS, Toronto, Ontario. Under the original name of Toronto Arenas, the club was one of the four league founder members in 1917 and was then the only club among them with facilities for mechanically frozen ice. Won their sixth championship title in 1963 but achieved greater distinction in the Stanley Cup, winning it for a 12th time in 1967. Home matches at the Maple Leaf Gardens, Toronto. Capacity: 12,291. Ice dimensions: 85 by 200 feet. The players train at Peterborough, Ontario. Outstanding players have included Syl Apps, Turk Broda, King Clancy, Red Horner, Harvey Jackson, Ted Kennedy and James Mortson. Colours: blue and white.

BUFFALO and VANCOUVER augmented the N.H.L. in 1970–71.

STANLEY CUP WINNERS

1894 Montreal A.A.A.	1911 Ottawa Senators
1895 Montreal Victorias	1912 Quebec Bulldogs
1896 Winnipeg Victorias	1913 Quebec Bulldogs
1897 Montreal Victorias	1914 Toronto Ontarios
1898 Montreal Victorias	1915 Vancouver Millionaires
1899 {Montreal Shamrocks / Montreal Victorias}	1916 Montreal Canadiens
	1917 Seattle Metropolitans
1900 Montreal Shamrocks	1918 Toronto Arenas
1901 Winnipeg Victorias	1919 No Competition
1902 Montreal A.A.A.	1920 Ottawa Senators
1903 Ottawa Silver Seven	1921 Ottawa Senators
1904 Ottawa Silver Seven	1922 Toronto St Pats
1905 Ottawa Silver Seven	1923 Ottawa Senators
1906 Montreal Wanderers	1924 Montreal Canadiens
1907 {Montreal Wanderers / Kenora Thistles}	1925 Victoria Cougars
	1926 Montreal Maroons
1908 Montreal Wanderers	1927 Ottawa Senators
1909 Ottawa Senators	1928 New York Rangers
1910 Montreal Wanderers	1929 Boston Bruins

STANLEY CUP WINNERS—*continued*

1930 Montreal Canadiens
1931 Montreal Canadiens
1932 Toronto Maple Leafs
1933 New York Rangers
1934 Chicago Black Hawks
1935 Montreal Maroons
1936 Detroit Red Wings
1937 Detroit Red Wings
1938 Chicago Black Hawks
1939 Boston Bruins
1940 New York Rangers
1941 Boston Bruins
1942 Toronto Maple Leafs
1943 Detroit Red Wings
1944 Montreal Canadiens
1945 Toronto Maple Leafs
1946 Montreal Canadiens
1947 Toronto Maple Leafs
1948 Toronto Maple Leafs
1949 Toronto Maple Leafs
1950 Detroit Red Wings

1951 Toronto Maple Leafs
1952 Detroit Red Wings
1953 Montreal Canadiens
1954 Detroit Red Wings
1955 Detroit Red Wings
1956 Montreal Canadiens
1957 Montreal Canadiens
1958 Montreal Canadiens
1959 Montreal Canadiens
1960 Montreal Canadiens
1961 Chicago Black Hawks
1962 Toronto Maple Leafs
1963 Toronto Maple Leafs
1964 Toronto Maple Leafs
1965 Montreal Canadiens
1966 Montreal Canadiens
1967 Toronto Maple Leafs
1968 Montreal Canadiens
1969 Montreal Canadiens
1970 Boston Bruins
1971 Montreal Canadiens

NATIONAL LEAGUE WINNERS

1918 Toronto Arenas
1919 Montreal Canadiens
1920 Ottawa Senators
1921 Ottawa Senators
1922 Toronto St Pats
1923 Ottawa Senators
1924 Montreal Canadiens
1925 Montreal Canadiens
1926 Montreal Maroons
1927 Ottawa Senators
1928 New York Rangers
1929 Boston Bruins
1930 Boston Bruins
1931 Montreal Canadiens
1932 New York Rangers
1933 Toronto Maple Leafs
1934 Detroit Red Wings
1935 Toronto Maple Leafs
1936 Detroit Red Wings
1937 Detroit Red Wings

1938 Toronto Maple Leafs
1939 Boston Bruins
1940 Boston Bruins
1941 Boston Bruins
1942 New York Rangers
1943 Detroit Red Wings
1944 Montreal Canadiens
1945 Montreal Canadiens
1946 Montreal Canadiens
1947 Montreal Canadiens
1948 Toronto Maple Leafs
1949 Detroit Red Wings
1950 Detroit Red Wings
1951 Detroit Red Wings
1952 Detroit Red Wings
1953 Detroit Red Wings
1954 Detroit Red Wings
1955 Detroit Red Wings
1956 Montreal Canadiens
1957 Detroit Red Wings

Roger Staub
(Switzerland),
1960 Olympic
giant slalom
champion

Jean-Claude Killy (France),
1968 Olympic triple gold medallist

Karl Schranz (Austria),
twice World Alpine Ski Cup winner

Emmerich Danzer (Austria), thrice world figure skating champion

Left: Figure skater Gary Visconti (U.S.A.), 1965 North American champion

Sonja Henie (Norway) won ten world and three Olympic figure skating titles. Her ten feature films accelerated the sport's worldwide popularity

High on the Scottish Cairngorms, where the snow can be ridged and flu
of skis w

the air crystal clear, that 'away from it all' feeling is truly enjoyed on a pair
1 company

A cross-country ski racer passes the impressive Holmenkollen ski jump, only 20 minutes from Oslo, capital of Norway. To nordic skiing enthusiasts, Holmenkollen means what Wimbledon does to tennis players or Cowes to yachtsmen

A brilliant ice hockey save by Jim Henry, goalkeeper for New York Rangers in the 1930s

Mid-air ecstasy at the United States winter resort of Sun Valley, Idaho

Right: Alpine ski racer Traudl Hecher (Austria)

NATIONAL LEAGUE WINNERS—*continued*

1958 Montreal Canadiens
1959 Montreal Canadiens
1960 Montreal Canadiens
1961 Montreal Canadiens
1962 Montreal Canadiens
1963 Toronto Maple Leafs
1964 Montreal Canadiens
1965 Detroit Red Wings
1966 Montreal Canadiens
1967 Chicago Black Hawks

1968 East: Montreal Canadiens
     West: Philadelphia Flyers
1969 East: Montreal Canadiens
     West: St Louis Blues
1970 East: Chicago Black Hawks
     West: St Louis Blues
1971 East: Boston Bruins
     West: Chicago Black Hawks

Nordic Ski Racing

Sixten Jernberg, greatest cross-country skier of the post-World War II era, was greeted by 12,000 spectators with cheers of sentimental admiration as the seemingly indefatigable Swedish veteran panted in to win the energy-sapping 50 kilometres marathon in 2 hours, 43 minutes and 52.6 seconds. More than a full minute ahead of the next man, he won the 1964 Olympic title. What a fantastic stayer was this Jernberg, then 35. In three Olympics, the powerful blond Lima salesman accumulated no fewer than four gold, three silver and two bronze medals.

Nordic ski races, as opposed to alpine events, comprise long-distance cross-country ski running on terrain generally most suitable in Scandinavia. Special skis and bindings are required which are lighter, longer and narrower than those used for the alpine style. The bindings allow for freer vertical heel movement and the sticks are also longer. It is necessary to have a good knowledge of the right kinds of wax to use on the skis to assist the varying degrees of climbing and descending involved.

Senior men's races are contested mainly over 15, 30 and 50 kilometres distances, equivalent to 9.3, 18.6 and 31 miles respectively. The main women's distances are 5 and 10 kilometres (3.1 and 6.2 miles). Relay races are also an exciting feature, four times 10 kilometres for men and three times 5 kilometres for women. The course, marked by flags, is roughly circular, finishing at the same point as the start. An average speed of 10 m.p.h. (16 k.p.h.) corresponds to a good performer's time.

Nordic (*langlauf*) ski racing is one of the most gruelling of sports, demanding long and arduous training. Strenuous and fatiguing though it may be, it is less hazardous than alpine downhill racing. Accidents serious enough to cause broken bones are few and far between. One can be successful later in life than in alpine racing.

The required stamina is acquired more readily around the age of 30, just as it is in ordinary marathon running.

Peak fitness and dedicated training are essential conditions to reaching the top. Deep, steady breathing, harmonious co-ordination of movement and the will to keep going when there seem many good reasons for pulling out – all this adds up to a tough he-man's sport which few women have attempted outside Russia and Scandinavia.

Although the sport has been primarily a northern European skill, Americans and Canadians have taken a progressively more active interest since the early 1960s and the Swiss have provided some good courses at popular resorts.

'It's as simple as walking' is a phrase one can often hear in Scandinavia, where the nature of the snow-covered countryside in winter has prompted many locals to learn the art from infancy. A long, rhythmic stride, with emphasis on the bent front knee and a full arm swing, controls the basic pendulum action. Turns are achieved by a relatively simple skating movement, with weight on the inside ski. The art of using the sticks most effectively for added thrust is in itself a technique of no little importance and one gradually learns to transform every stride into a rhythmic, energy-economising movement.

Cross-country rules lay down that the course shall consist of ever-varying sections of uphill, downhill and flat terrain. Climbs which are too long and steep, very difficult and risky downhill sections and monotonous open stretches should be avoided. Artificial obstacles are not permitted.

In order to avoid undue strain as far as possible, the first section of the course should be comparatively easy. The most strenuous part should occur about halfway or in the third quarter of the course. Changes of direction should not be arranged so close together that the competitor's rhythm is broken or his stride hampered.

In world and Olympic championships, the competitors start one at a time at half-minute intervals, each participant being timed to the nearest tenth of a second. In addition to the usual cross-country and jumping events at nordic meetings, a nordic combination event is included – consisting of a cross-country race, usually over 15 kilometres, and a jumping competition – contested by all-round performers proficient in both, with final positions decided on a points basis.

Major cross-country championships are normally held at different venues to those chosen for alpine events, few centres being ideally suited for both types of skiing. The International Ski Federation instituted the first world and Olympic championships at Chamonix in 1924.

The outstanding performers before World War II came, not surprisingly, from Sweden, Finland and Norway. Veli Saarinen (Finland) and Nils Englund (Sweden) were particularly prominent, each winning world titles at both 18 kilometres and 50 kilometres distances. In post-war world championships the same three countries continued to excel, Sweden's Sixten Jernberg and Finland's Veikko Hakulinen being especially successful. The Soviet Union has also staked a claim to distinction since the mid-1950s.

International women's events date from the first 10 kilometres race in 1952 in Oslo. Russian girls have predominated. In 1964, at Seefeld, Claudia Boyarskikh came first in all three women's events, including the team relay, and she was again outstanding in Oslo in 1966. But the girl of the 1968 Winter Olympics was a Swede, Toini Gustafsson, winning both individual events and coming second in the team relay.

Nordic ski racing is the oldest form of competitive skiing and its ancestry is embedded in Norwegian history. Although races of a kind took place in Norway as early as 1767, the modern version really originated from the invention of ski bindings in the 1880s by Sondre Nordheim, the Norwegian pioneer who, in 1868, demonstrated possibilities by skiing to Oslo from Morgedal, in Telemark, a distance of 115 miles (185 kilometres). Norway's and the world's first ski club was founded at Trysil in 1861 and, by 1880, some 4,000 Norwegians had become racers. By the turn of the century, they had introduced their sport to every continent.

Pleasure Skating

Once dependent on natural ice and, therefore, hard winters, pleasure skating during the 20th century dramatically changed from a strictly seasonal pastime to a highly organised year-long recreation after electrical refrigeration and covered rinks provided congenial comfort.

The public ice rink is becoming as commonplace as the theatre or swimming pool in many towns. Skating has been accepted in many places as a part of the school sports curriculum and civic authorities have become keener to instal their own rinks.

Skating is believed to have originated some 3,000 years ago in Scandinavia and is mentioned in Scandinavian literature of the 2nd century. Like skiing, it first developed as a mode of transport. It has been widely practised on the canals of Holland since the Middle Ages. The first known art illustration of the sport was a Dutch wood carving printed in 1498, depicting St Lydwina of Schiedam, who, in 1396, fell and broke a rib when skating at the age of 16. She died in 1433 and subsequently became known as the patron saint of skaters. Samuel Pepys described in his diary skating which he saw in 1662 on the frozen lake in St James's Park, London. Pepys danced on the ice with Nell Gwynn in London during the Great Frost of 1683.

The first skating club was formed in Edinburgh in 1742. The first international book on skating was written by Captain Robert Jones and published in London in 1772. Skating became fashionable in the French Court around 1776, when Marie-Antoinette was among the participants. In 1791 Napoleon Bonaparte, then a student at the *École Militaire*, narrowly escaped drowning while skating on the moat of the fort at Auxerre, France.

The Skating Club in London was founded in 1842 and the sport was introduced shortly afterwards into the United States and Canada by British servicemen. It developed particularly in Philadelphia, where the first American skating club was started in 1849 and a well-known painter, Benjamin West, became one of the earliest known American skaters of ability.

In 1858, the first properly maintained rink was organised on the lake in New York's Central Park. The New York Skating Club was formed in 1860 and, two years afterwards, it organised the first skating carnival on the frozen Union Pond in Brooklyn. Jackson Haines, an American from Chicago, developed a spectacular freestyle technique and impressed Europe with exhibitions from 1864. The first rink in Canada opened in 1868 at Toronto. A rink at Davos, Switzerland, was opened in 1877. Partly influenced by the performances of Haines, serious skating thrived from 1880 in Scandinavia.

The first mechanically refrigerated rink was a small private one, the Glaciarium near King's Road, Chelsea built by John Gamgee in 1876 with an ice surface measuring 40 by 24 feet (12 by 7.3 metres).

A public rink opened in Manchester the following year and clubs quickly multiplied in Britain before the end of the 19th century. Ice rinks began to appear in many cities and towns on both sides of the Atlantic, notably Baltimore, Brighton, Brooklyn, Brussels, London, Munich, New York, Paris, Philadelphia and Southport. Australia's first ice rink, the Melbourne Glaciarium, opened in 1904 and South Africa's at Johannesburg in 1909.

The sport's first federation, the National Skating Association of Great Britain, was instituted in 1879. The United States Figure Skating Association was inaugurated in 1886 and that of the Canadians in 1888. Other countries followed suit and these national associations collaborated in 1892 to found the International Skating Union, the world's governing administrative body, which by 1970 had 30 member nations. The Union has since supervised and standardised regulations in the three main variants of the sport, figure skating, ice dancing and speed skating.

The revolutionary demand for pleasure skating stimulated by electric refrigeration is well illustrated by the installation since 1950 of many artificial rinks at high altitude winter sports resorts. Natural ice is now much less acceptable and not reliable enough to satisfy the steadily increasing wishes of holiday skaters.

Most beginners probably find the initial public skating session a little frightening, the older ones perhaps the more so as one is frequently more self-conscious. Seeing the comical antics of other beginners striving to remain perpendicular with one hand on the barrier rail may cause one to hesitate.

Though not essential, the personal service of a junior instructor for 20 minutes is well worth the small outlay at this stage, because he or she should rapidly impart an earlier confidence and sense of balance sufficient to enable one to skate unaided to the centre of the rink on a second visit.

So long as one is content just to skate round the rink for the sheer pleasure of it, there is no pressing need to employ an instructor after the first time out unless or until more advanced ambitions are envisaged. Once able to skate away from the barrier without aid, it is easily possible to teach oneself elementary forward and backward skating and – very important – how to stop.

After learning fundamentally to skate forwards and backwards and to brake with a reasonable degree of comfort, one becomes more conscious of the importance of the fact that the figure skate is hollow-ground, each skating blade having two edges which run the length of the skate, the inside edge and the outside edge. From then on, the skater should normally think in terms of skating on a particular edge, and there are thus four – and *only* four – moves on either foot: forward on the outside edge; forward on the inside edge; backward on the outside edge; backward on the inside edge. All skating figures, however simple or advanced, are based on those four movements.

Skating on an edge entails a lean of the body over that edge sufficient to cause a forward or backward movement in a curve. Smoothness without jerking throughout any skating movement is necessarily the aim, and the only way to achieve that is by patient practice and repetition. Once armed with knowledge of the basic movements, practical experience is the best and quickest teacher.

The essential skating equipment purchase is that of boots with skates, which can be obtained either together as a set, or for the more discerning, separately. In the latter case, any good retailer would screw together the skates and boots selected by the customer.

Skating sets can be hired for a nominal charge per session at most rinks and, although one's own are naturally to be preferred, it is prudent not to buy a pair before becoming conscious of a definite desire to persevere with the sport.

The skate itself for normal pleasure purposes should be a 'figure' skate. It should be screwed to the boot so that the blade runs between the big toe and the second toe – in other words, very slightly inside the centre line that runs from toe to heel of the boot. Men's black leather boots should be preserved by regular use of a suitable polish or cream. Most women's boots nowadays are made of white suède or nubuck and need white liquid non-spirit cleaners.

Men normally begin to skate in long trousers and an ordinary jacket or sweater. Special tighter-fitting trousers and short, smartly cut jackets are favoured by many of the more seasoned male performers. For the feet, light wool socks are best.

Any 19th-century picture showing the apparel then worn by women skaters, particularly the long, near-ankle-length skirts, today is almost unbelievable and certainly, by present standards, quite impractical. Today, long narrow skirts are as out of place on a skating rink as they are on a tennis court.

Even when learning at the barrier-clinging stage, it looks less adversely conspicuous to dress in the accepted manner of the expert skater. Ideal are a light knitted woollen sweater and a full, circular, pleated or gored skirt which flares from the hip line and is cut so that it falls several inches above the knee-cap, and with matching, close-fitting panties.

It is a good idea also to wear woollen gloves, both for warmth and as a protection to the hands in the event of falling. If the weather is warm enough, bare legs look and feel better, but woollen stockings or tights should be worn in the colder weather, and at all times a pair of light ankle socks.

Shops are stocking more and more attractive skating outfits these days. To complete the costume, anything accentuating a general streamline effect and which at the same time allows full freedom of movement should be the guiding factor. Close-fitting beret-type headgear, if any, is best.

The beginner should be warned not to associate ideas of ice with cold necessarily, remembering that skating in heated indoor rinks is a vastly different proposition from outdoor frozen lakes.

Ski-Bobbing

'How to succeed on skis without really trying' has been an apt dub for ski-bobbing, which did not become an organised sport until the early 1950s, when a ski-bob suitable for competitions was introduced in Austria by Englebert Brenter.

Made of wood, metal or plastic, a ski-bob looks like a bicycle frame, with handlebars and with short skis where the wheels should be. The rider wears miniature foot-skis which only slightly overlap the length of his boots. The foot-skis are fitted with metal claws at the heel to assist braking. Complete equipment costs about the same as a pair of skis and clothing is similar to that used for ordinary skiing.

The first known 'ski-bike' was patented by Stevens, an American from Hartford, Connecticut, in 1892. It evolved as a utilitarian transport in Alpine villages, particularly for use by Swiss, Austrian and German delivery boys.

The great joy about riding a ski-bob is that it is so easy. Within ten minutes of first sitting astride it and coasting down the nursery snow slopes, the rider starts looking for somewhere steeper. The ski-bobber can take the steepest descents in much the same way as the skier, even to the extent of jumps around 20 feet (6 metres).

The sport undoubtedly attracts many non-skiers who lack either the time or patience to learn the major snow sport and want to get the thrill of speeding down a slope without spending hours in a skiing school.

The four points of ground contact make injury rare. Coaches are available but initial instruction is hardly essential and many winter resorts have made special provision for the sport, designating specific areas and arranging hire facilities. Speeds of around 60 m.p.h. (96 k.p.h.) are frequently attained and experts have been timed in excess of 100 m.p.h. (160 k.p.h.). Most ski-bobs partially fold and can be carried in cable cars and on chair lifts.

The International Ski-Bob Federation was formed at Innsbruck in 1961, with Austrians, West Germans and Swiss then primarily concerned, swelling to more than 20 member nations within the next five years. The first official world championships, held biennially, took place at Bad Hofgastein, Austria, in 1967. Combined titles are awarded for best overall performances in downhill and slalom events. The first two men's world champions were an Austrian, Sylvester Schauberger, and a Swiss, Pierre Bonvin. Gerhilde Schiff-korn (Austria) was the outstanding women racer on both occasions.

Ski-Jumping

It is doubtful whether any other sport is so spectacular and awe-inspiring as ski jumping, in which courage and grace combine so closely. Even the most experienced jumper feels apprehensive during the last nerve-racking moments at the lofty take-off tower. It is strangely quiet. The wind can muffle everything, even the buzzing of the thousands waiting expectantly below. What pluck these specialists must possess as each in turn steps firmly into the twin, icy-slick grooves, curls into a taut ball and gather momentum down the long ramp – reaching up to 75 m.p.h. (120 k.p.h.) – until seeming to explode into the air.

The man who jumps farthest does not necessarily win. In the air he soars to greatness or fades to obscurity, watched by five discerning pairs of eyes in the judging tower. Marks for style are awarded, somewhat similar to figure skating but, unlike the latter, the highest and lowest judges' marks are afterwards discarded, the middle three sets of marks being those which finally count.

Posture and technique are important factors. Points keenly assessed are whether the jumper reduces speed on his way down the ramp and whether his spring is properly timed, neither unduly late nor premature. Once the jumper is airborne, the judges look for straight knees, an extreme forward lean from the ankles – the *vorlage* position – with only a very slight curve of the hips and back. The skis should be held parallel and, during the final part of the flight, they should be inclined slightly upwards at an acute angle to the trajectory, so that the air resistance presses under the skis.

Obvious faults are penalised, such as an unsteady or oblique position of the body or arms, a curved or hollow back, bent knees or unsteady skis. The jumper maintains his forward lean all the way on to the landing slope. Officials, stationed an arm's length apart, record the middle point between the feet of the jumper where he lands.

125

As carefully as an airplane pilot prepares for a touch-down during the last seconds before landing, the ski jumper moves one foot forward into the telemark position, with knees bent to absorb the shock. Any unsteadiness or stiffness here can still lose valuable points. As connection is made with the snow, the arms are spread as stabilisers and every effort is made to avoid contacting the ground with the hands. Finally, the jumper skis along the flat 'outrun' and skids to a halt.

Wind resistance problems naturally preclude any thought of the jumper using ski sticks – regarded by the alpine downhill performer as essential equipment – and the very sight of a skier without them must put the ski jumper among the most daring-looking stars in sport.

Organised ski jumping meetings originated near Oslo, Norway, in 1866 at Iverslokka. The nearby Huseby hill was used for the major Norwegian events from 1879 to 1891, transferring to Holmenkollen in 1892.

Major international ski jump hills have been erected at Innsbruck, Austria; Vysoké Tatry, Czechoslovakia; Lahti, Finland; Chamonix and St Nizier, France; Cortina, Italy; Sapporo, Japan; Holmenkollen and Vikersund, Norway; Zakopane, Poland; Östersund, Sweden; St Moritz, Switzerland; Lake Placid and Squaw Valley, U.S.A.; and Garmisch and Oberstdorf, West Germany.

Because there are variations in the height and general construction of these and other jump hills, the records set at each are not fairly comparable. Oberstdorf, in the Bavarian Alps, possesses particularly favourable conditions for long jumps because it has a vertical height of 161 metres (528 feet).

The most famous ski jumping site is still Oslo's Holmenkollen Hill and the Holmenkollen Week each March is the highlight of the Scandinavian winter sports season. What Wimbledon means to lawn tennis players, Cowes to yachtsmen or Wembley to soccer fans is what Holmenkollen means to Nordic skiing enthusiasts. For more than three quarters of a century, the Holmenkollen competitions have been the most popular ski meetings in the world. The final jumping each year draws crowds of well over 100,000, usually headed by the Norwegian royal family.

The hill is situated in a typical villa district in the Frognerseter hills, only 20 minutes by train from the centre of Oslo. *Holmen* is the name of a large farm nearby and *koll* is Norwegian for hill. A tourist attraction on its own merits, the Holmenkollen ski tower is an impressive building of steel and concrete, over 42 metres (140 feet) high, built for the 1952 Winter Olympic Games and considerably improved for the 1966 world nordic skiing championships. It contains a ski museum where, among many interesting exhibits, one can see Fridtjof Nansen's and Roald Amundsen's polar exploration equipment.

The distance from the edge of the jump to the take-off platform is 83 metres (270 feet) and the slope is 33 degrees. On both sides of the jump, permanent stands have been built to seat 7,000. Around the flat finishing run at the bottom of the hill, additional seats have been built in the shape of a horseshoe (from which this area derives its name) where there is accommodation for another 13,000, with surrounding standing space for 130,000.

The first Olympic and world championships were won concurrently by Jacob Tullin-Thams (Norway) at Chamonix in 1924. Only one all-jumping event continued in the Olympic programmes until 1964, when two separate events were introduced, one from a height of 90 metres (295 feet) and the other from 70 metres (230 feet).

The most successful jumper has been Birger Ruud (Norway), with five world and two Olympic titles to his credit. Although the top honours of the sport are no longer a Norwegian prerogative, as a nation Norway still produces the greatest number of star performers.

The longest recorded jumps have exceeded 150 metres (492 feet). The first to break this barrier was Lars Grini (Norway) in 1967 at Oberstdorf. In 1969, Manfred Wolf (East Germany) cleared 165 metres (541 feet) at Planica. The world record in 1879 was 23 metres (75 feet) by Troj Hammestweit (Norway) at Huseby. In 1915, Amble Amundsen (Norway) passed 50 metres (164 feet) with a leap of 54 metres (177 feet) at Holmenkollen. First to exceed 100 metres (328 feet) was Sepp Bradl (Austria) with 101 metres (331 feet) at Planica in 1936.

Because, in recent years, television cameras have brought this dramatic sport to the homes of so many non-skiers, it is perhaps well to emphasise that jumping is highly specialised and is not practised by the holiday skier any more than high diving is pursued by the average swimmer.

The nordic combination is an event devised to test the overall ability of skiers in jumping and in 15 kilometres (9.3 miles) cross-country racing, winners being determined on a points basis after the two contests. Thorleif Haug (Norway) won the first world and Olympic titles, at Chamonix in 1924. Outstanding performers in the combination have been Johan Gröttumsbraaten (Norway), winning two Olympiç and three world titles; Oddbjorn Hagen (Norway), with one Olympic and three world successes; Heikki Hasu (Finland), Sverre Stenersen (Norway) and Georg Thoma (West Germany), each of the last three having collected one Olympic and two world titles.

A ski jumper in graceful soaring action, with skis ideally parallel and inclined

Robert Paul and Barbara Wagner (Canada), 1960 Olympic pair skating gold medallists and four times world champions

Ice dancers John Carrell and Lorna Dyer (U.S.A.)

Speed Skating

Ice speed skating record holders are the fastest self-propelled humans over level terrain. Ice racers in fact have averaged nearly 30 miles per hour in the shortest races. Over a mile, the speed skater has been approximately one minute faster than the athletics track runner. In 1969, the fastest track athlete at 5,000 metres was six minutes slower than the best time on ice.

Speed skating at top level is inevitably performed on open-air ice, if only because the large area required is impracticable to house under cover. Electrically refrigerated rinks, though few in number because of the high maintenance costs, are used for most major championships.

A more restricted form of the sport is conducted at indoor ice arenas but their area limitations mean insufficient length for adequate speeds and bends that are too sharp for reasonable cornering. There is thus a wide division in technique between indoor and outdoor racing.

There is only one way for a racer to make the top grade. Every year, one must spend several months in countries which can provide good tracks as well as enough ice. This means that many racers need to travel long distances to get suitable training. Norway is particularly well provided and the sport in that country commands a spectator following comparable to that of association football in other lands.

Leading international 400 metres circuits have been established at Cortina d'Ampezzo, Italy; Davos, Switzerland; Deventer, Holland; Gothenburg, Sweden; Grenoble, France; Helsinki, Finland; Innsbruck, Austria; Inzell, West Germany; Medeo, U.S.S.R.; Oslo, Norway, and Sapporo, Japan.

Good ice conditions are not the only ideal to seek in training. The thinner air at high altitudes is another aid to performance. It is no coincidence that most world records have been set on mountain rinks situated higher than 500 metres (1,640 feet). The time of each competitor being the factor deciding results, international championship competitors race only in pairs and in separate lanes, but pack-style racing has been prevalent in the United States.

The short indoor rinks, giving twelve or sixteen laps to the mile, which American, British and many other racers have to use, develop bad habits. The way in which the blade strikes the ice is very important. The toe is pointed almost straight down in sprints, to get more ride out of the blade. For distance races the blade is placed on the ice at a ten-degree angle forward, with the upper body following. The upper body relaxes above the leg over which it glides. So, when the skater pushes off his right skate he should collapse his upper body over his left thigh. The angle of the legs should be almost straight to the ice – and the straighter line one skates the better it is.

International championship meetings are normally of two days' duration, the usual practice being to stage 500 metres and 5,000 metres events on the first day and 1,500 and 10,000 metres the following day. The best all-round performer over these four distances, calculated on a points basis, is hailed as the overall individual champion.

So although, as in running, a speed skater soon becomes recognised as primarily either a sprinter or a distance performer, in international events an individual champion on the ice is still determined by his overall ability over the four recognised championship distances, perhaps an outdated tradition when considering that 10,000 metres is twenty times as far as 500.

On outdoor ice, the stars in action certainly present a thrilling spectacle. Over the longer distances the skater often races with his hands clasped behind his back to conserve energy, making his labour look much more effortless than it is. Each gliding stroke commences on the outside edge of the special steel blade and is rolled over to the inside edge by the end of the stride, a style which dictates an impressive body-roll quite fascinating to watch.

Clad in woollen tights, sweater and protective headgear, these racers – their slightly bent shadows often grotesquely magnified in the reflected light – take the bends with consummate artistry. It gives a highly exhilarating feeling, affording a dramatic sensation that it is not the skater but the ice beneath him that is moving.

The skates and boots are the only essential equipment for the average racer. Ice speed blades are thinner and appreciably longer –

12 to 18 inches (30 to 45 centimetres) – than those used for figures, while speed boots, with lower heel supports, are more like shoes than boots in appearance. While outdoor ice racing often attracts very large crowds, the sport indoors has remained basically a participants' preoccupation, perhaps partly because of the confusion to spectators when, because of the necessarily small circuit, competitors are frequently lapped and, in short-leg relays, it is difficult to follow the interchanging racers.

Ice speed skating began to evolve on the canals of Holland from the middle of the 13th century. Some kind of competition took place as early as 1676. Among pioneering Dutch events, the first known women's competition, with an entry of 130, was organised in 1805 on a straight course at Leeuwarden. Notable early men's straight course races were held at Woutdsend in 1823, Dokkum in 1840 and Amsterdam in 1864. After this, tracks became U-shaped, with one sharp bend and an overall length of 160 to 200 metres (175 to 220 yards).

During the early 19th century, with racing then more usually organised on a two-man basis, the Dutch took the sport to their closest neighbours, Germany, France and Austria. The Frieslanders of North Holland introduced it to England in the area extending from Cambridge to the Wash known as the Fens, where recorded competitions date from 1814.

A *Handbook of Fen Skating*, published in London in 1882, contained a drawing of a speed skating contest at Chatteris in 1823, watched by top-hatted spectators in a passing horse-drawn stage coach. Outstanding British professional skaters of the 19th century were William and George Smart, champions from 1854 to 1864 and from 1879 to 1889 respectively. The formation of the National Skating Association of Great Britain in 1879 led to an organised distinction between professionals and amateurs. British amateur championships, over one and a half miles, began at the Welsh Harp, Hendon, in 1800.

Some 10,000 spectators watched the first recorded competition in Norway in 1863. The first in Sweden took place in 1882, in Finland in 1883 and in Russia the following year. The sport also spread to North America in the mid-1800s and the earliest outstanding United States racer was Tim Donoghue, from 1863 to 1875. The first U.S. championships were staged in 1879 and Joseph Donoghue was a particularly prominent American performer in the 1890s. Norwegians who did much to popularise speed skating internationally around this time were Axel Paulsen, Harald Hagen and Carl Werner.

The first international speed skating competition was in Hamburg in 1885. World championships for men, though first held in 1889 at Amsterdam, were not officially recognised until 1893, the year after the International Skating Union was formed, when Jaap Eden (Netherlands) went on record as the first title holder.

Separate European men's championships also officially date from 1893, when Rudolf Ericsson (Sweden) became the first winner, in Berlin. The first women's world title was contested at Stockholm in 1936 and won by Kit Klein (U.S.A.). Men's speed skating gained Olympic status in 1924, when the first Winter Olympics were staged at Chamonix, but women's Olympic speed skating was not added until 1960 at Squaw Valley, U.S.A.

The most successful men's champions have been Oscar Mathisen (Norway), five times world champion; Clas Thunberg (Finland), who won five world titles and four Olympic gold medals; Ivar Ballangrud (Norway), with a tally of four world victories and four Olympic golds; and Hjalmar Andersen (Norway), three times world champion and the only male speed skater to win three gold medals in one Olympic meeting.

The four outstanding women, all Russians, have been Inga Artamonova, four times world title holder; Maria Isakova and Valentina Stenina, each world champions three times; and Lydia Skoblikova, who took six gold medals in two Winter Olympics, including all four in 1964.

70 YEARS' SPEED SKATING

	1900 RECORD	1970 RECORD
500 metres	45.2 seconds	38.46 seconds
1,500 metres	2 minutes 22.6 seconds	2 minutes 1.9 seconds
5,000 metres	8 minutes 37.6 seconds	7 minutes 13.2 seconds
10,000 metres	17 minutes 50.6 seconds	15 minutes 3.6 seconds

World Champions

Alpine Combination

1932	Otto Fürrer	(Switzerland)	Cortina
1933	Anton Seelos	(Austria)	Innsbruck
1934	David Zogg	(Switzerland)	St Moritz
1935	Anton Seelos	(Austria)	Mürren
1936	Rudolf Rominger	(Switzerland)	Innsbruck
1937	Emile Allais	(France)	Chamonix
1938	Emile Allais	(France)	Engelberg
1939	Josef Jennewein	(Germany)	Zakopane
1940–47	No competition		
1948	Henri Oreiller	(France)	St Moritz
1949–53	No competition, subsequently held every other year		
1954	Stein Eriksen	(Norway)	Åre
1956	Toni Sailer	(Austria)	Cortina
1958	Toni Sailer	(Austria)	Bad Gastein
1960	Guy Perillat	(France)	Squaw Valley
1962	Karl Schranz	(Austria)	Chamonix
1964	Ludwig Leitner	(Germany)	Innsbruck
1966	Jean-Claude Killy	(France)	Portillo
1968	Jean-Claude Killy	(France)	Chamrousse
1970	Bill Kidd	(U.S.A.)	Val Gardena

Downhill

1931	Walter Prager	(Switzerland)	Mürren
1932	Guzzi Lantschner	(Austria)	Cortina
1933	Walter Prager	(Switzerland)	Innsbruck
1934	David Zogg	(Switzerland)	St Moritz
1935	Franz Zingerle	(Austria)	Mürren
1936	Rudolf Rominger	(Switzerland)	Innsbruck
1937	Emile Allais	(France)	Chamonix
1938	James Couttet	(France)	Engelberg

133

Downhill—*continued*

1939	Helmut Lantschner	(Germany)	Zakopane
1940–47	No competition, subsequently held every other year		
1948	Henri Oreiller	(France)	St Moritz
1950	Zeno Colo	(Italy)	Aspen
1952	Zeno Colo	(Italy)	Oslo
1954	Christian Pravda	(Austria)	Åre
1956	Toni Sailer	(Austria)	Cortina
1958	Toni Sailer	(Austria)	Bad Gastein
1960	Jean Vuarnet	(France)	Squaw Valley
1962	Karl Schranz	(Austria)	Chamonix
1964	Egon Zimmerman	(Austria)	Innsbruck
1966	Jean-Claude Killy	(France)	Portillo
1968	Jean-Claude Killy	(France)	Chamrousse
1970	Bernhard Russi	(Switzerland)	Val Gardena

Slalom

1932	Friedl Daüber	(Germany)	Cortina
1933	Anton Seelos	(Austria)	Innsbruck
1934	Franz Pfnür	(Germany)	St Moritz
1935	Anton Seelos	(Austria)	Mürren
1936	Rudi Matt	(Austria)	Innsbruck
1937	Amile Allais	(France)	Chamonix
1938	Rudolf Rominger	(Switzerland)	Engelberg
1939	Rudolf Rominger	(Switzerland)	Zakopane
1940–47	No competition, subsequently held every other year		
1948	Edi Reinalter	(Switzerland)	St Moritz
1950	Georges Schneider	(Switzerland)	Aspen
1952	Othmar Schneider	(Austria)	Oslo
1954	Stein Eriksen	(Norway)	Åre
1956	Toni Sailer	(Austria)	Cortina
1958	Josl Rieder	(Austria)	Bad Gastein
1960	Ernst Hinterseer	(Austria)	Squaw Valley
1962	Charles Bozon	(France)	Chamonix
1964	Josef Stiegler	(Austria)	Innsbruck
1966	Carlo Senoner	(Italy)	Portillo
1968	Jean-Claude Killy	(France)	Chamrousse
1970	Jean-Noël Augert	(France)	Val Gardena

Giant Slalom

Held every other year

1950	Zeno Colò	(Italy)	Aspen
1952	Stein Eriksen	(Norway)	Oslo
1954	Stein Eriksen	(Norway)	Åre

Giant Slalom—*continued*

1956	Toni Sailer	(Austria)	Cortina
1958	Toni Sailer	(Austria)	Bad Gastein
1960	Roger Staub	(Switzerland)	Squaw Valley
1962	Egon Zimmermann	(Austria)	Chamonix
1964	Francois Bonlieu	(France)	Innsbruck
1966	Guy Périllat	(France)	Portillo
1968	Jean-Claude Killy	(France)	Chamrousse
1970	Karl Schranz	(Austria)	Val Gardena

WOMEN'S ALPINE SKIING

Alpine Combination

1932	Rösli Streiff	(Switzerland)	Cortina
1933	Inge Wersin-Lantschner	(Austria)	Innsbruck
1934	Christel Cranz	(Germany)	St Moritz
1935	Christel Cranz	(Germany)	Mürren
1936	Evelyn Pinching	(Gt Britain)	Innsbruck
1937	Christel Cranz	(Germany)	Chamonix
1938	Christel Cranz	(Germany)	Engelberg
1939	Christel Cranz	(Germany)	Zakopane
1940–53	No competition, subsequently held every other year		
1954	Ida Schöpfer	(Switzerland)	Åre
1956	Madeleine Berthod	(Switzerland)	Cortina
1958	Frieda Danzer	(Switzerland)	Bad Gastein
1960	Guy Perillat	(France)	Squaw Valley
1962	Marielle Goitschel	(France)	Chamonix
1964	Marielle Goitschel	(France)	Innsbruck
1966	Marielle Goitschel	(France)	Portillo
1968	Nancy Greene	(Canada)	Chamrousse
1970	Michele Jacot	(France)	Val Gardena

Downhill

1931	Esmé Mackinnon	(Gt Britain)	Mürren
1932	Paula Wiesinger	(Italy)	Cortina
1933	Inge Wesin-Lantschner	(Austria)	Innsbruck
1934	Anny Rüegg	(Switzerland)	St Moritz
1935	Christel Cranz	(Germany)	Mürren
1936	Evelyn Pinching	(Gt Britain)	Innsbruck
1937	Christel Cranz	(Germany)	Chamonix
1938	Lisa Resch	(Germany)	Engelberg
1939	Christel Cranz	(Germany)	Zakopane
1940–47	No competition, subsequently held every other year		
1948	Hedy Schlunegger	(Switzerland)	St Moritz

135

Downhill—*continued*

1950	Trude Jochum-Beiser	(Austria)	Aspen
1952	Trude Jochum-Beiser	(Austria)	Oslo
1954	Ida Schöpfer	(Switzerland)	Åre
1956	Madeleine Berthod	(Switzerland)	Cortina
1958	Lucile Wheeler	(Canada)	Bad Gastein
1960	Heidi Biebl	(Germany)	Squaw Valley
1962	Christl Haas	(Austria)	Chamonix
1964	Christl Haas	(Austria)	Innsbruck
1966	Erika Schinegger	(Austria)	Portillo
1968	Olga Pall	(Austria)	Chamrousse
1970	Annerösl Zryd	(Switzerland)	Val Gardena

Slalom

1931	Esmé Mackinnon	(Gt Britain)	Mürren
1932	Rösli Streiff	(Switzerland)	Cortina
1933	Inge Wersin-Lantschner	(Austria)	Innsbruck
1934	Christel Cranz	(Germany)	St Moritz
1935	Anny Rüegg	(Switzerland)	Mürren
1936	Gerda Paumgarten	(Austria)	Innsbruck
1937	Christel Cranz	(Germany)	Chamonix
1938	Christel Cranz	(Germany)	Engelberg
1939	Christel Cranz	(Germany)	Zakopane
1940–47	No competition, subsequently held every other year		
1948	Gretchen Frazer	(U.S.A.)	St Moritz
1950	Dagmar Rom	(Austria)	Aspen
1952	Andrea Mead-Lawrence	(U.S.A.)	Oslo
1954	Trude Klecker	(Austria)	Åre
1956	Renée Colliard	(Switzerland)	Cortina
1958	Inger Björnbakken	(Norway)	Bad Gastein
1960	Anne Heggveit	(Canada)	Squaw Valley
1962	Marianne Jahn	(Austria)	Chamonix
1964	Christine Goitschel	(France)	Innsbruck
1966	Annie Famose	(France)	Portillo
1968	Marielle Goitschel	(France)	Chamrousse
1970	Ingrid Lafforgue	(France)	Val Gardena

Giant Slalom

Held every other year

1950	Dagmar Rom	(Austria)	Aspen
1952	Andrea Mead-Lawrence	(U.S.A.)	Oslo
1954	Lucienne Schmidt	(France)	Åre
1958	Lucille Wheeler	(Canada)	Bad Gastein
1960	Yvonne Rüegg	(Switzerland)	Squaw Valley
1962	Marianne Jahn	(Austria)	Chamonix

Giant Slalom—*continued*

1964	Marielle Goitschel	(France)	Innsbruck
1966	Marielle Goitschel	(France)	Portillo
1968	Nancy Greene	(Canada)	Chamrousse
1970	Betsy Clifford	(Canada)	Val Gardena

MEN'S NORDIC SKIING

Nordic Combination

1924	Thorleif Haug	(Norway)	Chamonix
1925	O. Nemecky	(Czechoslovakia)	Johannisbad
1926	Johan Gröttumsbraaten	(Norway)	Lahti
1927	R. Purkert	(Czechoslovakia)	Cortina
1928	Johan Gröttumsbraaten	(Norway)	St Moritz
1929	Hans Vinjarengen	(Norway)	Zakopane
1930	Hans Vinjarengen	(Norway)	Oslo
1931	Johan Gröttumsbraaten	(Norway)	Oberhof
1932	Johan Gröttumsbraaten	(Norway)	Lake Placid
1933	Sven Eriksson	(Sweden)	Innsbruck
1934	Oddbjorn Hagen	(Norway)	Sollefteå
1935	Oddbjorn Hagen	(Norway)	Hohe Tatra
1936	Oddbjorn Hagen	(Norway)	Garmisch
1937	Sigurd Röen	(Norway)	Chamonix
1938	Olaf Hoffsbakken	(Norway)	Lahti
1939	Gustl Berauer	(Germany)	Zakopane
1940–47	No competition, subsequently held every other year		
1948	Heikki Hasu	(Finland)	St Moritz
1950	Heikki Hasu	(Finland)	Lake Placid
1952	Simon Slättvik	(Norway)	Oslo
1954	Sverre Stenersen	(Norway)	Falun
1956	Sverre Stenersen	(Norway)	Cortina
1958	Paavo Korhonen	(Finland)	Lahti
1960	Georg Thoma	(Germany)	Squaw Valley
1962	Arne Larsen	(Norway)	Zakopane
1964	Tormod Knutsen	(Norway)	Innsbruck
1966	Georg Thoma	(W. Germany)	Oslo
1968	Franz Keller	(W. Germany)	Autrans
1970	Ladislaw Rygl	(Czechoslovakia)	Vysoké Tatry

18 or 15 Kilometres

1924	Thorleif Haug	(Norway)	Chamonix
1925	O. Nemecky	(Czechoslovakia)	Johannisbad
1926	No competition		
1927	J. Lindgren	(Sweden)	Cortina
1928	Johan Gröttumsbraaten	(Norway)	St Moritz
1929	Veli Saarinen	(Finland)	Zakopane

137

18 or 15 Kilometres—*continued*

1930	Arne Rustadstuen	(Norway)	Oslo
1931	Johan Gröttumsbraaten	(Norway)	Oberhof
1932	Sven Utterström	(Sweden)	Lake Placid
1933	Nils Englund	(Sweden)	Innsbruck
1934	Sulo Nurmela	(Finland)	Sollefteå
1935	Klaes Karppinen	(Finland)	Hohe Tatra
1936	Erik Larsson	(Sweden)	Garmisch
1937	Lars Bergendahl	(Norway)	Chamonix
1938	Pauli Pitkänen	(Finland)	Lahti
1939	Juho Kurikkala	(Finland)	Zakopane
1940–47	No competition, subsequently held every other year		
1948	Martin Lundström	(Sweden)	St Moritz
1950	Karl-Erik Aström	(Sweden)	Lake Placid
1952	Hallgeir Brenden	(Norway)	Oslo
1954	Veikko Hakulinen	(Finland)	Falun
1956	Hallgeir Brenden	(Norway)	Cortina
1958	Veikko Hakulinen	(Finland)	Lahti
1960	Haakon Brusveen	(Norway)	Squaw Valley
1962	Assar Rönnlund	(Sweden)	Zakopane
1964	Eero Mäntyranta	(Finland)	Innsbruck
1966	Gjermund Eggen	(Norway)	Oslo
1968	Harald Grönningen	(Norway)	Autrans
1970	Lars Åslund	(Sweden)	Vysoké Tatry

30 Kilometres

1926	M. Raivio	(Finland)	Lahti
1927–53	No competition, subsequently held every other year		
1954	Vladimir Kuzin	(U.S.S.R.)	Falun
1956	Veikko Hakulinen	(Finland)	Cortina
1958	Kalevi Hämäläinen	(Finland)	Lahti
1960	Sixten Jernberg	(Sweden)	Squaw Valley
1962	Eero Mäntyranta	(Finland)	Zakopane
1964	Eero Mäntyranta	(Finland)	Innsbruck
1966	Eero Mäntyranta	(Finland)	Oslo
1968	Franco Nones	(Italy)	Autrans
1970	Vjatsjerlav Vedenin	(U.S.S.R.)	Vysoké Tatry

50 Kilometres

1924	Thorleif Haug	(Norway)	Chamonix
1925	Franz Donth	(Czechoslovakia)	Johannisbad
1926	M. Raivio	(Finland)	Lahti
1927	J. Lindgren	(Sweden)	Cortina
1928	Per Hedlund	(Sweden)	St Moritz

50 Kilometres—*continued*

1929	Anselm Knuuttila	(Finland)	Zakopane
1930	Sven Utterström	(Sweden)	Oslo
1931	Ole Stenen	(Norway)	Oberhof
1932	Veli Saarinen	(Finland)	Lake Placid
1933	Veli Saarinen	(Finland)	Innsbruck
1934	Elis Wiklund	(Sweden)	Sollefteå
1935	Nils Englund	(Sweden)	Hohe Tatra
1936	Elis Wiklund	(Sweden)	Garmisch
1937	Pekka Niemi	(Finland)	Chamonix
1938	Kalle Jalkanen	(Finland)	Lahti
1939	Lars Bergendahl	(Norway)	Zakopane
1940–47	No competition, subsequently held every other year		
1948	Nils Karlsson	(Sweden)	St Moritz
1950	Gunnar Eriksson	(Sweden)	Lake Placid
1952	Veikko Hakulinen	(Finland)	Oslo
1954	Vladimir Kuzin	(U.S.S.R.)	Falun
1956	Sixten Jernberg	(Sweden)	Cortina
1958	Sixten Jernberg	(Sweden)	Lahti
1960	Kalevi Hämäläinen	(Finland)	Squaw Valley
1962	Sixten Jernberg	(Sweden)	Zakopane
1964	Sixten Jernberg	(Sweden)	Innsbruck
1966	Gjermund Eggen	(Norway)	Oslo
1968	Ole Ellefsaeter	(Norway)	Autrans
1970	Kalevi Oikarainen	(Finland)	Vysoké Tatry

4 × 10 Kilometres Team Relay

1933	Sweden	P. Hedlund, S. Utterström, N. Englund, H. Bergström	Innsbruck
1934	Finland	S. Nurmela, K. Karppinen, M. Lappalainen, V. Saarinen	Sollefteå
1935	Finland	M. Hasu, K. Karppinen, V. Liikunen, S. Nurmela	Hohe Tatra
1936	Finland	S. Nurmela, K. Karppinen, M. Lähde, K. Jalkanen	Garmisch
1937	Norway	A. Ryen, O. Fredriksen, S. Röen, L. Bergendahl	Chamonix
1938	Finland	J. Kurikkala, M. Lauronen, P. Pitkänen, K. Karppinen	Lahti
1939	Finland	P. Pitkänen, O. Alakulppi, E. Olkinuora, K. Karppinen	Zakopane
1940–47	No competition, subsequently held every other year		
1948	Sweden	N. Ostensson, N. Täpp, G. Eriksson, M. Lundström	St Moritz
1950	Sweden	N. Täpp, K. Åström, M. Lundström, E. Josefsson	Lake Placid

4 × 10 Kilometres Team Relay—*continued*

1952	Finland	H. Hasu, P. Lonkila, U. Korhonen, T. Mäkelä	Oslo
1954	Finland	A. Kiuru, T. Mäkelä, A. Viitanen, V. Hakulinen	Falun
1956	U.S.S.R.	F. Terentjev, P. Kolchin, N. Anikin, V. Kusin	Cortina
1958	Sweden	S. Jernberg, L. Larsson, S. Grahn, P. Larsson	Lahti
1960	Finland	T. Alatalo, E. Mäntyranta, V. Huhtala, V. Hakulinen	Squaw Valley
1962	Sweden	L. Olsson, S. Grahn, S. Jernberg, A. Rönnlund	Zakopane
1964	Sweden	K. Asph, S. Jernberg, J. Stefansson, A. Rönnlund	Innsbruck
1966	Norway	O. Martinsen, H. Grönningen, O. Ellefsaeter, G. Eggen	Oslo
1968	Norway	O. Martinsen, P. Tyldum, H. Grönningen, O. Ellefsaeter	Autrans
1970	U.S.S.R.	V. Voronkov, V. Tarakanov, F. Simasov, V. Vedenin	Vysoké Tatry

WOMEN'S NORDIC SKIING

10 Kilometres

Held every other year

1952	Lydia Wideman	(Finland)	Oslo
1954	Ljubovj Kozyreva	(U.S.S.R.)	Falun
1956	Ljubovj Kozyreva	(U.S.S.R.)	Cortina
1958	Alevtina Kolljina	(U.S.S.R.)	Lahti
1960	Marija Gusakova	(U.S.S.R.)	Squaw Valley
1962	Alevtina Koltjina	(U.S.S.R.)	Zakopane
1964	Claudia Boyarskikh	(U.S.S.R.)	Innsbruck
1966	Claudia Boyarskikh	(U.S.S.R.)	Oslo
1968	Toini Gustafsson	(Sweden)	Autrans
1970	Alevtina Oljunina	(U.S.S.R.)	Vysoké Tatry

5 Kilometres

Held every other year

1962	Alevtina Koltjina	(U.S.S.R.)	Zakopane
1964	Claudia Boyarskikh	(U.S.S.R.)	Innsbruck
1966	Alevtina Kotchina	(U.S.S.R.)	Oslo
1968	Toini Gustafsson	(Sweden)	Autrans
1970	Galina Kulakova	(U.S.S.R.)	Vysoké Tatry

3 × 5 Kilometres Team Relay

Held every other year

Year			
1954	U.S.S.R.	L. Kozyreva, M. Maslennikova, V. Tsareva	Falun
1956	Finland	S. Polkunen, M. Hietamies, S. Rantanen	Cortina
1958	U.S.S.R.	R. Eroshina, A. Koltjina, L. Kozyreva	Lahti
1960	Sweden	I. Johansson, B. Strandberg, S. Edström-Ruthström	Squaw Valley
1962	U.S.S.R.	L. Baranova, M. Gusakova, A. Koltjina	Zakopane
1964	U.S.S.R.	A. Koltjina, E. Mekshilo, C. Boyarskikh	Innsbruck
1966	U.S.S.R.	C. Boyarskikh, R. Achkina, A. Koltjina	Oslo
1968	Norway	I. Aufles, B. Enger-Damon, B. Mördre	Autrans
1970	U.S.S.R.	N. Fjodorova, G. Kulakova, A. Oljunina	Vysoké Tatry

BIATHLON

Year	Individual		Team	
1958	Adolf Wiklund	(Sweden)	Sweden	Saalfelden
1959	Vladimir Melanin	(U.S.S.R.)	U.S.S.R.	Courmayeur
1960	Klas Lestander	(Sweden)	—	Squaw Valley
1961	Kalevi Huuskonen	(Finland)	Finland	Umea
1962	Vladimir Melanin	(U.S.S.R.)	U.S.S.R.	Tavastehus
1963	Vladimir Melanin	(U.S.S.R.)	U.S.S.R.	Seefeld
1964	Vladimir Melanin	(U.S.S.R.)	—	Seefeld
1965	Olav Jordet	(Norway)	Norway	Elverum
1966	Jon Istad	(Norway)	Norway	Garmisch
1967	Viktor Mamatov	(U.S.S.R.)	Norway	Altenberg
1968	Magnar Solberg	(Norway)	U.S.S.R.	Autrans
1969	Alexandre Tikhonov	(U.S.S.R.)	U.S.S.R.	Zakopane
1970	Alexandre Tikhonov	(U.S.S.R.)	Norway	Östersund
1971	Dieter Speer	(E. Germany)	U.S.S.R.	Hammennlina

SKI JUMPING

Year			
1924	Jacob Tullin-Thams	(Norway)	Chamonix
1925	W. Dick	(Czechoslovakia)	Johannisbad
1926	Jacob Tullin-Thams	(Norway)	Lahti

Ski Jumping—*continued*

1927	T. Edman	(Sweden)	Cortina
1928	Alf Andersen	(Norway)	St Moritz
1929	Sigmund Ruud	(Norway)	Zakopane
1930	Gunnar Andersen	(Norway)	Oslo
1931	Birger Ruud	(Norway)	Oberhof
1932	Birger Ruud	(Norway)	Lake Placid
1933	Marcel Reymond	(Switzerland)	Innsbruck
1934	Kristian Johanson	(Norway)	Sollefteå
1935	Birger Ruud	(Norway)	Hohe Tatra
1936	Birger Ruud	(Norway)	Garmisch
1937	Birger Ruud	(Norway)	Chamonix
1938	Asbjörn Ruud	(Norway)	Lahti
1939	Josef Bradl	(Austria)	Zakopane
1940–47	No competition		
1948	Petter Hugstedt	(Norway)	St Moritz
1949	No competition		
1950	Hans Björnstad	(Norway)	Lake Placid
1952	Arnfinn Bergmann	(Norway)	Oslo
1954	Matti Pietikainen	(Finland)	Falun
1956	Antti Hyvärinen	(Finland)	Cortina
1957	No competition		
1958	J. Kärkinen	(Finland)	Lahti
1959	No competition		
1960	Helmut Recknagel	(E. Germany)	Zakopane
1961	No competition		
1962	Helmut Recknagel	(E. Germany)	Zakopane
1963	No competition		
1964	Toralf Engan	(Norway)	Innsbruck
1965	No competition		
1966	Bjorn Wirkola	(Norway)	Oslo
1967	Reinhold Bachler	(Austria)	Vikersund
1968	Vladimir Beloussov	(U.S.S.R.)	St Nizier
1969	No competition		
1970	Garij Napalkov	(U.S.S.R.)	Vysoké Tatry

SKI JUMPING

(Small Hill, 70 metres)

Held every other year

1962	Toralf Engan	(Norway)	Zakopane
1964	Veikko Kankkonen	(Finland)	Innsbruck
1966	Bjorn Wirkola	(Norway)	Oslo
1968	Jiri Raska	(Czechoslovakia)	Autrans
1970	Garij Napalkov	(U.S.S.R.)	Vysoké Tatry

MEN'S SKI-BOBBING

Held every other year

1967	Sylvester Schauberger	(Austria)	Bad Hofgastein
1969	Pierre Bonvin	(Switzerland)	Montana
1971	Josef Estner	(West Germany)	Reno

WOMEN'S SKI-BOBBING

Held every other year

1967	Gerhilde Schiffkorn	(Austria)	Bad Hofgastein
1969	Gerhilde Schiffkorn	(Austria)	Montana
1971	Gertrude Geberth	(Austria)	Reno

MEN'S FIGURE SKATING

1896	Gilbert Fuchs	(Germany)	St Petersburg
1897	Gustav Hügel	(Austria)	Stockholm
1898	Henning Grenander	(Sweden)	London
1899	Gustav Hügel	(Austria)	Davos
1900	Gustav Hügel	(Austria)	Davos
1901	Ulrich Salchow	(Sweden)	Stockholm
1902	Ulrich Salchow	(Sweden)	London
1903	Ulrich Salchow	(Sweden)	St Petersburg
1904	Ulrich Salchow	(Sweden)	Berlin
1905	Ulrich Salchow	(Sweden)	Stockholm
1906	Gilbert Fuchs	(Germany)	Munich
1907	Ulrich Salchow	(Sweden)	Vienna
1908	Ulrich Salchow	(Sweden)	Troppau
1909	Ulrich Salchow	(Sweden)	Stockholm
1910	Ulrich Salchow	(Sweden)	Davos
1911	Ulrich Salchow	(Sweden)	Berlin
1912	Fritz Kachler	(Austria)	Manchester
1913	Fritz Kachler	(Austria)	Vienna
1914	Gösta Sandahl	(Sweden)	Helsingfors
1915–21	No competition		
1922	Gillis Grafström	(Sweden)	Stockholm
1923	Fritz Kachler	(Austria)	Vienna
1924	Gillis Grafström	(Sweden)	Manchester
1925	Willy Böckl	(Austria)	Vienna
1926	Willy Böckl	(Austria)	Berlin
1927	Willy Böckl	(Austria)	Davos
1928	Willy Böckl	(Austria)	Berlin
1929	Gillis Grafström	(Sweden)	London
1930	Karl Schäfer	(Austria)	New York

143

Men's Figure Skating—*continued*

1931	Karl Schäfer	(Austria)	Berlin
1932	Karl Schäfer	(Austria)	Montreal
1933	Karl Schäfer	(Austria)	Zürich
1934	Karl Schäfer	(Austria)	Stockholm
1935	Karl Schäfer	(Austria)	Budapest
1936	Karl Schäfer	(Austria)	Paris
1937	Felix Kaspar	(Austria)	Vienna
1938	Felix Kaspar	(Austria)	Berlin
1939	Graham Sharp	(Gt Britain)	Budapest
1940–46	No competition		
1947	Hans Gerschwiler	(Switzerland)	Stockholm
1948	Richard Button	(U.S.A.)	Davos
1949	Richard Button	(U.S.A.)	Paris
1950	Richard Button	(U.S.A.)	London
1951	Richard Button	(U.S.A.)	Milan
1952	Richard Button	(U.S.A.)	Paris
1953	Hayes Jenkins	(U.S.A.)	Davos
1954	Hayes Jenkins	(U.S.A.)	Oslo
1955	Hayes Jenkins	(U.S.A.)	Vienna
1956	Hayes Jenkins	(U.S.A.)	Garmisch
1957	David Jenkins	(U.S.A.)	Colorado Springs
1958	David Jenkins	(U.S.A.)	Paris
1959	David Jenkins	(U.S.A.)	Colorado Springs
1960	Alain Giletti	(France)	Vancouver
1961	No competition		
1962	Donald Jackson	(Canada)	Prague
1963	Donald McPherson	(Canada)	Cortina
1964	Manfred Schnelldorfer	(W. Germany)	Dortmund
1965	Alain Calmat	(France)	Colorado Springs
1966	Emerich Danzer	(Austria)	Davos
1967	Emerich Danzer	(Austria)	Vienna
1968	Emerich Danzer	(Austria)	Geneva
1969	Tim Wood	(U.S.A.)	Colorado Springs
1970	Tim Wood	(U.S.A.)	Ljubljana
1971	Ondrej Nepela	(Czechoslovakia)	Lyons

WOMEN'S FIGURE SKATING

1906	Madge Syers	(Gt Britain)	Davos
1907	Madge Syers	(Gt Britain)	Vienna
1908	Lily Kronberger	(Hungary)	Troppau
1909	Lily Kronberger	(Hungary)	Budapest
1910	Lily Kronberger	(Hungary)	Berlin
1911	Lily Kronberger	(Hungary)	Vienna
1912	Meray Horváth	(Hungary)	Davos
1913	Meray Horváth	(Hungary)	Stockholm

Women's Figure Skating—*continued*

1914	Meray Horváth	(Hungary)	St Moritz
1915–21	No competition		
1922	Herma Plank-Szabo	(Austria)	Stockholm
1923	Herma Plank-Szabo	(Austria)	Vienna
1924	Herma Plank-Szabo	(Austria)	Oslo
1925	Herma Jaross-Szabo	(Austria)	Davos
1926	Herma Jaross-Szabo	(Austria)	Stockholm
1927	Sonja Henie	(Norway)	Oslo
1928	Sonja Henie	(Norway)	London
1929	Sonja Henie	(Norway)	Budapest
1930	Sonja Henie	(Norway)	New York
1931	Sonja Henie	(Norway)	Berlin
1932	Sonja Henie	(Norway)	Montreal
1933	Sonja Henie	(Norway)	Stockholm
1934	Sonja Henie	(Norway)	Oslo
1935	Sonja Henie	(Norway)	Vienna
1936	Sonja Henie	(Norway)	Paris
1937	Cecilia Colledge	(Gt Britain)	London
1938	Megan Taylor	(Gt Britain)	Stockholm
1939	Megan Taylor	(Gt Britain)	Prague
1940–46	No competition		
1947	Barbara Ann Scott	(Canada)	Stockholm
1948	Barbara Ann Scott	(Canada)	Davos
1949	Aja Vrzanova	(Czechoslovakia)	Paris
1950	Aja Vrzanova	(Czechoslovakia)	London
1951	Jeannette Altwegg	(Gt Britain)	Milan
1952	Jacqueline du Bief	(France)	Paris
1953	Tenley Albright	(U.S.A.)	Davos
1954	Gundi Busch	(Germany)	Oslo
1955	Tenley Albright	(U.S.A.)	Vienna
1956	Carol Heiss	(U.S.A.)	Garmisch
1957	Carol Heiss	(U.S.A.)	Colorado Springs
1958	Carol Heiss	(U.S.A.)	Paris
1959	Carol Heiss	(U.S.A.)	Colorado Springs
1960	Carol Heiss	(U.S.A.)	Vancouver
1961	No competition		
1962	Sjoukje Dijkstra	(Netherlands)	Prague
1963	Sjoukje Dijkstra	(Netherlands)	Cortina
1964	Sjoukje Dijkstra	(Netherlands)	Dortmund
1965	Petra Burka	(Canada)	Colorado Springs
1966	Peggy Fleming	(U.S.A.)	Davos
1967	Peggy Fleming	(U.S.A.)	Vienna
1968	Peggy Fleming	(U.S.A.)	Geneva
1969	Gabriele Seyfert	(E. Germany)	Colorado Springs
1970	Gabriele Seyfert	(E. Germany)	Ljubljana
1971	Trixi Schuba	(Austria)	Lyons

Pair Skating

1908	Heinrich Burger and Anna Hübler	(Germany)	St Petersburg
1909	James Johnson and Phyllis Johnson	(Gt Britain)	Stockholm
1910	Heinrich Burger and Anna Hübler	(Germany)	Berlin
1911	Walter Jakobsson and Ludowika Eilers	(Finland)	Vienna
1912	James Johnson and Phyllis Johnson	(Gt Britain)	Manchester
1913	Karl Mejstrik and Helene Engelmann	(Austria)	Stockholm
1914	Walter Jakobsson and Ludowika Jakobsson	(Finland)	St Moritz
1915–21	No competition		
1922	Alfred Berger and Helene Engelmann	(Austria)	Davos
1923	Walter Jakobsson and Ludowika Jakobsson	(Finland)	Oslo
1924	Alfred Berger and Helene Engelmann	(Austria)	Manchester
1925	Ludwig Wrede and Herma Jaross-Szabo	(Austria)	Vienna
1926	Pierre Brunet and Andrée Joly	(France)	Berlin
1927	Ludwig Wrede and Herma Jaross-Szabo	(Austria)	Vienna
1928	Pierre Brunet and Andrée Joly	(France)	London
1929	Otto Kaiser and Lily Scholz	(Austria)	Budapest
1930	Pierre Brunet and Andrée Brunet	(France)	New York
1931	Laszlo Szollas and Emilie Rotter	(Hungary)	Berlin
1932	Pierre Brunet and Andrée Brunet	(France)	Montreal
1933	Laszlo Szollas and Emilie Rotter	(Hungary)	Stockholm
1934	Laszlo Szollas and Emilie Rotter	(Hungary)	Helsingfors
1935	Laszlo Szollas and Emilie Rotter	(Hungary)	Budapest
1936	Ernst Baier and Maxi Herber	(Germany)	Paris

Pair Skating—*continued*

1937	Ernst Baier and Maxi Herber	(Germany)	London
1938	Ernst Baier and Maxi Herber	(Germany)	Berlin
1939	Ernst Baier and Maxi Herber	(Germany)	Budapest
1940–46	No competition		
1947	Pierre Baugniet and Micheline Lannoy	(Belgium)	Stockholm
1948	Pierre Baugniet and Micheline Lannoy	(Belgium)	Davos
1949	Ede Kiraly and Andrea Kekéssy	(Hungary)	Paris
1950	Peter Kennedy and Karol Kennedy	(U.S.A.)	London
1951	Paul Falk and Ria Baran	(Germany)	Milan
1952	Paul Falk and Ria Falk	(Germany)	Paris
1953	John Nicks and Jennifer Nicks	(Gt Britain)	Davos
1954	Norris Bowden and Frances Dafoe	(Canada)	Oslo
1955	Norris Bowden and Frances Dafoe	(Canada)	Vienna
1956	Kurt Oppelt and Sissy Schwarz	(Austria)	Garmisch
1957	Robert Paul and Barbara Wagner	(Canada)	Colorado Springs
1958	Robert Paul and Barbara Wagner	(Canada)	Paris
1959	Robert Paul and Barbara Wagner	(Canada)	Colorado Springs
1960	Robert Paul and Barbara Wagner	(Canada)	Vancouver
1961	No competition		
1962	Otto Jelinek and Maria Jelinek	(Canada)	Prague
1963	Hans-Jürgen Bäumler and Marika Kilius	(W. Germany)	Cortina
1964	Hans-Jürgen Bäumler and Marika Kilius	(W. Germany)	Dortmund
1965	Oleg Protopopov and Ludmila Protopopov	(U.S.S.R.)	Colorado Springs
1966	Oleg Protopopov and Ludmila Protopopov	(U.S.S.R.)	Davos

Pair Skating—*continued*

1967	Oleg Protopopov and Ludmila Protopopov	(U.S.S.R.)	Vienna
1968	Oleg Protopopov and Ludmila Protopopov	(U.S.S.R.)	Geneva
1969	Aleksej Ulanov and Irena Rodnina	(U.S.S.R.)	Colorado Springs
1970	Aleksej Ulanov and Irena Rodnina	(U.S.S.R.)	Ljubljana
1971	Aleksej Ulanov and Irena Rodnina	(U.S.S.R.)	Lyons

ICE DANCE SKATING

1952	Lawrence Demmy and Jean Westwood	(Gt Britain)	Paris
1953	Lawrence Demmy and Jean Westwood	(Gt Britain)	Paris
1954	Lawrence Demmy and Jean Westwood	(Gt Britain)	Oslo
1955	Lawrence Demmy and Jean Westwood	(Gt Britain)	Vienna
1956	Paul Thomas and Pamela Weight	(Gt Britain)	Garmisch
1957	Courtney Jones and June Markham	(Gt Britain)	Colorado Springs
1958	Courtney Jones and June Markham	(Gt Britain)	Paris
1959	Courtney Jones and Doreen Denny	(Gt Britain)	Colorado Springs
1960	Courtney Jones and Doreen Denny	(Gt Britain)	Vancouver
1961	No competition		
1962	Pavel Roman and Eva Romanova	(Czechoslovakia)	Prague
1963	Pavel Roman and Eva Romanova	(Czechoslovakia)	Cortina
1964	Pavel Roman and Eva Romanova	(Czechoslovakia)	Dortmund
1965	Pavel Roman and Eva Romanova	(Czechoslovakia)	Colorado Springs
1966	Bernard Ford and Diane Towler	(Gt Britain)	Davos
1967	Bernard Ford and Diane Towler	(Gt Britain)	Vienna
1968	Bernard Ford and Diane Towler	(Gt Britain)	Geneva

Ice Dancing Skating—*continued*

1969	Bernard Ford and Diane Towler	(Gt Britain)	Colorado Springs
1970	Aleksandre Gorshkov and Ljudmila Pakhomova	(U.S.S.R.)	Ljubljana
1971	Aleksandre Gorshkov and Ljudmila Pakhomova	(U.S.S.R.)	Lyons

MEN'S SPEED SKATING

(Decided over 500, 1,500, 5,000 and 10,000 metres)

1893	Jaap Eden	(Netherlands)	Amsterdam
1894	No competition		
1895	Jaap Eden	(Netherlands)	Hamar
1896	Jaap Eden	(Netherlands)	St Petersburg
1897	Jack McCullock	(Canada)	Montreal
1898	Peder Oestlund	(Norway)	Davos
1899	Peder Oestlund	(Norway)	Berlin
1900	Edvard Engelsaas	(Norway)	Christiania
1901	Franz Wathen	(Finland)	Stockholm
1902–3	No competition		
1904	Sigurd Mathisen	(Norway)	Christiania
1905	Coen de Koning	(Netherlands)	Groningen
1906–7	No competition		
1908	Oscar Mathisen	(Norway)	Davos
1909	Oscar Mathisen	(Norway)	Christiania
1910	Nicholas Strunikoff	(Russia)	Helsingfors
1911	Nicholas Strunikoff	(Russia)	Trondheim
1912	Oscar Mathisen	(Norway)	Christiania
1913	Oscar Mathisen	(Norway)	Helsingfors
1914	Oscar Mathisen	(Norway)	Christiania
1915–21	No competition		
1922	Harald Ström	(Norway)	Christiania
1923	Clas Thunberg	(Finland)	Stockholm
1924	Roald Larsen	(Norway)	Helsingfors
1925	Clas Thunberg	(Finland)	Oslo
1926	Ivar Ballangrud	(Norway)	Trondheim
1927	Bernt Evensen	(Norway)	Tammerfors
1928	Clas Thunberg	(Finland)	Davos
1929	Clas Thunberg	(Finland)	Oslo
1930	Michael Staksrud	(Norway)	Oslo
1931	Clas Thunberg	(Finland)	Helsingfors
1932	Ivar Ballangrud	(Norway)	Lake Placid
1933	Hans Engnestangen	(Norway)	Trondheim
1934	Bernt Evensen	(Norway)	Helsingfors
1935	Michael Staksrud	(Norway)	Oslo
1936	Ivar Ballangrud	(Norway)	Davos

149

Men's Speed Skating—*continued*

1937	Michael Staksrud	(Norway)	Oslo
1938	Ivar Ballangrud	(Norway)	Davos
1939	Birger Wasenius	(Finland)	Helsingfors
1940–46	No competition		
1947	Lauri Parkkinen	(Finland)	Oslo
1948	Odd Lundberg	(Norway)	Helsinki
1949	Kornel Pajor	(Hungary)	Oslo
1950	Hjalmar Andersen	(Norway)	Eskilstuna
1951	Hjalmar Andersen	(Norway)	Davos
1952	Hjalmar Andersen	(Norway)	Hamar
1953	Oleg Goncharenko	(U.S.S.R.)	Helsinki
1954	Boris Schilkov	(U.S.S.R.)	Sapporo
1955	Sigvard Ericsson	(Sweden)	Moscow
1956	Oleg Goncharenko	(U.S.S.R.)	Oslo
1957	Knut Johannesen	(Norway)	Östersund
1958	Oleg Goncharenko	(U.S.S.R.)	Helsinki
1959	Juhani Jarvinen	(Finland)	Oslo
1960	Boris Stenin	(U.S.S.R.)	Davos
1961	Hendrik Van Der Grift	(Netherlands)	Gothenburg
1962	Viktor Kosichken	(U.S.S.R.)	Moscow
1963	Jonny Nilsson	(Sweden)	Karuizawa
1964	Knut Johannesen	(Norway)	Helsinki
1965	Per Moe	(Norway)	Oslo
1966	Kees Verkerk	(Netherlands)	Gothenburg
1967	Kees Verkerk	(Netherlands)	Oslo
1968	Fred Maier	(Norway)	Gothenburg
1969	Dag Fornaess	(Norway)	Deventer
1970	Ard Schenk	(Netherlands)	Oslo
1971	Ard Schenk	(Netherlands)	Gothenburg

WOMEN'S SPEED SKATING

(Decided over 500, 1,000, 3,000 and 5,000 metres)

1936	Kit Klein	(U.S.A.)	Stockholm
1937	Laila Schou-Nilsen	(Norway)	Davos
1938	Laila Schou-Nilsen	(Norway)	Oslo
1939	Verne Lesche	(Finland)	Tammerfors
1940–46	No competition		
1947	Verne Lesche	(Finland)	Drammen
1948	Maria Isakova	(U.S.S.R.)	Turku
1949	Maria Isakova	(U.S.S.R.)	Königsberg
1950	Maria Isakova	(U.S.S.R.)	Moscow
1951	Eva Huttunen	(Finland)	Eskilstuna
1952	Lydia Selichova	(U.S.S.R.)	Kokkola
1953	Khalida Schegoleeva	(U.S.S.R.)	Lillehammer
1954	Lydia Selichova	(U.S.S.R.)	Östersund

Women's Speed Skating—*continued*

1955	Rimma Shukova	(U.S.S.R.)	Kuopio
1956	Sofia Kondakova	(U.S.S.R.)	Kvarnsveden
1957	Inga Artamonova	(U.S.S.R.)	Imatra
1958	Inga Artamonova	(U.S.S.R.)	Kristinehamn
1959	Tamara Rylova	(U.S.S.R.)	Sverdlovsk
1960	Valentina Stenina	(U.S.S.R.)	Östersund
1961	Valentina Stenina	(U.S.S.R.)	Tuzova
1962	Inga Artamonova	(U.S.S.R.)	Imatra
1963	Lydia Skoblikova	(U.S.S.R.)	Karuizawa
1964	Lydia Skoblikova	(U.S.S.R.)	Kristinehamn
1965	Inga Artamonova	(U.S.S.R.)	Piaksamaki
1966	Valentina Stenina	(U.S.S.R.)	Trondheim
1967	Stien Kaiser	(Netherlands)	Deventer
1968	Stien Kaiser	(Netherlands)	Helsinki
1969	Lasma Kauniste	(U.S.S.R.)	Grenoble
1970	Atje Keulen-Deelstra	(Netherlands)	West Allis
1971	Nina Statkevich	(U.S.S.R.)	Helsinki

ICE HOCKEY

1920	Canada	Antwerp
1921–23	No competition	
1924	Canada	Chamonix
1925–27	No competition	
1928	Canada	St Moritz
1929	No competition	
1930	Canada	Chamonix
1931	Canada	Krynica
1932	Canada	Lake Placid
1933	U.S.A.	Prague
1934	Canada	Milan
1935	Canada	Davos
1936	Great Britain	Garmisch
1937	Canada	London
1938	Canada	Prague
1939	Canada	Zürich
1940–46	No competition	
1947	Czechoslovakia	Prague
1948	Canada	St Moritz
1949	Czechoslovakia	Stockholm
1950	Canada	London
1951	Canada	Paris
1952	Canada	Oslo
1953	Sweden	Zürich
1954	U.S.S.R.	Stockholm
1955	Canada	Dusseldorf
1956	U.S.S.R.	Cortina

Ice Hockey—*continued*

1957	Sweden	Moscow
1958	Canada	Oslo
1959	Canada	Prague
1960	U.S.A.	Squaw Valley
1961	Canada	Geneva
1962	Sweden	Colorado Springs
1963	U.S.S.R.	Stockholm
1964	U.S.S.R.	Innsbruck
1965	U.S.S.R.	Tampere
1966	U.S.S.R.	Ljubljana
1967	U.S.S.R.	Vienna
1968	U.S.S.R.	Grenoble
1969	U.S.S.R.	Stockholm
1970	U.S.S.R.	Stockholm
1971	U.S.S.R.	Geneva

CURLING

(Silver Broom, formerly Scotch Cup)

1959	Canada	1965	U.S.A.
1960	Canada	1966	Canada
1961	Canada	1967	Scotland
1962	Canada	1968	Canada
1963	Canada	1969	Canada
1964	Canada	1970	Canada
		1971	Canada

TWO-MAN BOBSLEIGH

1931	Germany (H. Kilia, S. Huber)	Oberhof
1932	U.S.A. (J. Stevens, C. Stevens)	Lake Placid
1933	Rumania (A. Papana, D. Hubert)	Schreiberhau
1934	Rumania (A. Frim, V. Dimitriescu)	Engelberg
1935	Switzerland (R. Capadrutt, E. Diener)	Igls
1936	U.S.A. (I. Brown, A. Washbound)	Garmisch
1937	Great Britain (F. McEvoy, B. Black)	Cortina
1938	Germany (I. Fischer, R. Thielecke)	St Moritz
1939	Belgium (B. Lunden, J. Kuffer)	St Moritz
1940–46	No competition	
1947	Switzerland (F. Fcierabend, S. Waser)	St Moritz
1948	Switzerland (F. Endrich, F. Waller)	St Moritz
1949	Switzerland (F. Endrich, F. Waller)	Lake Placid

Two-Man Bobsleigh—*continued*

1950	Switzerland (F. Feierabend, S. Waser)	Cortina
1951	Germany (A. Ostler, L. Nieberl)	L'Alpe d'Huez
1952	Germany (A. Ostler, L. Nieberl)	Oslo
1953	Switzerland (F. Endrich, F. Stockli)	Garmisch
1954	Italy (G. Scheibmeier, A. Zambelli)	Cortina
1955	Switzerland (F. Feierabend, H. Warbourton)	St Moritz
1956	Italy (U. Dalla Costa, G. Conti)	Cortina
1957	Italy (E. Monti, R. Alvera)	St Moritz
1958	Italy (E. Monti, R. Alvera)	Garmisch
1959	Italy (E. Monti, R. Alvera)	St Moritz
1960	Italy (E. Monti, R. Alvera)	Cortina
1961	Italy (E. Monti, S. Siorpaes)	Lake Placid
1962	Italy (R. Ruatti, E. De Lorenzo)	Garmisch
1963	Italy (E. Monti, S. Zardini)	Igls
1964	Great Britain (A. Nash, R. Dixon)	Igls
1965	Great Britain (A. Nash, R. Dixon)	St Moritz
1966	Italy (E. Monti, S. Siorpaes)	Cortina
1967	Austria (E. Thaler, R. Durnthaler)	Alpe d'Huez
1968	Italy (E. Monti, L. De Paolis)	Alpe d'Huez
1969	Italy (N. De Zordo, A. Frassinelli)	Lake Placid
1970	West Germany (H. Floth, P. Bader)	St Moritz
1971	Italy (G. Gaspari, M. Armano)	Cervinia

FOUR-MAN BOBSLEIGH

1924	Switzerland (E. Scherrer, A. Neveu, A. Schlaeppi, H. Schlaeppi)	Chamonix
1925–26	No competition	
1927	Great Britain (5-man) (N. Martineau, P. Diggle, N. Milles, P. Reid, E. Hall)	St Moritz
1928	U.S.A. (5-man) (B. Fiske, N. Taker, G. Mason, C. Gray, P. Parke)	St Moritz
1929	No competition	
1930	Italy (F. Zanietta, G. Giasini, A. Dorini, G. Rossi)	Caux
1931	Germany (W. Zahn, R. Schmidt, F. Bock, E. Hinderfeld)	St Moritz
1932	U.S.A. (B. Fiske, E. Eagan, C. Gray, J. O'Brien)	Lake Placid
1934	Germany (H. Kilian, F. Schwarz, H. Valta, S. Huber)	Garmisch
1935	Germany (H. Kilian, A. Gruber, H. Valta, F. Schwarz)	St Moritz
1936	Switzerland (P. Musy, A. Gartmann, C. Bouvier, J. Beerli)	Garmisch

153

Four-Man Bobsleigh—*continued*

1937	Great Britain (F. McEvoy, D. Looker, C. Green, B. Black)	St Moritz
1938	Great Britain (F. McEvoy, D. Looker, C. Green, C. Mackintosh)	Garmisch
1939	Switzerland (F. Feierabend, H. Cattani, A. Hoerning, J. Beerli)	Cortina
1940–46	No competition	
1947	Switzerland (F. Feierabend, F. Waller, F. Endrich, S. Wasser)	St Moritz
1948	U.S.A. (F. Tyler, P. Martin, E. Rimkus, W. D'Amico)	St Moritz
1949	U.S.A. (S. Benham, P. Martin, W. Casey, W. D'Amico)	Lake Placid
1950	U.S.A. (S. Benham, P. Martin, J. Atkinson, W. D'Amico)	Cortina
1951	Germany (A. Ostler, L. Nieberl, Z. Leitl, M. Possinger)	Alpe d'Huez
1952	Germany (A. Ostler, L. Nieberl, F. Kuhn, F. Kemser)	Oslo
1953	U.S.A. (L. Johnson, P. Biesiadecki, H. Miller, J. Smith)	Garmisch
1954	Switzerland (F. Feierabend, A. Warburton, G. Diener, H. Angst)	Cortina
1955	Switzerland (F. Kapus, G. Diener, R. Alt, H. Angst)	St Moritz
1956	Switzerland (F. Kapus, G. Diener, R. Alt, H. Angst)	Cortina
1957	Switzerland (F. Zoller, H. Leu, R. Theler, R. Kuderli)	St Moritz
1958	Germany (H. Roesch, A. Hammer, W. Haller, T. Bauer)	Garmisch
1959	U.S.A. (A. Tyler, G. Sheffield, P. Vooris, T. Butler)	St Moritz
1960	Italy (E. Monti, F. Nordio, S. Siorpaes, R. Alvera)	Cortina
1961	Italy (E. Monti, F. Nordio, S. Siorpaes, R. Alvera)	Lake Placid
1962	W. Germany (F. Schelle, O. Goebl, J. Sterff, L. Siebert)	Garmisch
1963	Italy (S. Zardini, R. Bonagura, F. Dalla, T. Mocellini)	Igls
1964	Canada (V. Emery, D. Anakin, J. Emery, P. Kirby)	Igls
1965	Canada (V. Emery, P. Kirby, G. Presley, M. Young)	St Moritz

Four-Man Bobsleigh—*continued*

1968	Italy (E. Monti, L. De Paolis, R. Zandonella, M. Armano)	Alpe d'Huez
1969	W. Germany (W. Zimmerer, S. Geisreiter, W. Steinbauer, P. Utzschneider)	Lake Placid
1970	Italy (N. De Zordo, R. Zandonella, M. Armano, L. de Paolis)	St Moritz
1971	Switzerland (R. Stadler, M. Forster, H. Schaerer, P. Schaerer)	Cervinia

MEN'S LUGE TOBOGGANING

1955	Anton Salvesen	(Norway)	Oslo
1956	No competition		
1957	Hans Schaller	(W. Germany)	Davos
1958	Jerzy Wojnar	(Poland)	Krynica
1959	Herbert Thaler	(Austria)	Villard
1960	Helmuth Berndt	(W. Germany)	Garmisch
1961	Jerzy Wojnar	(Poland)	Girenbad
1962	Thomas Köhler	(E. Germany)	Krynica
1963	Fritz Nachmann	(W. Germany)	Imst
1964	Thomas Köhler	(E. Germany)	Igls
1965	Hans Plenk	(W. Germany)	Davos
1966	No competition		
1967	Thomas Köhler	(E. Germany)	Hammarstrand
1968	Manfred Schmid	(Austria)	Villard
1969	Josef Feistmantl	(Austria)	Königsee
1970	J. Fendt	(W. Germany)	Berchtesgaden
1971	K. Brunner	(Italy)	Valdaora

WOMEN'S LUGE TOBOGGANING

1955	Karla Kienzl	(Austria)	Oslo
1956	No competition		
1957	Maria Isser	(Austria)	Davos
1958	Maria Semczyszak	(Poland)	Krynica
1959	Elly Lieber	(Austria)	Villard
1960	Maria Isser	(Austria)	Garmisch
1961	Elisabeth Naegele	(Switzerland)	Girenbad
1962	Ilse Geisler	(E. Germany)	Krynica
1963	Ilse Geisler	(E. Germany)	Imst
1964	Ortrun Enderlein	(E. Germany)	Igls
1965	Ortrun Enderlein	(E. Germany)	Davos
1967	Ortrun Enderlein	(E. Germany)	Hammarstrand
1968	Erica Lechner	(Italy)	Villard
1969	Petra Tierlich	(W. Germany)	Königsee
1970	B. Piecha	(Poland)	Berchtesgaden
1971	E. Demleitner	(W. Germany)	Valdaora

Two-Seat Luge Tobogganing

1955	Hans Krausner and Josef Thaler	(Austria)	Oslo
1956	No competition		
1957	Josef Strillinger and Fritz Nachmann	(W. Germany)	Davos
1958	Josef Strillinger and Fritz Nachmann	(W. Germany)	Krynica
1959	No competition		
1960	Reinhold Frosch and Ewald Walch	(Austria)	Garmisch
1961	Giorgio Pichler and E. Prinot	(Italy)	Girenbad
1962	Johann Graber and Giampaolo Ambrosi	(Italy)	Krynica
1963	Ryszard Pedrak and Lucjan Kudzia	(Poland)	Imst
1964	Josef Feistmantl and Manfred Stengl	(Austria)	Igls
1965	Wolfgang Scheidel and Michael Köhler	(E. Germany)	Davos
1966	No competition		
1967	Thomas Köhler and Klaus Bonsack	(E. Germany)	Hammarstrand
1968	Thomas Köhler and Klaus Bonsack	(E. Germany)	Villard
1969	Manfred Schmid and Ewald Walch	(Austria)	Königsee
1970	Manfred Schmid and Ewald Walch	(Austria)	Berchtesgaden
1971	P. Hildgartner and K. Plainkner	(W. Germany)	Valdaora

Olympic Review

'May the Olympic Flame shed its light
on all generations and prove a blessing
to mankind on its journey ever upward
to a nobler and a braver world.'

PIERRE DE COUBERTIN

Every four years, skiers, skaters, bobsledders, tobogganists and ice hockey players mingle more than at any other time. The Winter Olympic Games are the highest common denominator of all the snow and ice sports and each Olympiad considerably furthers a mutual understanding and appreciation between participants and followers.

There is something about the Winter Olympic atmosphere which captures imaginations sufficiently to render annual or biennial world championships quite ordinary by comparison. Even world title holders undoubtedly regard an Olympic occasion as the zenith of their careers, each seeking an honour that would be treasured the most.

LONDON, England   October 28–29, 1908

Figure skating was included in the Olympic schedule before other ice and snow sports and 16 years before the first separate Winter Olympics were held. This was because skating has by far the oldest international organisation. The International Skating Union dates from 1892 and world skating championships were already in good order by the turn of the century.

The availability of a suitable indoor ice rink, built for the Prince's Skating Club in 1895, prompted acceptance of figure skating as a convenient part of the IVth summer Olympic Games, held in London in 1908. Participating in the three events were 20 skaters from six nations – Argentine, Germany, Great Britain, Russia, Sweden and U.S.A.

The Swede, Ulrich Salchow, at 31 only two-thirds of the way through his decade of world dominance, gained the men's title with superior figures. Although outpointed in the free-skating by his compatriot, Richard Johansson, Salchow finished with three of the five judges in his favour. Third placed Per Thorén made it a grand slam for Sweden.

The women's victory of Britain's Madge Syers was most impressive. In those days Mrs Syers compared favourably with most men and in fact competed with them in early world championships, coming second to Salchow in 1902. She outclassed her Olympic opponents to gain a unanimous judges' verdict over the German runner-up, Elsa Rendschmidt.

The pairs title was taken comfortably by the Germans, Heinrich Burger and Anna Hübler, against the below-form Britishers, James and Phyllis Johnson. A close third, Edgar Syers must have wondered how much better a pair skater his wife might have been had she not had to concentrate her major training for the singles.

ANTWERP, Belgium   April 23–29, 1920

With World War I intervening, the second Olympic contest in figure skating was not held until 1920, when further Olympic winter sports progress concerned the introduction of ice hockey to the programme at Antwerp Ice Palace, swelling the total ice events entries to 73 men and 12 women from 10 nations.

The ice hockey debut proved a great success, considerably furthering the European popularity of the sport. Seven teams entered and it mattered little that the Canadian winners and American

WINTER SPORTS IN THE IV SUMMER OLYMPIC GAMES 1908

FIGURE SKATING

	Gold	Silver	Bronze
Men	Ulrich Salchow (Sweden)	Richard Johansson (Sweden)	Per Thorén (Sweden)
Women	Madge Syers (Great Britain)	Elsa Rendschmidt (Germany)	Dorothy Greenhough-Smith (Great Britain)
Pairs	Heinrich Burger Anna Hübler (Germany)	James Johnson Phyllis Johnson (Great Britain)	Edgar Syers Madge Syers (Great Britain)

159

runners-up were in a class above Europe's best. The latter had far less experience but subsequently learned fast. That the Czechs and Swedes in turn stood out from the other European teams was a significant omen. Switzerland was humiliated 29–0 by the Americans, who lost 2–0 in their key encounter with Canada.

Following in the wake of his illustrious compatriot, Salchow, Sweden's Gillis Grafström, originator of the flying sit-spin, won the first of his three consecutive gold medals in the men's figure skating. Although shining more in the figures, he was also a clear leader in the freestyle. Salchow, still competing at 42, was fourth of nine competitors despite a knee injury.

Magda Julin-Mauroy set a hot early pace in the women's figures but lapsed badly through nerves in the freestyle. Her ultimate narrow victory was curious because, although none of the judges placed her first, their divided opinions of her rivals varied sufficiently to sway the verdict her way. Another Swede, Svea Norén, was runner-up but the third girl, Theresa Weld of the United States (later to become editor of the American magazine, *Skating*), was a deserving top marker in the free-skating, with jumps of higher quality than her figures.

The pairs event belonged unquestionably to the stylish Finns, Walter and Ludovika Jakobsson. The total skating entries comprised nine men, six women and eight pairs.

CHAMONIX, France   January 25–February 4, 1924

A competitor who finished last at Chamonix was later to become the most famous of all Winter Olympic entrants. It was the international debut of a tiny Norwegian schoolgirl at the incredible age of 11. Her name was Sonja Henie, afterwards to reign as queen of the ice with three Olympic and ten world championship crowns.

With suitable indoor ice available, figure skating had already formed part of the Olympic Games in London in 1908 and again at Antwerp in 1920, when ice hockey was also included. But other snow and ice sports did not gain Olympic status until 1924, when nordic skiers, bobsledders and speed skaters joined figure skaters and ice hockey players at Chamonix in the first self-contained, separate Winter Olympic programme.

It was indeed an historic occasion. It was also the first, but by no means last, Winter Olympics to cause much anxiety about the weather during preceding weeks. This, despite the French Alpine resort's

Stars for Britain – *Above:* Bernard Ford
and Diane Towler, four times world ice
dance champions. *Top left:* Jeannette
Altwegg, 1952 Olympic figure skating
champion. *Below:* Terry Malkin, the
nation's leading Olympic speed skater in
1964

A Norwegian mother and daughter share the happiness of learning to ski

Right: Uschi Stoll (West Germany), prominent ski-bobbing pioneer in the 1950s

WINTER SPORTS IN THE VI SUMMER OLYMPIC GAMES 1920

	Gold	Silver	Bronze
FIGURE SKATING			
Men	Gillis Grafström (Sweden)	Andreas Krogh (Norway)	Martin Stixrud (Norway)
Women	Magda Julin-Mauroy (Sweden)	Svea Norén (Sweden)	Theresa Weld (U.S.A.)
Pairs	Walter Jakobsson Ludovika Jakobsson (Finland)	Yngvar Bryn Alexia Bryn (Norway)	Basil Williams Phyllis Johnson (Great Britain)
ICE HOCKEY	Canada	U.S.A.	Czechoslovakia
	Robert Benson	Raymond Bonney	Adolf Dusek
	Wally Byron	Anthony Conroy	Karel Hartmann
	Frank Fredrickson	Herbert Drury	Vilém Loos
	Chris Fridfinnson	Edward Fitzgerald	Jan Pallausch
	Mike Goodman	George Geran	Jan Peka
	Haldor Halderson	Frank Goheen	Karel Pešek
	Konrad Johannesson	Joseph McCormick	Josef Šroubek
	Huck Woodman	Lawrence McCormick	Otakar Vindyš
		Frank Synott	
		Leon Tuck	
		Cyril Weidenborner	

F

favourable climatic record at the suitable altitude of 1,050 metres (3,443 feet).

A month beforehand, there was not an ounce of snow to be seen. Then, within 24 hours, the locals found three and a half feet had fallen during the night, virtually trapping them in their own homes. Modern snow ploughs and graders had yet to be invented but somehow 36,000 cubic metres (46,800 cubic yards, of snow were cleared from the ice rink into the river Arve.

Then, with a week to go, rain transformed the speed skating oval into a lake. But suddenly frosts returned to provide ideal conditions for a memorable opening ceremony. The official procession assembled outside the town hall and marched through the main streets before entering the first-ever specially built Olympic Ice Stadium.

Gaston Vidalm, French Under-Secretary of State, declared the Games open and the now familiar procedure of standard bearers separating from their teams to form a semi-circle preceded the Olympic oath, spoken by the French skier, Staff Sergeant C. Mandrillon, using similar words to those used ever since.

Fourteen titles were contested by 16 nations, represented by 283 competitors. These comprised 102 skiers, 82 ice hockey players, 39 bobsledders, 31 speed skaters and 29 figure skaters.

The latter group included the only women competitors in the Games, numbering 13, of whom five took part in the pairs as well as their solo event. Three of the men soloists also entered the pairs, making a total of eight figure skaters in dual roles, nowadays generally considered too difficult to attempt because the simultaneous training requirements would mean leaving one's partner too often on the sidelines.

The ice stadium, admirable by the standards of the time, was a complex arena including a 400-metres speed skating perimeter around two ice hockey rinks, with the end semi-circles used by figure skaters. It was an impressive beginning and more than 10,000 spectators watched the main events.

Taking the lion's share of medals, Norway dominated the skiing and Finland emerged the second strongest nation after particular success in the speed skating. The outstanding individuals were the Norwegian skier, Thorleif Haug, and the Finnish speed skater, Clas Thunberg. Each won three gold medals. In addition, Thunberg secured a silver and a bronze and Haug also collected a bronze.

One of Thunberg's gold medals was, in a sense, complimentary, because it was separately awarded for being the best overall performer in the four ice distances, the only time a combination award has been made for Olympic speed skating.

Haug ably spearheaded the Norwegian skiers, who in the 1920s were acknowledged world masters both of cross-country and jumping events. His superiority was most marked in the gruelling 50 kilometres. Only 21 of 33 contestants finished a difficult course made hazardous by several frozen downhill slopes.

Haug's three compatriots took the next places, the four separated by little more than five minutes, but the fifth-placed Swede, Torkel Persson, was more than 21 minutes slower than Haug, and the last to finish, a Pole named Witkowski, was over two and a half hours behind.

The story was much the same in the 18 kilometres. Haug led a Norwegian quartet into four of the top five places, split by a Finn, Tapani Niku, who took the bronze behind Johan Gröttumsbraaten, winner of three gold medals in the two subsequent Winter Olympics.

Haug's versatility was stressed by another comfortable victory in the nordic combination, a challenging test of overall cross-country and jumping skill in which, once more, the top four positions were all taken by Norwegians. A grand slam was also achieved in the specialised jump event on a hill erected with leaps of 60 metres in mind. But the jury shortened the inrun and so lessened the distance potential. Jacob Thams took the title with two leaps of 49 metres in the adjudged best style, though the longest clearance, 50 metres (164 feet), was made by an American, Anders Haugen, who finally finished fourth.

Successful though the Norwegians were in skiing, their eclipse in all the speed skating events was a major surprise because this was also a sport in which the nation had distinguished traditions.

Thunberg convincingly won the two middle distances, 1,500 and 5,000 metres, finishing second to his fellow Finn, Julius Skutnabb, in the 10,000, and tied for third place in the 500 metres sprint won by the American, Charles Jewtraw.

The best overall performance in all four distances gained a third title for Thunberg, but Olympic philosophy has always tended to favour the specialist and no titles for consistency in more than one event have been awarded in subsequent Games, such an honour probably being regarded as a somewhat superfluous bonus, even though overall world titles are still recognised today as the major distinction at speed skating world championship meetings.

The individual gold figure skating medals each went to respected greats in the sport's history. Gillis Grafström, of Sweden, placed first by only four of the seven judges, gained a narrow verdict over his competent Austrian rival, Willy Böckl.

Herma Plank-Szabó, one of the early Viennese stalwarts and world champion for five consecutive years from 1922, took the women's title by unanimous vote. Beatrix Loughran, the American runner-up, was followed by Britain's Ethel Muckelt, with an endearingly diminutive Sonja Henie last in a field of eight. But, even then, the connoisseur could detect unquestionable potential in the Norwegian's smoothly landed jumps and graceful spins.

In the pairs contest, Alfred Berger and Helene Engelmann struck another blow for the Viennese school of technique by outpointing the then better known Finns, Walter and Ludovika Jakobsson. The composition of the partnerships following them underlined the frequency in those days of doubling in solo and pairs events. Andrée Joly, third with Pierre Brunet, was also fifth among the women. The British pair who finished fourth were John Page, the fifth placed man, and Miss Muckelt, the women's bronze medallist.

Bobsledding was confined to one event, for crews of four or five riders. Two-man bobs did not enter the Olympic scene until 1932. The Chamonix bob run at the time was considered pretty hazardous and technically below the top international standards. The Swiss had mixed fortunes. Their number one sled had to withdraw after a serious crash but their second crew, driven by Eduard Scherrer, took the title.

Clocking the fastest times in each of the first three runs, Scherrer played for safety in his fourth descent, when the British number two sled, led by R. H. Broome, was faster but unable to make up the aggregate leeway. More than three full seconds finally separated the winners from the British silver medallists, who were nearly 14 seconds clear of the third placed Belgian crew. This emphasises the subsequent advance to higher speeds and closer times which now frequently differ by mere hundredths of a second.

The ice hockey tournament was, as always since, the big spectator draw and Europeans were dazzled by a transatlantic level which the Continental teams were unable to match. Goals galore in uneven games seldom failed to mesmerise onlookers, who admired and respected a brand of play to which they had not been accustomed.

Canada overwhelmed the rest and the United States team, even though overshadowed by the Canadians, also outclassed the best Europe could offer. The eight contenders were divided into two groups, the top two in each qualifying for a final pool of four, These were Canada, U.S.A., Great Britain and Sweden, finishing in that order.

Canada scored 33 goals without reply against Switzerland. This, not surprisingly, still stands as the Olympic scoring record – an astonishing average rate of less than two minutes per goal throughout 60 minutes' play.

The Canadians also defeated Czechoslovakia 30–0 and Sweden 22–0. Their least one-sided game was a 6–1 victory over U.S.A. – the Americans' only defeat. Great Britain, though losing 2–19, was the only side to score more than once against the champions. A 4–3 win against Sweden, the only match decided by the odd goal, earned Britain the bronze medal.

It is an Olympic tradition that the host country may present in the programme two additional sports as demonstration events, which do not count officially in the results and for which no medals are awarded. One such event is expected to be typical of that practised by the organising nation and the other one relatively strange to it.

At Chamonix, the chosen demonstration events were curling and a military patrol race. Three nations contested the curling, won by the British team led by T. S. Aikman, with Sweden runners-up. The more widely practised rules of Scottish origin were used, as distinct from the German version of curling which was also demonstrated at later Olympics.

The military patrol race, combining skiing and rifle marksmanship over a difficult 30 kilometres course, was a forerunner of the now officially included biathlon but had greater emphasis on team cohesion. The earlier sport had a more martial character than its successor and was especially popular in Switzerland, whose team narrowly defeated Finland, with France third of six nations represented.

A great start had been made in separate Winter Olympics but this was only the beginning. Skating had slipped easily into Olympic

165

gear because it had been internationally organised since the formation of the International Skating Union in 1892. Administratively, skiers were only starting to find their feet. Tobogganing and two-man bobsledding had yet to be included. Alpine skiing was not added until 1948. The biathlon and women's speed skating did not get in before 1960, while curling and dance skating still lobby eagerly for admission.

Now, more than double the number of nations represented at Chamonix send over five times the number of competitors to more than twice the number of events.

St Moritz, Switzerland   February 11–19, 1928

Skeleton tobogganing on the challenging Cresta Run was introduced in the 1928 programme, memorable for Gillis Grafström's third figure skating success and as the first, at the astonishing age of 15, of Sonja Henie's three triumphs – less sensational than it might have been had she not already prepared the way by winning the world championship the previous season.

A sharp increase in the number of entries for the second Winter Olympics reflected the substantial rise in popularity of winter sports during the four years since the first winter Games. Competitors totalling 494 from 25 countries took part. Despite the higher latitude of 1,850 metres (6,066 feet), an unseasonably mild westerly *föhn* wind caused a rapid thaw which affected some performances and caused the 10,000 metres speed skating to be cancelled.

In heavy conditions, Per Erik Hedlund's victory in the 50 kilometres cross-country ski race took 68 minutes longer than Haug in 1924. Swedes took all three medals in this event but it was Norway's turn for a grand slam in the 18 kilometres when, on a contrasting course crackling with frost, Johan Gröttumsbraaten finished two full minutes ahead of two compatriots. In convincing style, Gröttumsbraaten also won the nordic combination, when Norwegians once more monopolised the medals.

Hampered by a short in-run for the take-off, Alf Andersen clinched another gold for Norway in the jumping, after Jacob Tullin-Thams, the title defender, crashed when landing what would have been a winning leap.

The Finnish speed skater, Clas Thunberg, although nearly 35, proved still a master by winning two gold medals for the two shorter distances. But in the 500 metres sprint, Norwegian Bernt Evensen also took a gold with an equal time, the first winter Olympic occasion

THE I WINTER OLYMPIC GAMES 1924

	Gold	Silver	Bronze
NORDIC SKIING			
18 kilometres	Thorleif Haug (Norway)	Johan Gröttumsbraaten (Norway)	Tapani Niku (Finland)
50 kilometres	Thorleif Haug (Norway)	Thoralf Strömstad (Norway)	Johan Gröttumsbraaten (Norway)
Jumping	Jacob Thams (Norway)	Narve Bonna (Norway)	Thorleif Haug (Norway)
Combined	Thorleif Haug (Norway)	Thoralf Strömstad (Norway)	Johan Gröttumsbraaten (Norway)
FIGURE SKATING			
Men	Gillis Grafström (Sweden)	Willy Böckl (Austria)	Georges Gautschi (Switzerland)
Women	Herma Plank-Szabó (Austria)	Beatrix Loughran (U.S.A.)	Ethel Muckelt (Great Britain)
Pairs	Alfred Berger Helene Engelmann (Austria)	Walter Jakobsson Ludovika Jakobsson (Finland)	Pierre Brunet Andrée Joly (France)
SPEED SKATING			
500 metres	Charles Jewtraw (U.S.A.)	Oskar Olsen (Norway)	Roald Larsen (Norway)
1,500 metres	Clas Thunberg (Finland)	Roald Larsen (Norway)	Clas Thunberg (Finland)
5,000 metres	Clas Thunberg (Finland)	Julius Skutnabb (Finland)	Sigurd Moen (Norway)
10,000 metres	Julius Skutnabb (Finland)	Clas Thunberg (Finland)	Roald Larsen (Norway) Roald Larsen (Norway)

	Gold	Silver	Bronze
BOBSLEDDING 4–5-man bobs	Switzerland Eduard Scherrer Alfred Neveu Alfred Schläppi Heinrich Schläppi	Great Britain R. Broome T. Arnold H. Richardson Rodney Soher	Belgium Charles Mulder René Mortiaux Paul van der Broeck V. Verschueren H. Willems
ICE HOCKEY	Canada Jack Cameron Ernest Collett Albert McCaffery Harold McMunn Duncan Munro Beattie Ramsay Cyril Slater Reginald Smith Harry Watson	U.S.A. Clarence Abel Herbert Drury Alphonse Lacroix John Langley John Lyons Justin McCarthy Willard Rice Irving Small Frank Synott	Great Britain W. Anderson Lorne Carr-Harris Colin Carruthers Eric Carruthers Guy Clarkson Ross Cuthbert George Holmes Hamilton Jukes Edward Pitblado Blane Sexton

when two golds were awarded for an individuals' event. The 5,000 metres revealed the early world-beating class of yet another Norwegian, Ivar Ballangrud, later to be recognised as an all-time great.

The figure skating saw the last of Gillis Grafström's three men's victories for Sweden and the first of Sonja Henie's three women's wins for Norway – a master at his peak and a prodigy on the way up. The Austrian, Willy Böckl, closely challenged Grafström all the way while Miss Henie enjoyed a more comfortable passage and introduced a refreshingly more athletic element in women's freestyle. In the pairs event, Pierre Brunet and Andrée Joly set a high standard in well timed lifts.

Despite their home course advantage, the Swiss were disappointing in the five-man bobsleigh event, contested by 23 teams from 14 countries. The thawing course allowed only two runs instead of the usual four. The American sleds took the first two placcs. Jennison Heaton, who drove the second bob, won the first Olympic skeleton toboggan event on the separate Cresta Run, with his brother John in second place, ahead of the British Earl of Northesk.

The ice hockey tournament emphasised the still wide gulf between the Canadians and the ten other competing nations. U.S.A. did not enter and, because of their obvious superiority, the Canadians were granted exemption until the semi-finals, against Sweden, Switzerland and Great Britain. Scoring double figures without conceding a goal against each of the other three (an aggregate of 38–0), Canada displayed complete mastery while the Swedes proved best of the rest by defeating third placed Switzerland 4–0 and Great Britain 3–1. The Swiss beat the British 4–0 to take the bronze medal.

A military patrol ski event was demonstrated at these Games and was a basic forerunner of the biathlon, to be included in 1960. But perhaps the most significant development at St Moritz really took place at the conference table, for it was here that Britain's Arnold Lunn seized an opportunity to persuade the then nordic-biased International Ski Federation to agree in principle on the future Olympic inclusion of alpine skiing, even though the motion took another eight years to reach reality. As someone observed at the time, Lunn's achievement was comparable to a Norwegian getting the rules of cricket changed.

169

THE II WINTER OLYMPIC GAMES 1928

	Gold	Silver	Bronze
NORDIC SKIING			
18 kilometres	Johan Gröttumsbraaten (Norway)	Ole Hegge (Norway)	Reidar Ödegaard (Norway)
50 kilometres	Per Hedlund (Sweden)	Gustaf Jonsson (Sweden)	Volger Andersson (Sweden)
Jumping	Alf Andersen (Norway)	Sigmund Ruud (Norway)	Rudolf Burkert (Czechoslovakia)
Combined	Johan Gröttumsbraaten (Norway)	Hans Vinjarengen (Norway)	John Snersrud (Norway)
FIGURE SKATING			
Men	Gillis Grafström (Sweden)	Willy Böckl (Austria)	Robert van Zeebroeck (Belgium)
Women	Sonja Henie (Norway)	Fritzi Burger (Austria)	Beatrix Loughran (U.S.A.)
Pairs	Pierre Brunet Andrée Joly (France)	Otto Kaiser Lilly Scholz (Austria)	Ludwig Wrede Melitta Brunner (Austria)
SPEED SKATING			
500 metres	Clas Thunberg (Finland) Bernt Evensen (Norway)		John Farrell (U.S.A.) Roald Larsen (Norway) Jaakko Friman (Finland)
1,500 metres	Clas Thunberg (Finland)	Bernt Evensen (Norway)	Ivar Ballangrud (Norway)
5,000 metres	Ivar Ballangrud (Norway)	Julius Skutnabb (Finland)	Bernt Evensen (Norway)

	Gold	Silver	Bronze
BOBSLEDDING			
5-man bobs	U.S.A.	U.S.A.	Germany
	William Fiske	Jennison Heaton	Hanns Kilian
	Nion Tocker	David Granger	Valentin Krempl
	Charles Mason	Lyman Hine	Hans Hess
	Clifford Gray	Thomas Doe	Sebastian Huber
	Richard Parke	Jay O'Brien	Hans Nägle
SKELETON TOBOGGANING	Jennison Heaton	John Heaton	Earl of Northesk
	(U.S.A.)	(U.S.A.)	(Great Britain)
ICE HOCKEY	Canada	Sweden	Switzerland
	Charles Delahey	Carl Abrahamsson	Giannin Andreossi
	Frank Fisher	Emil Bergman	Mezzi Andreossi
	Louis Hudson	Birger Holmqvist	Robert Breiter
	Norbert Mueller	Gustaf Johansson	Louis Dufour
	Herbert Plaxton	Henry Johansson	Charles Fasel
	Hugh Plaxton	Nils Johansson	Albert Geromini
	Roger Plaxton	Ernst Karlberg	Fritz Kraatz
	John Porter	Erik Larsson	Arnold Martignoni
	Frank Sullivan	Bertil Linde	Heini Meng
	Joseph Sullivan	Sigurd Öberg	Anton Morosani
	Ross Taylor	Vilhelm Petersen	Luzius Rüedi
	David Trottier	Kurt Sucksdorff	Richard Torriani

LAKE PLACID, U.S.A.   February 4–15, 1932

A gold medal in each of four consecutive Winter Olympic meetings has never been achieved by one person, but perhaps only a slight injury narrowly prevented this happening in 1932.

The third Winter Olympic Games were the first to be held outside Europe and, because this entailed much longer travel and greater expense for the majority, entries were drastically pruned. The five sports staged were contested by 93 nordic skiers, 39 figure skaters, 41 speed skaters, 41 bobsledders and 48 ice hockey players, a total of only 262 competitors, from 17 nations, compared to 494 from 25 countries for the 1928 gathering at St Moritz.

Scandinavians dominated the four nordic ski events at Lake Placid, at an altitude around 1,860 feet (558 metres) in the northern part of New York State. There were Norwegian grand slams both in the jumping and the combination contests. In unfavourable thawing conditions Birger Ruud, possible the best jumper of all time, came dramatically from behind to pip Hans Beck after the latter had jumped five metres further in his first leap. Beck in his second descent played, as he thought, for safety and Ruud outjumped him by 5.5 metres. Ruud was to add a second gold and a silver in the two subsequent winter Games.

Versatile Johan Gröttumsbraaten, another of Norway's giants, crowned a glorious career by winning the nordic combination for the second time, having also finished third at his first attempt eight years previously.

The 50 kilometres cross-country marathon provided the closest and most exciting duel between the two Finns, Veli Saarinen and Väinö Liikkanen. After nearly four-and-a-half hours of gruelling skiing, Saarinen was just 20 seconds faster than his compatriot, with the third man nearly five minutes behind them. The 18 kilometres was far less close, with Sven Utterström coming in a clear two minutes ahead of his fellow Swede, Axel Wikström.

Sonja Henie, at the zenith of her form, won the second of her three Olympic figure skating victories at these Games, with a unanimous judges' verdict over Fritzi Burger, the Austrian runner-up. But even Sonja's magnetism was overshadowed by the fascinated interest in the men's event. Could that remarkable Swede, Gillis Grafström, win for a fourth successive time at the incredible age of 38?

The new man of the moment was Austrian Karl Schäfer, at 22 a babe by comparison. Schäfer won a thrilling tussle by a 5–2 decision and went on to succeed again four years later. In fairness to Grafström, it must be recorded that a knee injury hampered his performance and probably cost him the distinction of becoming the only person to win an Olympic event for a fourth time. As it was, he still finished clearly ahead of the third placed Canadian, Montgomery Wilson.

The pairs title was retained by the French couple, Pierre and Andrée Brunet, who had married since their previous victory. Their nearest challengers, Americans Sherwin Badger and Beatrix Loughran, came close enough to take better marks from two of the seven judges.

American successes over all four speed skating distances – two each by John Shea and Irving Jaffee – were gained with more than ordinary home ice advantages. For the only time in any Olympic or world speed skating championship, the customary international rules of racing in pairs were temporarily suspended in deference to the American-style 'pack' starts with heats and finals. This meant a revolution in tactics so far as the European competitors were concerned, the strategy of spurting and the use of elbowing technique being completely new to them. The redoubtable Finn, Clas Thunberg, declined to compete in these controversial circumstances and the only two Europeans able to gain medals were the Norwegians, Ivar Ballangrud – the outstanding racer of that era – and Bernt Evensen, second in the 10,000 and 500 metres respectively.

Shea equalled the Olympic record for the 500 metres with a time of 43.4 seconds. But his victory in the 1,500 metres and both the Jaffee longer distance wins were the slowest Olympic successes ever recorded. The Americans were significantly outpaced during the annual world championships, held later on the same track under the normal two-at-a-time racing rules, when Ballangrud won every event.

The ice hockey tournament, a third success in this event for Canada, was notable for a closer American challenge than before and for the smallest entry the Olympic series has ever had. With Germany and Poland Europe's sole representatives, only four teams competed – each playing the other twice. In the two Canada-U.S.A. matches which settled the issue, the Canadians won the first 2–1 in extra time and drew the other 2–2 after three additional periods.

The bobsleigh course, well sited on Mount Van Hoevenberg in the

Adirondacks, was longer and more dangerous than the one there today. Stretching a mile and a half instead of the since more generally approved mile, this was a challenging, snake-like track demanding particular skill at the now famous Shady Corner and Zigzag turns.

Training crashes put one German sled and crew out of action. An American bob was substituted and extra riders were hastily recruited from German residents in the United States. The status of bobsledding increased with the Olympic debut of two-man sleds, only events for four-man bobs having been held at the two previous winter Games.

With the obvious advantage of home track familiarity, U.S. bobs won both events. Retaining the four-man title gained in 1928, William Fiske steered cleverly for his second victory in two Winter Olympics. One of Fiske's crew, Clifford Gray, had also shared in the earlier triumph and the two thus became the first bobsledders to win second gold medals. The American number two crew, led by Henry Homburger, took an aggregate 2.2 seconds longer for the four runs to clinch the silver. In the two-man event, the American brothers, Hubert and Curtis Stevens, had only 1.44 seconds in hand over the runner-up Swiss bob guided by Reto Capadrutt.

The supporting demonstration events at Lake Placid, contested only by Americans and Canadians, comprised a curling tournament, dogsleigh races and women's speed skating.

GARMISCH, Germany   February 6–16, 1936

A disbelieving 14,000 packed the elaborate new Olympic Ice Stadium to watch Carl Erhardt lead Britain's ice hockey players in an historic defeat of Canada, the acknowledged masters of the game who had won every previous Olympic contest. This dramatic form upset was brought about by beating the Canadians 2–1 and, in the final game, holding the United States to a scoreless draw sufficient for overall victory.

In those pre-television days Bob Giddens, then a distinguished writer on the sport, recorded how Britain received the news from the B.B.C. radio commentator, Bob Bowman. 'Almost hysterical but brilliantly fluent, Bowman poured excited words into his mike which told folks with their heads halfway down their loudspeakers that now, before his eyes, the British team had achieved a miracle. By beating Canada, Britain had cured the complex, so deeply bedded in European minds, that Canada was invincible.'

THE III WINTER OLYMPIC GAMES 1932

	Gold	Silver	Bronze
NORDIC SKIING			
18 kilometres	Sven Utterström (Sweden)	Axel Wikström (Sweden)	Veli Saarinen (Finland)
50 kilometres	Veli Saarinen (Finland)	Väinö Liikkanen (Finland)	Arne Rustadstuen (Norway)
Jumping	Birger Ruud (Norway)	Hans Beck (Norway)	Karre Wahlberg (Norway)
Combined	Johan Gröttumsbraaten (Norway)	Ole Stenen (Norway)	Hans Vinjarengen (Norway)
FIGURE SKATING			
Men	Karl Schäfer (Austria)	Gillis Grafström (Sweden)	Montgomery Wilson (Canada)
Women	Sonja Henie (Norway)	Fritzi Burger (Austria)	Maribel Vinson (U.S.A.)
Pairs	Pierre Brunet Andrée Brunet (France)	Sherwin Badger Beatrix Loughran (U.S.A.)	László Szollás Emilia Rotter (Hungary)
SPEED SKATING			
500 metres	John Shea (U.S.A.)	Bernt Evensen (Norway)	Alexander Hurd (Canada)
1,500 metres	John Shea (U.S.A.)	Alexander Hurd (Canada)	William Logan (Canada)
5,000 metres	Irving Jaffee (U.S.A.)	Edward Murphy (U.S.A.)	William Logan (Canada)
10,000 metres	Irving Jaffee (U.S.A.)	Ivar Ballangrud (Norway)	Frank Stack (Canada)

	Gold	Silver	Bronze
BOBSLEDDING			
2-man bobs	U.S.A.	Switzerland	U.S.A.
	Hubert Stevens	Reto Capadrutt	John Heaton
	Curtis Stevens	Oscar Geier	Robert Minton
4-man bobs	U.S.A.	U.S.A.	Germany
	William Fiske	Henry Homburger	Hanns Kilian
	Edward Eagan	Percy Bryant	Max Ludwig
	Clifford Gray	Francis Stevens	Hans Mehlhorn
	Jay O'Brien	Edmund Horton	Sebastian Huber
ICE HOCKEY	Canada	U.S.A.	Germany
	William Cockburn	Osborn Anderson	Rudi Ball
	Clifford Crowley	John Bent	Alfred Heinrich
	Albert Duncanson	John Chase	Erich Herker
	George Garbutt	John Cookman	Gustav Jaenecke
	Roy Hinkel	Douglas Everett	Werner Korff
	Victor Lindquist	Franklin Farrell	Walter Leinweber
	Norman Malloy	Joseph Fitzgerald	Erich Römer
	Walter Monson	Edward Frazier	Marquardt Slevogt
	Kenneth Moore	John Garrison	Martin Schröttle
	Romeo Rivers	Gerard Hallock	Georg Strobl
	Harold Simpson	Robert Livingston	
	Hugh Sutherland	Francis Nelson	
	Stanley Wagner	Winthrop Palmer	
	Aliston Wise	Gordon Smith	

With fewer reserves carried than today, a 12-strong team accomplished what had seemed an impossible task – Sandy Archer, James Borland, Ed Brenchley, Jimmy Chappell, John Coward, Gordon Dailley, John Davey, Carl Erhardt, Jimmy Foster, John Kilpatrick, Archie Stinchcombe and Bob Wyman.

The fourth Winter Olympic Games, staged in and around the picturesque Bavarian resort of Garmisch-Partenkirchen, attracted a then record entry of 755 competitors from 28 nations, with Australia, Bulgaria, Greece, Liechtenstein, Spain and Turkey participating for the first time.

The undoubted success of a separate winter Olympic meeting and the greatness of its potential were now clearly evident. With the host country intent on prestige, money was available to organise on a scale hitherto unparalleled. The easily accessible location, midway between Munich and Innsbruck, enabled half a million spectators to attend the 17 events.

Baron Pierre de Coubertin, founder of the modern Olympic series, for the first time excused himself from attending the opening ceremony. It was Hitler's turn to inaugurate the Games and, though no serious political incident occurred, the appearance of the swastika ominously heralded what was to be the last Winter Olympics for 12 years.

Alpine skiing was included for the first time and, when a crowd of 70,000 turned up to see the men's slalom, Britain's pioneering Arnold Lunn, who was referee, must have been a very proud man to see his brain child so enthusiastically acclaimed. Men's and women's downhill and slalom contests were held, but medals were awarded only to the best overall performers. The combination winners, Franz Pfnür and Christel Cranz, were both Germans – and Fräulein Cranz was thus victor of the first Olympic skiing event for women.

Women were not yet represented in nordic skiing or speed skating, which probably deprived a remarkably versatile Norwegian girl of greater fame. Schou Nilsen, only 16, dominated the downhill and took the bronze medal in the alpine combination. It was a sensational achievement for a prominent tennis player of the day who held no fewer than five world women's speed skating records as well.

Scandinavians, not surprisingly, monopolised the nordic skiing honours. Swedes won both the individual cross-country races, the gruelling 50 kilometres test of endurance going to Elis Wiklund and the relatively short 18 kilometres to Erik Larsson. A Finnish quartet took the first Olympic relay title to be contested, beating the Norwegians by only six seconds – a small margin indeed after four legs of 10 kilometres each.

Oddbjörn Hagen retained the nordic combination for Norway. His stylish compatriot, Birger Ruud, with leaps of 75 and 77.5 metres, withstood a spirited challenge from the Swede, Sven Eriksson, in the special ski jumping. For this, 150,000 awe-struck onlookers clustered round the 'horse-shoe' below the impressive, newly constructed Olympic jump tower, which remains to this day a spectacular landmark overlooking Garmisch.

After four Olympiads, Norway proudly remained undefeated in ski jumping, thanks to Ruud. But the real star of the Garmisch Games was Norwegian speed skater Ivar Ballangrud. In his third Olympics and less than a month from his 32nd birthday, Ballangrud won three gold medals, for the 500, 5,000 and 10,000 metres, and also took the silver in the 1,500 metres, just one second slower than his fellow countryman, Charles Mathiesen.

The figure skating inevitably will be remembered most for the third Olympic victory of Sonja Henie, who became a legend in her own time. But whereas the great Sonja had clearly dominated four years previously, the gap between her rivals had now decreased. Though eight years Sonja's junior, Britain's Cecilia Colledge, who was to become world champion the following season, proved a dangerous challenger. No longer did Sonja enjoy a unanimous verdict, one judge placing the two girls equal, and the Norwegian was probably wise to turn professional soon afterwards.

Karl Schäfer, a star pupil of the Vienna Skating School's most glorious era, comfortably retained the men's crown he had captured in 1932. His nearest challenger, Ernst Baier, was compensated with a hard-earned victory for Germany in the pairs contest, partnered by his future wife, Maxi Herber.

It was something of a cliff-hanger, with a young Viennese brother and sister, Erik and Ilse Pausin, stealing the spectators' hearts with a skilful interpretation of a lilting Strauss waltz. The Germans' more experienced technique split the judges 7–2 in their favour.

The new, steeply banked Riessersee bobsleigh course did not see the home success which many had expected. With Alan Washbond as brakeman, Ivan Brown piloted the United States boblet to victory, just half a second clear of the Swiss sled driven by Fritz Feierabend.

The Swiss made no mistake in the four-man event, their second and first crews – led by Pierre Musy and Reto Capadrutt respectively – taking gold and silver medals in that order, with Fred McEvoy guiding the British sled home for the bronze.

Two demonstration events, as had now become a customary feature of the Winter Olympics, were a ski military patrol race, forerunner of the present-day biathlon, and German-style curling. No medals are awarded for these supporting contests. The skiing and shooting, over a 25 kilometres course, produced an unexpected Italian victory led by Capt. Silvestri. The curling honours went to Austria.

ST MORITZ, Switzerland   January 30–February 8, 1948
The fifth Winter Olympic meeting was originally scheduled for 1940 at Sapporo, Japan, but World War II intervened and Sapporo had to wait another 32 years. The selection of St Moritz for a second time was influenced by early post-war conditions when the Games were resumed in 1948.

The Swiss resort's already existing facilities appealed, as did its geographical and political suitability. The atmosphere throughout the programme appeared to be that of a brave front being put up by Europeans still suffering in many respects from the aftermath of war, but the important thing was that the Olympic flame could be re-kindled in spite of countless frustrations.

In the circumstances, the entry of 28 nations was encouraging, equal to that of 1936, though the total number of competitors, 636 men and 77 women, fell 40 short of the Garmisch figures – understandably, in view of various travel and financial problems which also greatly reduced the numbers of spectators. For the first time, there were Chilean, Danish, Icelandic, Korean and Lebanese competitors.

The development of alpine skiing since 1936 justified the extension of medals for these competitions to include separate awards for downhill, slalom and combined. Significantly, 25 nations were represented in the downhill – 10 more than in any nordic ski event. Ideal weather was temporarily interrupted by a thawing *föhn* wind, less severe than 20 years previously, but sufficient to affect the 10,000 metres speed skating and some of the ice hockey matches. Fortunately, no event had to be cancelled.

The Swedes proved supreme in the cross-country skiing, taking all three medals in the 18 kilometres, first two places in the 50 kilo-

THE IV WINTER OLYMPIC GAMES 1936

	Gold	Silver	Bronze
NORDIC SKIING			
18 kilometres	Erik Larsson (Sweden)	Oddbjörn Hagen (Norway)	Pekka Niemi (Finland)
50 kilometres	Elis Wiklund (Sweden)	Axel Wikström (Sweden)	Nils Englund (Sweden)
Relay, 4 × 10 kilometres	Sulo Nurmela, Klaes Karppinen, Matti Lähde, Kalle Jalkanen — Finland	Oddbjörn Hagen, Olav Hoffsbakken, Sverre Brodahl, Bjarne Iversen — Norway	John Berger, Erik Larsson, Artur Häggblad, Martin Matsbo — Sweden
Jumping	Birger Ruud (Norway)	Sven Eriksson (Sweden)	Reidar Andersen (Norway)
Combined	Oddbjörn Hagen (Norway)	Olaf Hoffsbakken (Norway)	Sverre Brodahl (Norway)
ALPINE SKIING: MEN			
Combined	Franz Pfnür (Germany)	Gustav Lantschner (Germany)	Emile Allais (France)
ALPINE SKIING: WOMEN			
Combined	Christel Cranz (Germany)	Käthe Grasegger (Germany)	Laila Nilsen (Norway)
FIGURE SKATING			
Men	Karl Schäfer (Austria)	Ernst Baier (Germany)	Felix Kaspar (Austria)
Women	Sonja Henie (Norway)	Cecilia Colledge (Great Britain)	Vivi-Anne Hultén (Sweden)
Pairs	Ernst Baier, Maxi Herber (Germany)	Erik Pausin, Ilse Pausin (Austria)	László Szollás, Emilia Rotter (Hungary)
SPEED SKATING			
500 metres	Ivar Ballangrud (Norway)	Georg Krog (Norway)	Leo Freisinger (U.S.A.)

		Gold	Silver	Bronze
SPEED SKATING	1,500 metres	Charles Mathiesen (Norway)	Ivar Ballangrud (Norway)	Birger Wasenius (Finland)
	5,000 metres	Ivar Ballangrud (Norway)	Birger Wasenius (Finland)	Antero Ojala (Finland)
	10,000 metres	Ivar Ballangrud (Norway)	Birger Wasenius (Finland)	Max Stiepl (Austria)
BOBSLEDDING	2-man bobs	U.S.A. Ivan Brown Alan Washbond	Switzerland Fritz Feierabend Joseph Beerli	U.S.A. Gilbert Colgate Richard Lawrence Great Britain Frederick McEvoy James Cardno Guy Dugdale Charles Green
	4-man bobs	Switzerland Pierre Musy Arnold Gartmann Charles Bouvier Joseph Beerli	Switzerland Reto Capadrutt Hans Aichele Fritz Feierabend Hans Bütikofer	
ICE HOCKEY		Great Britain Alex Archer James Borland Edgar Brenchley James Chappell John Coward Gordon Dailley John Davey Carl Erhardt James Foster John Kilpatrick Archie Stinchcombe Robert Wyman	Canada Maxwell Deacon Hugh Farquharson Kenneth Farmer James Haggarty Walter Kitchen Raymond Milton Francis Moore Herman Murray Arthur Nash David Neville Ralph St Germain Alex Sinclair William Thomson	U.S.A. John Garrison August Kammer Philip La Batte John Lax Thomas Moone Eldridge Ross Paul Rowe Francis Shaughnessy Gordon Smith Francis Spain Frank Stubbs

181

metres, and leading the Finnish runners-up by nine seconds in the team relay.

Martin Lundström, victor of the 18 kilometres, got his second gold medal in the relay but the Swedish strength in depth was underlined by the ability to win the latter without the services of Nils Karlsson, an impressive 50 kilometres champion despite being more troubled than most by an altitude to which he was unaccustomed.

The all-round ability of two Finns earned gold and silver in the nordic combination for Heikki Hasu and Martti Huhtala. Switzerland's Niklaus Stump, fourth, achieved the highest nordic place yet by a central European, with the best Norwegian sixth.

The Norwegians re-asserted their traditional supremacy in the jumping, taking all the medals for an event in which they had yet to concede first place. The winner, Petter Hugsted, owed his victory more to near-perfect style than to sheer distance, his longest leap falling three metres short of the 138 metres covered by the fourth placed Finn, Matti Pietikainen, whose posture cannot have pleased the judges. At 36, Birger Ruud gained a noteworthy silver medal 16 years after his first gold for the same event.

In the men's alpine skiing, a downhill triumph with more than four seconds in hand and third place in the slalom gave the Frenchman Henri Oreiller, the academic combined title to total two gold medals and a bronze. Edi Reinalter won the slalom for Switzerland with an aggregate for the two runs just half a second faster than another Frenchman, James Couttet.

The women's honours were shared by three nations. Hedy Schlunegger took the downhill for Switzerland. Gretchen Frazer, at 29, was a surprise American slalom winner – the first skiing medal to be won by the United States. Austrian Trude Beiser, second in the downhill, was unplaced in the slalom but her overall performance was just good enough to pip Miss Frazer for the combined title.

The figure skating saw a transatlantic freestyle eclipse by American Dick Button and Canadian Barbara Ann Scott. They gave Europe a first glimpse of the new American school of theatrical athleticism in jumps. Displaying physical strength and suppleness, Button was the forerunner of a revolutionary trend that was to characterise future men's free-skating.

The more orthodox Swiss, Hans Gerschwiler, held second place only by virtue of his figures, outpointed in freestyle by another American, John Lettengarver. Miss Scott serenely withstood fierce pressure from Britain's Jeannette Altwegg in the figures and by the Austrian, Eva Pawlik, in the free-skating.

The Belgians, Pierre Baugniet and Micheline Lannoy, a gracefully authentic partnership, clinched the pairs title after a resolute Hungarian bid from Ede Király and Andrea Kékessy.

Norwegians won three of the four speed skating events. Finn Helgesen snatched the 500 metres by a tenth of a second from his compatriot, Thomas Byberg, and the two Americans, Ken Bartholomew and Robert Fitzgerald, whose equal times earned the first Winter Olympic triple tie for silver medals.

Sverre Farstad won the 1,500 metres and Reidar Liaklev the 5,000. But the Swede, Åke Seyffarth, was the most noteworthy speed skater on view. Decisive winner of the 10,000 metres with nearly ten seconds to spare, he was also runner-up in the 1,500 – a powerful racer who had passed his peak form, having established world records over two distances during the war years.

An intimate knowledge of their home course enabled the Swiss to secure gold and silver medals in the two-man bobsleigh event. The Americans took first and third places in their four-man sleds, separated by a Belgian crew in second spot.

Skeleton tobogganing made its second Olympic appearance on the Cresta Run. The event provided Italy's first gold medal in winter sports, thanks to the rare skill of Nino Bibbia, the cleverest exponent the course had known, due largely to his being a St Moritz resident. Also regularly familiar with the course, American John Heaton gained a notable silver medal – repeating his achievement of 20 years previously, when runner-up to his brother Jennison.

The Canadians recaptured the ice hockey title, avenging their unexpected defeat by the British in 1936, but only by a goal-average verdict over the Czechs. Each won seven of their eight matches, their direct encounter ending in a rare goal-less stalemate. The Czech line-up included a player who gained greater fame as a tennis player, Jaroslav Drobny.

There was confusion and embarrassment concerning the American ice hockey entry. Two United States teams arrived at St Moritz and the one eventually allowed to compete finished fourth, only to be disqualified by the I.O.C. because it was not affiliated to the American Olympic Association.

Two supporting demonstration events were a military patrol ski race, won by the host nation in a field of eight teams, and an enterprising winter pentathlon, comprising cross-country skiing, pistol shooting, a downhill race, fencing and horse-riding. In this widely varied combination the Swedes proved best.

This second St Moritz Winter Olympic presentation determinedly overcame unenviable difficulties and emphasised the compactness and easy access of all the sites, in very favourable comparison to some of the subsequent venues. The palpable will to revive the Games was a heartening element.

OSLO, Norway   February 14–25, 1952

With the first winter Olympic events to be staged near a capital city, the Oslo Games drew a new record entry of 30 nations, including the first post-war return of Germany and Japan and the debuts of New Zealand and Portugal. But the total number of competitors, 623 men and 109 women, fell slightly short of the 1936 figures.

The cross-country races and ski jumping at Holmenkollen were only a few miles from the city centres. The slalom events were held at the nearby Rödkleiva slope. All the ice sports were within the Oslo area but the downhill and giant slalom had to be run at Norefjell, 120 kilometres (75 miles) north-west of Oslo.

It was the first time the Games had gone to the country which pioneered sport on skis and, appropriately, the Olympic flame was lit not in Greece, as had been the custom, but in Morgedal, the village in the Norwegian province of Telemark where Sondre Nordheim, 'the father of skiing', had been born 127 years previously.

Ninety-four un-named skiers carried the torch along the 220 kilometres (137 miles) route to Oslo, where Eigil Nansen, grandson of the Norwegian explorer, Fridtjof Nansen, ran the final lap in the Bislet Stadium. In an emotional opening, the Norwegian flag was lowered to half-mast while a minute's silence respected news of the death of Britain's King George VI, the first Olympic occasion on which anything of the kind had happened.

Attendance statistics were remarkable. There were 541,407 paying spectators. More than 130,000 watched the four speed skating competitions, 110,000 attended ice hockey matches at the new Jordal Amfi rink. Over 28,000 packed the Bislet arena for each figure skating final and the opening and closing ceremonies; 10,000 lined the cross-country ski courses, 25,000 saw the slalom and 130,000 gathered for the ski jumping finale.

THE V WINTER OLYMPIC GAMES 1948

	Gold	Silver	Bronze
NORDIC SKIING			
18 kilometres	Martin Lundström (Sweden)	Nils Östensson (Sweden)	Gunnar Eriksson (Sweden)
50 kilometres	Nils Karlsson (Sweden)	Harald Eriksson (Sweden)	Benjamin Vanninen (Finland)
Relay, 4 × 10 kilometres	Sweden	Finland	Norway
	Nils Östensson Nils Täpp Gunnar Eriksson Martin Lundström	Lauri Silvennoinen Teuvo Laukkanen Sauli Rytky August Kiuru	Erling Evensen Olaf Økern Reidar Nyborg Olav Hagen
Jumping	Petter Hugsted (Norway)	Birger Ruud (Norway)	Thorleif Schjelderup (Norway)
Combined	Heikki Hasu (Finland)	Martti Huhtala (Finland)	Sven Israelsson (Sweden)
ALPINE SKIING: MEN			
Downhill	Henri Oreiller (France)	Franz Gabl (Austria)	Karl Molitor (Switzerland) Rolf Olinger (Switzerland)
Slalom	Edi Reinalter (Switzerland)	James Couttet (France)	Henri Oreiller (France)
Combined	Henri Oreiller (France)	Karl Molitor (Switzerland)	James Couttet (France)
ALPINE SKIING: WOMEN			
Downhill	Hedy Schlunegger (Switzerland)	Trude Beiser (Austria)	Resi Hammerer (Austria)
Slalom	Gretchen Frazer (U.S.A.)	Antoinette Meyer (Switzerland)	Erika Mahringer (Austria)

	Gold	Silver	Bronze
ALPINE SKIING: WOMEN			
Combined	Trude Beiser (Austria)	Gretchen Frazer (U.S.A.)	Erika Mahringer (Austria)
FIGURE SKATING			
Men	Richard Button (U.S.A.)	Hans Gerschwiler (Switzerland)	Edi Rada (Austria)
Women	Barbara Scott (Canada)	Eva Pawlik (Austria)	Jeannette Altwegg (Great Britain)
Pairs	Pierre Baugniet Micheline Lannoy (Belgium)	Ede Király Andrea Kékessy (Hungary)	Wallace Diestelmeyer Suzanne Morrow (Canada)
SPEED SKATING			
500 metres	Finn Helgesen (Norway)	Kenneth Bartholomew (U.S.A.) Thomas Byberg (Norway) Robert Fitzgerald (U.S.A.)	
1,500 metres	Sverre Farstad (Norway)	Åke Seyffarth (Sweden)	Odd Lundberg (Norway)
5,000 metres	Reidar Liaklev (Norway)	Odd Lundberg (Norway)	Göthe Hedlund (Sweden)
10,000 metres	Åke Seyffarth (Sweden)	Lauri Parkkinen (Finland)	Pentti Lammio (Finland)
BOBSLEDDING			
2-man bobs	Switzerland Felix Endrich Fritz Waller U.S.A.	Switzerland Fritz Feierabend Paul Eberhard Belgium	U.S.A. Fred Fortune Schuyler Carron U.S.A.

	Gold	Silver	Bronze
SPEED SKATING			
4-man bobs	Francis Tyler	Max Houben	James Bickford
	Patrick Martin	Freddy Mansveld	Thomas Hicks
	Edward Rimkus	Georges Niels	Donald Dupree
	William D'Amico	Jacques Mouvet	William Dupree
SKELETON TOBOGGANING			
	Nino Bibbia	John Heaton	John Crammond
	(Italy)	(U.S.A.)	(Great Britain)
ICE HOCKEY			
	Canada	Czechoslovakia	Switzerland
	Murray Dowey	Vladimir Bouzek	Hans Bänninger
	Bernard Dunster	Augustin Bubnik	Alfred Bieler
	Orval Gravelle	Jaroslav Drobny	Heinrich Boller
	Patrick Guzzo	Přemysl Hajny	Ferdinand Cattini
	Walter Halder	Zdenek Jarkovsky	Hans Cattini
	Thomas Hibbert	Stanislav Konopásek	Hans Dürst
	Ross King	Bohumil Modry	Walter Dürst
	Henri Laperrire	Miloslav Pokorny	Emil Handschin
	John Lecompte	Václav Rozinák	Heini Lohrer
	George Mara	Miroslav Sláma	Werner Lohrer
	Albert Renaud	Karel Stibor	Reto Perl
	Reginald Schroeter	Vilém Štovik	Gebhard Poltera
		Ladislav Troják	Ulrich Poltera
		Josef Trousilek	Beat Rüedi
		Oldřich Zábrodsky	Otto Schubiger
		Vladimir Zábrodsky	Richard Torriani
			Hans Trepp

187

Hallgeir Brenden regained the 18 kilometres ski sprint title for Norway for the first time since Gröttumsbraaten's success in 1928. Simon Slattvik scored another home triumph in the nordic combination, but Finland took the honours in the team relay and the 50 kilometres, when the great Veikko Hakulinen finished a full five minutes ahead of the field to lay the foundation of an impressive career. All three medals also went to Finns in the first Olympic women's cross-country ski race, over 10 kilometres, won by the robust and well-schooled Lydia Wideman.

A Scandinavian monopoly of the nordic events was not so surprising as the significant success of the stylish Norwegian alpine skier, Stein Eriksen. His giant slalom gold and slalom silver epitomised the rising skill of north Europeans in this kind of skiing. Othmar Schneider gained slalom gold and downhill silver for Austria, but the downhill was won by an Italian, Zeno Colò. Twenty-seven nations were represented in the men's downhill and slalom, more than in any other event.

Andrea Mead-Lawrence was the most successful woman alpine racer, winning both the slalom and the giant slalom, but a crash put paid to her chances in the downhill, won by the Austrian, Trude Jochum-Beiser.

The outstanding individual of these Games was the Norwegian speed skater, Hjalmar Andersen, who took three gold medals for the 1,500, 5,000 and 10,000 metres, setting new Olympic times for the two longest distances. His strength at the time is underlined by the fact that, only a week previously at Hamar, Norway, he set a world record for 10,000 metres which stood until 1960. Ken Henry won the 500 metres sprint for the United States.

Dick Button repeated his 1948 success in the men's figure skating, when the stress and strain of arduous practice led to his achieving the first real triple loop jump in a comfortable victory. Excellent figure tracings, perhaps the nearest to perfection yet achieved, gained the women's gold medal for Britain's Jeannette Altwegg, even though she was surpassed in freestyle by the spectacular French girl, Jacqueline du Bief, and two Americans, Tenley Albright and Virginia Baxter.

This was Miss Altwegg's farewell championship appearance and, instead of following the vogue to capitalise in professional ranks, she won worldwide admiration by accepting a post at the Pestalozzi children's village in Trogen, Switzerland. The pair skating went to the German husband and wife team, Paul and Ria Falk, whose precision timing in lifts and skilful 'shadow' jumps and spins was superb.

Germans also excelled in the bobsleigh events, cashing in on their then quite legitimate weight advantage. Driver Anderl Ostler and brakeman Lorenz Nieberl were in both winning crews. In each case, the issue was decided by a winning margin of more than two seconds.

The Americans and Swiss were second and third in both events, each time guided by Stan Benham and Fritz Feierabend respectively. The result prompted the International Bobsleigh Federation to amend the rules, limiting maximum combined weights of sleds and riders to create more equal conditions.

Nine nations contested the ice hockey tournament, again won by the Canadians, but this sixth success in seven Olympics was to prove their last for a very long time. In eight games Canada conceded only one point, in a tie with U.S.A. The Americans were runners-up after losing one match to the Swedes, who finished level third on points with the Czechs. In an exciting bronze medal decider, Sweden won 5–3 after the Czechs had established a three-goal lead.

In interesting contrast, bandy – the 11-a-side skating ball game with curved-bladed sticks – was chosen for an official demonstration competition. In this, Sweden emerged victorious from a triple contest against Norway and Finland.

The ski jumping at Holmenkollen was a fitting climax to the Games. As a people's sporting festival, it could in some ways be likened to England's Derby Day at Epsom. Gay laughter among countless privately organised parties on the snow heralded the main proceedings, but in the great horse-shoe shaped area of spectators massed at the foot of the famous hill there was rapt attention when, one by one, the world's greatest exponents made their appearance in a fascinating succession of graceful arcs described by jumpers borne on the wings of applause. Happily for the majority present, local hero Arnfinn Bergmann retained the title for Norway.

CORTINA, Italy   January 26–February 5, 1956

More competitors from more nations took part in more events than in any previous Winter Olympics when the seventh quadrennial programme was colourfully staged in and around the picturesque Italian resort of Cortina d'Ampezzo, overlooked by magnificent snow-

THE VI WINTER OLYMPIC GAMES 1952

	Gold	Silver	Bronze
NORDIC SKIING: MEN			
18 kilometres	Hallgeir Brenden (Norway)	Tapio Mäkelä (Finland)	Paavo Lonkila (Finland)
50 kilometres	Veikko Hakulinen (Finland)	Eero Kolehmainen (Finland)	Magnar Estenstad (Norway)
Relay, 4 × 10 kilometres	Finland	Norway	Sweden
	Heikki Hasu	Magnar Estenstad	Nils Täpp
	Paavo Lonkila	Mikal Kirkholt	Sigurd Andersson
	Urppo Korhonen	Martin Stokken	Enar Josefsson
	Tapio Mäkelä	Hallgeir Brenden	Martin Lundström
Jumping	Arnfinn Bergmann (Norway)	Torbjörn Falkanger (Norway)	Karl Holmström (Sweden)
Combined	Simon Slåttvik (Norway)	Heikki Hasu (Finland)	Sverre Stenersen (Norway)
NORDIC SKIING: WOMEN			
10 kilometres	Lydia Wideman (Finland)	Mirja Hietamies (Finland)	Siiri Rantanen (Finland)
ALPINE SKIING: MEN			
Downhill	Zeno Colò (Italy)	Othmar Schneider (Austria)	Christian Pravda (Austria)
Slalom	Othmar Schneider (Austria)	Stein Eriksen (Norway)	Guttorm Berge (Norway)
Giant Slalom	Stein Eriksen (Norway)	Christian Pravda (Austria)	Toni Spiess (Austria)
ALPINE SKIING: WOMEN			
Downhill	Trude Jochum-Beiser (Austria)	Annemarie Buchner (Germany)	Giuliana Minuzzo (Italy)

	Gold	Silver	Bronze
ALPINE SKIING WOMEN:			
Slalom	Andrea Mead-Lawrence (U.S.A.)	Ossi Reichert (Germany)	Annemarie Buchner (Germany)
Giant Slalom	Andrea Mead-Lawrence (U.S.A.)	Dagmar Rom (Austria)	Annemarie Buchner (Germany)
FIGURE SKATING			
Men	Richard Button (U.S.A.)	Helmut Seibt (Austria)	James Grogan (U.S.A.)
Women	Jeannette Altwegg (Great Britain)	Tenley Albright (U.S.A.)	Jacqueline du Bief (France)
Pairs	Paul Falk Ria Falk (Germany)	Michael Kennedy Karol Kennedy (U.S.A.)	László Nagy Marianna Nagy (Hungary)
SPEED SKATING			
500 metres	Kenneth Henry (U.S.A.)	Donald McDermott (U.S.A.)	Arne Johansen (Norway) Gordon Audley (Canada)
1,500 metres	Hjalmar Andersen (Norway)	Willem van der Voort (Netherlands)	Roald Aas (Norway)
5,000 metres	Hjalmar Andersen (Norway)	Kees Broekman (Netherlands)	Sverre Haugli (Norway)
10,000 metres	Hjalmar Andersen (Norway)	Kees Broekman (Netherlands)	Carl-Erik Asplund (Sweden)
BOBSLEDDING	Germany	U.S.A.	Switzerland

191

	Gold	Silver	Bronze
BOBSLEDDING			
2-man bobs	Andreas Ostler	Stanley Benham	Fritz Feierabend
	Lorenz Nieberl	Patrick Martin	Stephan Waser
	Germany	U.S.A.	Switzerland
4-man bobs	Andreas Ostler	Stanley Benham	Fritz Feierabend
	Friedrich Kuhn	Patrick Martin	Albert Madörin
	Lorenz Nieberl	Howard Crossett	André Filippini
	Franz Kemser	James Atkinson	Stephan Waser
ICE HOCKEY	Canada	U.S.A.	Sweden
	George Abel	Ruben Bjorkman	Göte Almqvist
	John Davies	Leonard Ceglarski	Hans Andersson
	William Dawe	Joseph Czarnota	Stig Andersson
	Robert Dickson	Richard Desmond	Åke Andersson
	Donald Gauf	Andre Gambucci	Lars Björn
	William Gibson	Clifford Harrison	Göte Blomqvist
	Ralph Hansch	Gerald Kilmartin	Thord Flodqvist
	Robert Meyers	John Mulhern	Erik Johansson
	David Miller	John Noah	Gösta Johansson
	Eric Paterson	Arnold Oss	Rune Johansson
	Thomas Pollock	Robert Rompre	Sven Johansson
	Allan Purvis	James Sedin	Åke Lassas
	Gordon Robertson	Allen Van	Holger Nurmela
	Louis Secco	Donald Whiston	Hans Öberg
	Francis Sullivan	Kenneth Yackel	Lars Pettersson
	Robert Watt		Lars Svensson
			Sven Thunman

clad peaks of the majestic Dolomite mountains, many of which are more than 10,000 feet (3,000 metres) high.

Profits from Italy's nationalised football pools largely subsidised the elaborately erected sites and it mattered little that the 231 million lire, netted from 157,000 admission tickets, repaid only a proportion of the £2½ million promotional costs.

As the first Winter Olympics to be internationally televised, worldwide publicity of the meeting brought substantial long-term commercial benefits to snow and ice sports, to Italy in general and Cortina in particular. Such obvious assets ensured no shortage of applicants to stage subsequent Olympics.

The newly built four-decker grandstands of the lavish £750,000 ($1,785,000) Olympic Ice Stadium were packed with 13,000 gaily expectant onlookers when President Giovanni Gronchi of Italy declared the Games open. Guido Caroli, the Italian ice racer, skated the final lap with the Olympic Flame, which had been brought 500 miles in relays from Rome's ruined Temple of Jupiter. The diminutive Italian skier, Juliana Minuzzo, took the Olympic oath on behalf of the competitors.

One outstanding performer emerges from most Olympic meetings and Cortina was no exception. The big name on this occasion was the Austrian alpine skier, Toni Sailer, a 20-year-old plumber from Kitzbühel, the winter resort famed for Tyrolese yodelling and *schuhplattler* dancing.

Sailer was hailed as the most brilliant and daring alpine skier yet seen, not just because he won all three of his events, but because of the impressive, hip-swinging style and decisive time margins which quite outclassed the opposition. His giant slalom time was 6.2 seconds better than that of the runner-up, fellow Austrian Anderl Molterer. In the slalom, 4 clear seconds separated him from the American-based Chiharu Igaya, the first Japanese to win an Olympic Winter Games medal. The icy, wind-swept downhill gave Sailer a 3.5 seconds lead over the second placed Swiss, Raymond Fellay.

But the Swiss had more glory in the women's events. Dairymaid Madeleine Berthod was the most successful, winning the downhill and coming fifth in the slalom. Her compatriot, Renée Colliard, triumphed in the slalom but Ossi Reichert, a German hotelier's daughter, took the giant slalom.

Competing for the first time in the Winter Olympics, the Russians

G

took the lion's share of medals and earned respect as an obviously strengthening force. Their well balanced nordic ski team earned a convincing relay win but the individual cross-country stars were the seemingly indefatigable Swede, Sixten Jernberg, and the never flagging Finn, Veikko Hakulinen.

Jernberg's medals tally – a gold, two silver and a bronze – was even one more than Sailer's. The Norwegian special jumping dominance in all six previous Winter Olympics was at last cracked by a Finn, Antti Hyvärinen, with a winning new aerodynamic drop style.

An unprecedented spate of speed skating records on the outdoor circuit at Lake Misurina was due to rapidly improving techniques at high altitude. In the four events, three skaters set new world records. Seventy-three competitors were inside the previous best Olympic times for their distances and 41 new national records were established.

Soviet racers got four gold medals for winning three events because compatriots Jurij Mikailov and Eugenii Grischin tied in the 1,500 metres, each clocking a new world record time. Grischin, the outstanding ice sprinter of his day, also established a fresh world time to win the 500 metres. For the first time since 1932, Norway failed to get a speed skating first.

The technical and spectacular highlight of the figure skating was undoubtedly the freestyle of the men's dominant American trio, Hayes Jenkins, Ronnie Robertson and David Jenkins, who finished in that order. Hayes Jenkins won by virtue of a slender lead in the figures, and though his free-style was excellent, the contents of his programme were not quite as ambitious as those displayed by Robertson, who was a sensational, at times almost acrobatic free-skater. He gave everything he had on this occasion. He touched a hand down when landing a triple loop jump, then completed a triple salchow to perfection and concluded with a fast cross-toe spin, altogether a thrilling programme for the mesmerised audience.

In the women's contest Tenley Albright, runner-up in the previous Winter Olympics to Britain's Jeannette Altwegg, presented a wonderfully delicate programme, dramatically timed to *Tales of Hoffman* in a seemingly effortless, graceful style, ending worthily with a rapid cross-foot spin. But if a miracle was needed by Carol Heiss to overtake her brilliant compatriot, this she so nearly achieved. Very speedy and impressive, she not only scored almost as many marks as Tenley, but was actually placed first in the freestyle by five of the eleven judges.

The elegant Viennese partnership, Kurt Oppelt and Sissy Schwarz, gained a controversial verdict over Canada's Norris Bowden and Frances Dafoe in the pairs event, both couples synchronising superbly.

The ice hockey, as usual, drew the greatest number of spectators. At their first attempt, the Russians emerged victorious and unbeaten in their five final pool matches against the previously fancied United States runners-up, third placed Canada, Sweden, Czechoslovakia and Germany. Scoring 25 goals and conceding only five, the Soviet players never looked unduly ruffled. Their clever stick-handling and superior skating, both in defence and attack, decided the issue in the two games that mattered most, defeating U.S.A. 4–0 and Canada 2–0.

Franz Kapus, 46, became the oldest gold medallist in any Winter Olympics when he cannily piloted the Swiss sled to victory in the four-man bobsleigh event, 1.26 seconds ahead of the Italian ace, Eugenio Monti. In his two-man boblet, Monti was again pipped, but this time by his fellow Italian, Dalla Costa – a popular home success and a triumph for the new Podar-designed sleds, which nearly every nation afterwards adopted.

SQUAW VALLEY, U.S.A.   February 18–28, 1960

'The gamble which came off' is a phrase aptly describing the choice of venue for the eighth Winter Olympics. In face of keen competition from three well established European resorts, the I.O.C. voted for an empty, scarcely known Californian site where everything had to be built from scratch.

On the eastern side of the Sierra Nevada, 200 miles (320 kilometres) from San Francisco and at an altitude of 6,230 feet (1,900 metres), it all seemed like a risky throw of the dice. But Alexander Cushing, who owned the land used, insisted with oratorial conviction that the compactness would be a key feature – and so it proved.

As pageantry committee chairman, filmdom's Walt Disney supervised all the ceremonial arrangements and did not miss a trick. But the miracle of these Games was the weather. After weeks of rain which had threatened to wash away the courses, snow and wind threatened to ruin the elaborately planned opening by Vice-President Nixon. Then, with only 15 minutes to go, as if by magic the clouds cleared, the sun shone and only the humorist attributed this dramatic effect to Disney.

195

THE VII WINTER OLYMPIC GAMES 1956

	Gold	Silver	Bronze
NORDIC SKIING: MEN			
15 kilometres	Hallgeir Brenden (Norway)	Sixten Jernberg (Sweden)	Pavel Koltschin (U.S.S.R.)
30 kilometres	Veikko Hakulinen (Finland)	Sixten Jernberg (Sweden)	Pavel Koltschin (U.S.S.R.)
50 kilometres	Sixten Jernberg (Sweden)	Veikko Hakulinen (Finland)	Fjodor Terentjev (U.S.S.R.)
Relay, 4 × 10 kilometres	U.S.S.R. Fjodor Terentiev Pavel Koltschin Nikolaj Anikin Vladimir Kusin	Finland August Kiuru Jormo Kortelainen Arvo Viitanen Veikko Hakulinen	Sweden Lennart Larsson Gunnar Samuelsson Per-Erik Larsson Sixten Jernberg
Jumping	Antti Hyvärinen (Finland)	Aulis Kallakorpi (Finland)	Harry Glass (Germany)
Combined	Sverre Stenersen (Norway)	Bengt Eriksson (Sweden)	Franciszek Gron-Gasienica (Poland)
NORDIC SKIING: WOMEN			
10 kilometres	Ljubov Kozyreva (U.S.S.R.)	Radja Jeroschina (U.S.S.R.)	Sonja Edström (Sweden)
Relay, 3 × 5 kilometres	Finland Sirkka Polkunen Mirja Hietamies Siiri Rantanen	U.S.S.R. Ljubov Kozyreva Alevtina Koltschina Radja Jeroschina	Sweden Irma Johansson Anna-Lisa Eriksson Sonja Edström
ALPINE SKIING: MEN			
Downhill	Toni Sailer (Austria)	Raymond Fellay (Switzerland)	Anderl Molterer (Austria)
Slalom	Toni Sailer (Austria)	Chiharu Igaya (Japan)	Stig Sollander (Sweden)

	Gold	Silver	Bronze
ALPINE SKIING: MEN			
Giant Slalom	Toni Sailer (Austria)	Anderl Molterer (Austria)	Walter Schuster (Austria)
ALPINE SKIING: WOMEN			
Downhill	Madeleine Berthod (Switzerland)	Frieda Danzer (Switzerland)	Lucille Wheeler (Canada)
Slalom	Renée Colliard (Switzerland)	Regina Schöpf (Austria)	Jevgenija Sidorova (U.S.S.R.)
Giant Slalom	Ossi Reichert (Germany)	Puzzi Frandl (Austria)	Dorothea Hochleitner (Austria)
FIGURE SKATING			
Men	Hayes Jenkins (U.S.A.)	Ronald Robertson (U.S.A.)	David Jenkins (U.S.A.)
Women	Tenley Albright (U.S.A.)	Carol Heiss (U.S.A.)	Ingrid Wendl (Austria)
Pairs	Kurt Oppelt Elisabeth Schwarz (Austria)	Norris Bowden Frances Dafoe (Canada)	László Nagy Marianna Nagy (Hungary)
SPEED SKATING			
500 metres	Eugenii Grischin (U.S.S.R.)	Rafael Gratsch (U.S.S.R.)	Alv Gjestvang (Norway)
1,500 metres	Eugenii Grischin (U.S.S.R.) Jurij Mikailov (U.S.S.R.)		Toivo Salonen (Finland)
5,000 metres	Boris Shilkov (U.S.S.R.)	Sigvard Ericsson (Sweden)	Oleg Gontscharenko (U.S.S.R.)
10,000 metres	Sigvard Ericsson (Sweden)	Knut Johannesen (Norway)	Oleg Gontscharenko (U.S.S.R.)

BOBSLEDDING

2-man bobs

Gold	Silver	Bronze
Italy	Italy	Switzerland
Lamberto Dalla Costa	Eugenio Monti	Max Angst
Giacomo Conti	Renzo Alverà	Harry Warburton

4-man bobs

Gold	Silver	Bronze
Switzerland	Italy	U.S.A.
Franz Kapus	Eugenio Monti	Arthur Tyler
Gottfried Diener	Ulrico Girardi	William Dodge
Robert Alt	Renzo Alvera	Charles Butler
Heinrich Angst	Renato Mocellini	James Lamy

ICE HOCKEY

Gold	Silver	Bronze
U.S.S.R.	U.S.A.	Canada
Eugenyi Babitsch	Wendell Anderson	Denis Brodeur
Vsevolod Bobrov	Wellington Burnett	Charles Brooker
Nikolaj Chlystov	Eugene Campbell	William Colvin
Aleksej Guryschev	Gordon Christian	Alfred Horne
Jurij Krylov	William Cleary	Arthur Hurst
Alfred Kutschevskij	Richard Dougherty	Byrle Klinck
Valentin Kusin	Willard Ikola	Paul Knox
Grigorij Mkrttschan	John Matchefts	Kenneth Laufman
Viktor Nikiforov	John Mayasich	Howard Lee
Jurij Pantjuchov	Daniel McKinnon	James Logan
Nikolaj Putschkov	Richard Meredith	Floyd Martin
Viktor Schuvalov	Weldon Olson	Jack McKenzie
Genrich Sidorenkov	John Petroske	Donald Rope
Nikolaj Sologubov	Kenneth Purpur	Georges Scholes
Ivan Tregubov	Donald Rigazio	Gerald Theberge
Dmitrij Ukolov	Richard Rodenhiser	Robert White
Aleksandr Uvarov	Edward Sampson	Keith Woodall

Throughout the entire 11-day meeting, warm Californian sunshine on incongruous-looking snow and ice dominated the proceedings. The great asset of Squaw Valley and a boon to the spectators was that, except for the cross-country ski courses 17 miles (27 kilometres) away on the McKinney Creek, everything was within short walking distance. Sometimes it was possible to watch speed skating, figure skating, ice hockey, downhill skiing and ski jumping from the same spot – and one could not do that anywhere else in the world.

There was some dissension because no bobsleigh or tobogganing runs were built, but this was the only real shortcoming, somewhat atoned by the friendly spirit so prevalent among competitors and spectators. Andrea Mead-Lawrence, the U.S. alpine skier, carried the torch on its last ski-borne relay, having been lit at Mordegal, Norway, as in 1952. The American ice racer, Ken Henry, skated a final lap with the torch before igniting the sacred flame.

Five inside the world record, eight inside the Olympic record and 12 inside their national records – *all* in one event. That, in the history-making 10,000 metres, was the speed skating highlight. Norwegian Knut Johannesen fairly whistled through to chop 46 seconds off the 1952 record established by the great Hjalmar Andersen. Even Britain's Terence Monaghan, who came fifth, was a full second faster than Andersen's previous world's best.

Eugenii Grischin equalled his own world record time of 40.2 seconds in winning the 500 metres for U.S.S.R., emphasising that, at 28, he still had no peers as a sprinter. He also tied with the Norwegian, Roald Aas, to share the 1,500 metres gold medal award. In the 5,000 metres, Russian Viktor Kosischkin was nearly 10 seconds faster than Johannesen.

Women's speed skating was included for the first time and another Russian, Lydia Skoblikova, had the distinction of being the only contestant in the Games to win two individual golds, for the 1,500 metres and the 3,000 metres, setting a new world record in the former. The 500 metres was won by Helga Haase, of Germany, and the 1,000 by Klara Guseva, of U.S.S.R.

In the men's figure skating at the architectural prize-winning Blyth Arena, American David Jenkins included high triple and double jumps of a standard which no European could match, overhauling a lead in the figures by the Czech, Karol Divin. Jenkins's compatriot and future sister-in-law, Carol Heiss, won the women's event by a comfortable margin and the Canadian combination,

Robert Paul and Barbara Wagner, were equally convincing in the pairs.

The United States clinched the ice hockey issue with a 2–1 upset of the form favourites, Canada. It was the first U.S.A. win over Canada in any major international competition since 1956 and only the third since 1920. The Canadians also defeated the Russians 8–5, the Soviet side suffering a clear setback after their 1956 triumph.

No outstanding alpine skier hogged the honours. Roger Staub won the men's giant slalom for Switzerland, Ernst Hinterseer took the slalom for Austria and Jean Vuarnet, of France, came first in the downhill. Another Frenchman, Guy Périllat, was the most consistent performer, gaining a bronze in the downhill and finishing sixth in each of the other two events.

Canadian Anne Heggtveit, victor of the women's slalom, did well enough in the other races to register the best all-round performance. Yvonne Ruegg, a downhill specialist, confounded the experts by winning the giant slalom for Switzerland. Heidi Biebl took the downhill for Germany and Americans came second in all three events. Penny Pitou got silvers for the downhill and giant slalom – pipped in the latter by a mere tenth of a second – and Betsy Snite was runner-up in the slalom.

The cross-country skiing showed the two Olympic veterans, Sixten Jernberg and Veikko Hakulinen, to be still among the best. Sweden's Jernberg scored a gold and a silver in the two shorter distances and came fifth in the marathon 50 kilometres, won by the Finn, Kalevi Hämäläinen. Hakulinen gained the 50 kilometres silver, got a bronze in the 15 kilometres sprint, won by Norway's Haakon Brusveen, and was hero of Finland's remarkable victory in the relay. In a dramatic duel on the last 10 kilometres leg, Hakulinen made up a 22 seconds leeway to pass Brusveen and win by just the length of a ski.

While the men's cross-country events continued very much as the prerogative of Scandinavia, there was a major surprise when a German postman, Georg Thoma, emerged as winner of the nordic combination, a stern test of all-round skill in cross-country and ski jumping. It was the first time a non-Scandinavian had won the event.

But Germany was to defy the critics still more. Few expected Helmut Recknagel to win the spectacular 80 metres jumping, but he did it by a comfortable margin, impressing with his extra rapid take-off and an outmoded orthodox arms-forward style. The sunshine on this calm day showed enormous shadows ahead of each silent jumper, further enhancing the theatrical effect which fascinated the awe-inspired crowds thronging the foot of that impressive hill.

The newly introduced biathlon, combining cross-country ski running and rifle marksmanship, was won by Klas Lestander, of Sweden, whose 20 shots without a miss made up for a lagging pace along the track.

Four Russians, headed by Marija Gusakova, filled the first four places in the women's 10 kilometres race. The Soviet team's defeat by the Swedes in the relay was consequently sensational, but due mainly to a Russian racer falling and breaking a ski during the first leg, costing irretrievable time.

The entry for these Games, the second to be held outside Europe, totalled 521 men and 144 women from 30 countries, not as many as at Cortina because many nations pruned their numbers to reduce travel costs. But an increase of 13 countries since the Lake Placid Games of 1932 reflected the widening of winter sports interest through three decades.

Nobody discovered why the mountain used for the men's slalom and women's downhill was called KT-22, but there was no lack of suggestions – ranging from that of the 22 kick-turns it took the first skier to get down it to that of an historic fight with redskins which resulted in these words being carved on a tree: 'Killed by Tomahawk, 22'. They say the tree is still there, but perhaps the etchings were obliterated by snow. . . .

INNSBRUCK, Austria   January 29–February 9, 1964
The first Olympic meeting to award four gold medals to one person. Two members of a family alternately first and second to each other. Victories for countries without courses of their own. More nations, more competitors, more spectators. These were highlights of the ninth Winter Olympic Games at Innsbruck, outstandingly successful despite an alarming dearth of snow.

Just under a million spectators saw the events during the 12 days' programme. Many paid nearly £3 10s ($8 or 250 Austrian schillings) for a seat at the Olympic Ice Stadium, where the capacity 11,000 would have been more than doubled for all the three figure skating events and for at least one ice hockey game each day if space had permitted. The Games drew a record entry of 1,186 participants (986 men and 200 women) from 36 nations.

THE VIII WINTER OLYMPIC GAMES 1960

	Gold	Silver	Bronze
NORDIC SKIING: MEN			
15 kilometres	Haakon Brusveen (Norway)	Sixten Jernberg (Sweden)	Veikko Hakulinen (Finland)
30 kilometres	Sixten Jernberg (Sweden)	Rolf Rämgård (Sweden)	Nikolai Anikin (U.S.S.R.)
50 kilometres	Kalevi Hämäläinen (Finland)	Veikko Hakulinen (Finland)	Rolf Rämgård (Sweden)
Relay, 4 × 10 kilometres	Toimi Alatalo Eero Mäntyranta Väinö Huhtala Veikko Hakulinen Finland	Harald Grönningen Halgeir Brenden Einar Östby Haakon Brusveen Norway	Anatolii Scheljuchin Gennadii Vagenov Aleksei Kusnetsov Nikolai Anikin U.S.S.R.
Jumping	Helmut Recknagel (Germany)	Niilo Halonen (Finland)	Otto Leodolter (Austria)
Combined	Georg Thoma (Germany)	Tormod Knutsen (Norway)	Nikolai Gusakov (U.S.S.R.)
Biathlon	Klas Lestander (Sweden)	Antti Tyrväinen (Finland)	Aleksandr Privalov (U.S.S.R.)
NORDIC SKIING: WOMEN			
10 kilometres	Marija Gusakova (U.S.S.R.) Sweden	Liubov Baranova (U.S.S.R.) U.S.S.R.	Radia Eroschina (U.S.S.R.) Finland
Relay, 3 × 5 kilometres	Irma Johansson Britt Strandberg Sonja Ruthström-Edström	Radia Eroschina Marija Gusakova Liubov Baranova	Siiri Rantanen Eeva Ruoppa Toini Pöysti
ALPINE SKIING: MEN			
Downhill	Jean Vuarnet (France)	Hans Lanig (Germany)	Guy Perillat (France)
Slalom	Ernst Hinterseer (Austria)	Matthias Leitner (Austria)	Charles Bozon (France)

	Gold	Silver	Bronze
ALPINE SKIING: MEN			
Giant Slalom	Roger Staub (Switzerland)	Josef Stiegler (Austria)	Ernst Hinterseer (Austria)
ALPINE SKIING: WOMEN			
Downhill	Heidi Biebl (Germany)	Penny Pitou (U.S.A.)	Traudl Hecher (Austria)
Slalom	Anne Heggtveit (Canada)	Betsy Snite (U.S.A.)	Barbi Henneberger (Germany)
Giant Slalom	Yvonne Rüegg (Switzerland)	Penny Pitou (U.S.A.)	Giuliana Minuzzo-Chenal (Italy)
FIGURE SKATING			
Men	David Jenkins (U.S.A.)	Karol Divin (Czechoslovakia)	Donald Jackson (Canada)
Women	Carol Heiss (U.S.A.)	Sjoukje Dijkstra (Netherlands)	Barbara Roles (U.S.A.)
Pairs	Robert Paul Barbara Wagner (Canada)	Hans Bäumler Marika Kilius (Germany)	Ronald Ludington Nancy Ludington (U.S.A.)
SPEED SKATING: MEN			
500 metres	Eugenii Grischin (U.S.S.R.)	William Disney (U.S.A.)	Rafael Gratsch (U.S.S.R.)
1,500 metres	Roald Aas (Norway) Eugenii Grischin (U.S.S.R.)		Boris Stenin (U.S.S.R.)
5,000 metres	Viktor Kosichkin (U.S.S.R.)	Knut Johannesen (Norway)	Jan Pesman (Netherlands)
10,000 metres	Knut Johannesen (Norway)	Viktor Kosichkin (U.S.S.R.)	Kjell Bäckman (Sweden)

203

	Gold	Silver	Bronze
SPEED SKATING: WOMEN			
500 metres	Helga Haase (Germany)	Natalia Donchenko (U.S.S.R.)	Jeanne Ashworth (U.S.A.)
1,000 metres	Klara Guseva (U.S.S.R.)	Helga Haase (Germany)	Tamara Rylova (U.S.S.R.)
1,500 metres	Lydia Skoblikova (U.S.S.R.)	Elvira Seroczynska (Poland)	Helena Pilejczyk (Poland)
3,000 metres	Lydia Skoblikova (U.S.S.R.)	Valentina (U.S.S.R.)	Eevi Huttunen (Finland)
ICE HOCKEY	U.S.A.	Canada	U.S.S.R.

U.S.A.
Roger Christian
William Christian
Robert Cleary
William Cleary
Eugene Grazia
Paul Johnson
John Kirrane
John Mayasich
Jack McCartan
Robert McVey
Richard Meredith
Weldon Olson
Edwyn Owen
Rodney Paavola
Lawrence Palmer
Richard Rodenhiser
Thomas Williams

Canada
Bob Attersley
Moe Benoit
Jim Connelly
Jack Douglas
Fred Etcher
Bob Forhan
Don Head
Harold Hurley
Kenneth Laufman
Floyd Martin
Bob McKnight
Clifford Pennington
Donald Rope
Bob Rousseau
George Samolenko
Harry Sinden
Darryl Sly

U.S.S.R.
Veniamin Aleksandrov
Aleksandr Alimetov
Jurii Baulin
Michail Bytschkov
Vladimir Grebennikov
Eugenii Groschev
Viktor Jakuschev
Eugenii Jerkin
Nikolai Karpov
Alfred Kutschevski
Konstantin Loktev
Stanislav Petruchov
Viktor Priaschtschnikov
Nikolai Putschkov
Genrich Siderenkov
Nikolai Solugubov
Jurii Tsitsinov

With no previous experience of staging Olympic events, the Austrian organisers promoted this series with an efficiency belying their financial limitations. 'Simple' is how they described their plans, but this proved to be false modesty. That the unexpectedly sparse snow and high temperatures did not cause any event to be cancelled – during the mildest first week of February that the ancient Tyrolean city had experienced for 58 years – was a tribute to astute re-planning and considerable Army co-operation. IBM computers provided results with unprecedented speed.

For the first time in the history of the Winter Olympics, the opening ceremony was not held at an ice rink but in the natural amphitheatre which formed the base of the scenic Bergisel ski jump, enabling more than 60,000 to watch. A short silence was observed in memory of the British tobogganist, Kay Skrzypecki, and the Australian skier, Ross Milne, both killed while training the week previously.

While U.S.S.R. convincingly captured the lion's share of medals (11 gold, 8 silver and 6 bronze), the numerical might of U.S.A., with the largest team present, achieved comparatively few of the spoils, and the non-appearance of Switzerland in the medals table reflected a lean era of star material in a country whose name is synonymous with winter sports.

The dominant individual in these Games was the Russian speed skater, Lydia Skoblikova, the first competitor ever to win four gold medals at one Winter Olympics. It was not this alone, but the fact that three of her four times were new Olympic records – and all in the space of four days – which caused this 24-year-old blonde Soviet flyer to be acclaimed the greatest woman ice racer seen.

Two more Olympic ice speed records were shattered by the men. An American barber, Richard McDermott, shaved a tenth of a second off the old 500 metres time, a full half second ahead of three who tied for second place, including the respected Russian sprinter, Eugenii Grischin. The other speed record was set by the veteran Norwegian, Knut Johannesen, over 5,000 metres.

Queen Juliana of the Netherlands saw an inspired Sjoukje Dijkstra capture her country's first Olympic gold medal in any sport since Fanny Blankers-Koen's athletics riumph in 1948. For technical merit, six of the nine judges gave the powerful Dutch figure skater 5.9 marks out of a possible six. Manfred Schnelldorfer took the men's title for Germany after seeing his French rival, Alain Calmat, twice fall heavily.

In the pairs event, the classically smooth Russian partnership, Oleg Protopopov and Ludmila Belousova, pipped the German world title holders, Hans Bäumler and Marika Kilius, in a thrillingly close tussle between the two best partnerships to be seen for many years. Protopopov's strength in lifts and his partner's acute-angled edges were rare sights for the connoisseur.

Five of the six alpine ski races were staged at Axamer Lizum, about 10 miles south-west of Innsbruck, and the men's downhill was held on the Patscherkofel mountain, near Igls. French and Austrian skiers monopolised the top honours and a unique women's double was scored by the French sisters, Marielle and Christine Goitschel. In the slalom, Christine beat her sister by nearly a second over the two runs, with American Jean Saubert third. In the giant slalom, it was Marielle's turn for a gold, and this time Christine shared second place with Miss Saubert.

In the three men's events, Ludwig Leitner, the best all-rounder, emphasised a growing German strength and two Americans, William Kidd and James Heuga, shone in the slalom. Austrian Karl Schranz, who had lapsed surprisingly in 1960, recaptured some of his old form to take the giant slalom silver, but the most successful Austrian men were Egon Zimmermann, the downhill winner, and Josef Stiegler, first in the slalom and third in the giant slalom, with François Bonlieu triumphant for France in the latter.

It seemed appropriate that the grand old man of *langlauf*, Sixten Jernberg, should win another gold medal in the final nordic ski race, the 4 × 10 kilometres relay, as this was also the farewell event of his brilliant career spanning three Olympiads. Cheers of sentimental admiration had earlier greeted his finishing spurt in the strenuous 50 kilometres marathon at Seefeld, on the eve of his 35th birthday. What a fantastic stayer was this Jernberg, the Stanley Matthews of skiing who in three Olympics accumulated four gold medals, three silver and two bronze.

Sharing his glory in the cross-country skiing was that symbol of female Russian stamina, Claudia Boyarskikh, who came first in all three women's events, including the relay. Yet another Russian success came in the biathlon, introduced experimentally in 1960 at Squaw Valley when few believed it would survive, and now voted for retention at the 1968 Games.

The Commonwealth successes of Britain and Canada in the two bobsleigh events at Igls were, as the winning Canadian four-men driver, Vic Emery, pointed out, a 'triumph for countries without a single course of their own'. In the two-man contest, Tony Nash and Robin Dixon took the all-important ninth turn at Hexenkessel Corner 'just under the second "O" in the Coca-Cola sign above', exactly as Nash had planned after much trial and error in training.

Precisely 12 hundredths of a second faster than the Italians, Sergio Zardini and Romano Bonagura, this determined pair spent much time and money from their own pockets to merit only the fourth Olympic gold medal awards ever made to Britain for winter sports. The previous winners were figure skater Madge Syers in 1908, the national ice hockey team in 1936, and figure skater Jeannette Altwegg in 1952.

Germans took all the men's singles tobogganing medals at Igls. The total winning time of Thomas Köhler was less than three tenths of a second faster than the runner-up, Klaus Bonsack. In the two-seater contest, Josef Feistmantl and Manfred Stengl scored for the host nation, but in the women's singles another German, Ortrun Enderlein, defeated the world champion, Ilse Geisler.

In contrast to the forward-prone position of a skeleton Cresta rider, it was for many a new spectacle to see these luge tobogganists adopt a sitting posture, steering by clever weight-transference and delicate control of the sharp-edged runners. It was the first lugeing to be included in an Olympic programme. Perhaps because of this, some of the less experienced competitors made it look a highly hazardous sport, while, in contrast, the Austrian and German experts seldom gave cause for anxiety.

Although the final table suggested that U.S.S.R. won the ice hockey with plenty to spare, in fact the title was decided by a 3–2 defeat of Canada in their final game. Had the Canadians won that match, the two nations would have finished equal on points, in which case by Olympic rules the victorious team in the match between the two would have been champions.

But there is no question that victory was well merited by the only team to win all seven of its matches and the one with the most goals for and the least against. Keys to the Soviet success were superb fitness, which made them dominant in the final period of every match; superior skating skill, which gave them quicker manoeuvrability, and their forwards' technique of keeping possession until the right scoring chance came.

The thrilling spectacle of 52 ski jumpers soaring silently above the

Bergisel Hill provided a colourful highlight for well over 60,000 entranced onlookers. After the Finn, Veikko Kankkonen, had won the newly introduced 'little' 70 metres jump at Seefeld, the Norwegian, Toralf Engan, proved supreme in the traditional 90 metres event. What courage these specialists must have possessed as each in turn appeared to explode into the air, to describe graceful arcs high above the snow – with the awesome sight below of an Innsbruck cemetery!

That no event had to be cancelled was a testimonial to the Austrian organisers. Somehow, snow which had fallen earlier was preserved and laboriously augmented on the alpine and nordic ski courses. When necessary, bobsleigh and toboggan events were held very early in the mornings, before the sun got to work on the steeply banked runs.

GRENOBLE, France   February 6–18, 1968
A crowd of 60,000 filled a spacious amphitheatre temporarily constructed at Grenoble for the ceremonial opening by President de Gaulle. This arena was not used for any of the competitions and its elaborate stands were dismantled afterwards, emphasising the efforts made by the host country to provide spectacular presentation.

The pageantry was updated when showers of artificial roses, emblematic of the French city, descended from helicopters; the five symbolic rings were weaved by aircraft in appropriately coloured smoke trails, and Olympic flags fluttered down under miniature parachutes. Recorded musical accompaniment prompted incongruous thoughts of astronauts and, for once, no traditional military march helped the 1,560 competitors from 37 nations as they entered the parade.

Alain Calmat, the former French world figure skating champion, brought in the torch which had been carried in relays from Olympia, Greece, and Leo Lacroix, the French alpine skier, took the oath of amateurism on behalf of the participants. There were 623,680 spectators during the 13 days of the Games and probably more than 100 million televiewers saw the highlights. Unseasonably mild weather, though pleasurable for the skaters, affected the bobsleigh, luge and alpine ski courses enough to cause some tiresome timetable adjustments.

An individual has tended to dominate each Winter Olympics and the tenth Games at Grenoble were no exception. This time it was

THE IX WINTER OLYMPIC GAMES 1964

	Gold	Silver	Bronze
NORDIC SKIING: MEN			
15 kilometres	Eero Mäntyranta (Finland)	Harald Grönningen (Norway)	Sixten Jernberg (Sweden)
30 kilometres	Eero Mäntyranta (Finland)	Harald Grönningen (Norway)	Igor Vorontschichin (U.S.S.R.)
50 kilometres	Sixten Jernberg (Sweden)	Assar Rönnlund (Sweden)	Arto Tiainen (Finland)
Relay, 4 × 10 kilometres	Sweden — Karl Asph, Sixten Jernberg, Janne Stefansson, Assar Rönnlund	Finland — Vaeinoe Huhtala, Arto Tiainen, Kalevi Laurila, Eero Mäntyranta	U.S.S.R. — Ivan Utrobin, Gennady Vaganov, Igor Vorontschichin, Pavel Kolchin
70 metres Jumping	Veikko Kankkonen (Finland)	Toralf Engan (Norway)	Torgeir Brandtzaeg (Norway)
90 metres Jumping	Toralf Engan (Norway)	Veikko Kankkonen (Finland)	Torgeir Brandtzaeg (Norway)
Combined	Tormod Knutsen (Norway)	Nikolai Kiselev (U.S.S.R.)	Georg Thoma (Germany)
Biathlon	Vladimir Melanin (U.S.S.R.)	Aleksandr Privalov (U.S.S.R.)	Olav Jordet (Norway)
NORDIC SKIING: WOMEN			
5 kilometres	Claudia Boyarskikh (U.S.S.R.)	Mirja Lehtonen (Finland)	Alevtina Koltschina (U.S.S.R.)
10 kilometres	Claudia Boyarskikh (U.S.S.R.)	Eudokia Mekshilo (U.S.S.R.)	Maria Gusakova (U.S.S.R.)

	Gold	Silver	Bronze
NORDIC SKIING: WOMEN			
Relay, 3 × 5 kilometres	U.S.S.R. Alevtina Koltschina Eudokia Mekshilo Claudia Boyarskikh	Sweden Barbro Martinsson Britt Strandberg Toini Gustafsson	Finland Senja Pusula Toini Poeysti Mirja Lehtonen
ALPINE SKIING: MEN			
Downhill	Egon Zimmermann (Austria)	Leo Lacroix (France)	Wolfgang Bartels (Germany)
Slalom	Josef Stiegler (Austria)	William Kidd (U.S.A.)	James Heuga (U.S.A.)
Giant Slalom	François Bonlieu (France)	Karl Schranz (Austria)	Josef Stiegler (Austria)
ALPINE SKIING: WOMEN			
Downhill	Christl Haas (Austria)	Edith Zimmermann (Austria)	Traudl Hecher (Austria)
Slalom	Christine Goitschel (France)	Marielle Goitschel (France)	Jean Saubert (U.S.A.)
Giant Slalom	Marielle Goitschel (France)	Christine Goitschel (France) Jean Saubert (U.S.A.)	
FIGURE SKATING			
Men	Manfred Schnelldorfer (Germany)	Alain Calmat (France)	Scott Allen (U.S.A.)
Women	Sjoukje Dijkstra (Netherlands)	Regine Heitzer (Austria)	Petra Burka (Canada)
Pairs	Oleg Protopopov Ludmila Belousova (U.S.S.R.)	Hans Bäumler Marika Kilius (Germany)	Guy Revell Debbi Wilkes (Canada)

	Gold	Silver	Bronze
SPEED SKATING: MEN			
500 metres	Richard McDermott (U.S.A.)	Eugenii Grischin (U.S.S.R.) Vladimir Orlov (U.S.S.R.) Alv Gjestvang (Norway)	
1,500 metres	Ants Antson (U.S.S.R.)	Kees Verkerk (Netherlands)	Villy Haugen (Norway)
5,000 metres	Knut Johannesen (Norway)	Per Moe (Norway)	Anton Maier (Norway)
10,000 metres	Jonny Nilsson (Sweden)	Anton Maier (Norway)	Knut Johannesen (Norway)
SPEED SKATING: WOMEN			
500 metres	Lydia Skoblikova (U.S.S.R.)	Irina Yegorova (U.S.S.R.)	Tatiana Sidorova (U.S.S.R.)
1,000 metres	Lydia Skoblikova (U.S.S.R.)	Irina Yegorova (U.S.S.R.)	Kaija Mustonen (Finland)
1,500 metres	Lydia Skoblikova (U.S.S.R.)	Kaija Mustonen (Finland)	Berta Kolokoltseva (U.S.S.R.)
3,000 metres	Lydia Skoblikova (U.S.S.R.)	Valentina Stenina (U.S.S.R.) Pil Han (Korea)	
BOBSLEDDING			
2-man bobs	Great Britain Tony Nash Robin Dixon	Italy Sergio Zardini Romano Bonagura	Italy Eugenio Monti Sergio Siorpaes

211

	Gold	Silver	Bronze
BOBSLEDDING			
4-man bobs	Canada	Austria	Italy
	Vic Emery	Erwin Thaler	Eugenio Monti
	Peter Kirby	Adolf Koxeder	Sergio Siorpaes
	Douglas Anakin	Josef Nairz	Benito Rigoni
	John Emery	Reinhold Durnthaler	Gildo Siorpaes
LUGE TOBOGGANING: MEN			
Single	Thomas Köhler (Germany)	Klaus Bonsack (Germany)	Hans Plenk (Germany)
2-seater	Austria	Austria	Italy
	Josef Feistmantl	Reinhold Senn	Walter Aussendorfer
	Manfred Stengl	Helmut Thaler	Sigisfredo Mair
LUGE TOBOGGANING: WOMEN			
Single	Ortrun Enderlein (Germany)	Ilse Geisler (Germany)	Helene Thurner (Austria)
ICE HOCKEY	U.S.S.R.	Sweden	Czechoslovakia
	Veniamin Alexandrov	Anders Andersson	Vlastimil Bubnik
	Aleksandr Almetov	Gert Blomé	Josef Cerny
	Vitali Davidov	Lennart Häggroth	Jiri Dolana
	Anatolii Firsov	Lennart Johansson	Vlado Dzurila
	Eduard Ivanov	Nils Johansson	Josef Golonka
	Victor Konovalenko	Sven Johansson	Frantisek Gregor
	Victor Kuzkin	Lars Lundvall	Jiri Holik
	Konstantin Loktev	Eilert Määttä	Jaroslav Jirik
	Boris Maiorov	Hans Mild	Jan Klapac
	Eugenii Maiorov	Nils Nilsson	Vladimir Nadrchal
	Stanislav Petuchov	Bert Nordlander	Rudolf Potsch

ICE HOCKEY

Gold

Alexandre Ragulin
Boris Saitsev
Oleg Saitsev
Viatches Starchinov
Leonid Volkov
Victor Yakushev

Silver

Carl Oberg
Uno Ohrlund
Ronald Pettersson
Ulf Sterner
Roland Stoltz
Kjell Svensson

Bronze

Stanislav Pryl
Ladislav Smid
Stanislav Sventek
Frantisek Tikal
Miroslav Vlach
Jaroslav Walter

Jean-Claude Killy, of France, because of the consistent form with which he won all three gold medals for the men's alpine skiing. But he could have been denied this triple triumph if a protest after the slalom had been upheld. Karl Schranz, the evergreen Austrian whose impressive career had stretched to its eleventh season, asked for an enquiry after being disqualified for allegedly missing a gate during a second slalom descent which gave him a faster overall time than Killy. Doubts were raised and feelings ran high, but the jury decided in the Frenchman's favour.

The Schranz appeal was not the only skiing controversy. Another threatened the sport's very future in the Olympics. An unenforced demand by the I.O.C. president, Avery Brundage, that trade-names on skis be removed, escalated a sensitive situation concerning still unresolved problems of professional involvement.

But none of this marred the real Killy glory. Visibility was sometimes impaired on the challenging Chamrousse courses, though the runs were otherwise good, technically difficult and a fair test to the world's best. In an awesome-looking downhill, Killy exceeded 60 m.p.h. (96 k.p.h.) with a confident style epitomising the French hip-swinging technique with an accentuated forward lean. His giant slalom victory was the easiest, with more than two seconds in hand over the Swiss runner-up, Willi Favre. But even with Killy's greatness and the second downhill place of his compatriot, Guy Périllat, France lacked some of the dominance which had been so palpable in the world championships two years previously at Portillo, Chile. This time the Swiss, led by Favre, Jean Daetwyler and Dumeng Giovanoli, and the Austrians, notably Heinrich Messner as well as Schranz, posed more constant danger to the tricolour.

Nancy Greene, of Canada, was the most successful woman alpine racer despite a suspect ankle which had marred her prior engagements. Winner of the first World Alpine Ski Cup the previous season, the courageous Ottawa student regained peak form to take giant slalom gold and slalom silver.

In the twilight of a momentous career, Marielle Goitschel, perhaps the greatest woman skier the world has known, was seen at her best only when winning the slalom. Starting each run with incredible speed but exercising shrewd caution as she neared the finish, the French girl's turning technique was a model of alert anticipation and extreme but safe-looking body-sway. If Miss Goitschel's success suggested the value of a physically large and powerful frame, such theories were confounded by her contrastingly light and diminutive compatriot, Annie Famose, who came second in the giant slalom and third in the slalom.

Isabelle Mir, runner-up in the downhill, was yet another French medallist but the Austrians shone more in the downhill, with Olga Pall and veteran Christl Haas first and third respectively. Spearheading a resurgence of British strength, Gina Hathorn, fourth in the slalom, frustratingly missed a bronze medal by a mere three-hundredths of a second.

Just as Killy was the man of this meeting, the outstanding woman without doubt was the Swedish cross-country skier, Toini Gustafsson. She left all opposition well in her wake to win the 5 kilometres with over three seconds in hand but took the 10 kilometres with more than a minute to spare. To her two gold medals Miss Gustafsson added a silver as the anchor-girl of the Swedish relay trio, which came second to Norway in the 3 × 5 kilometres.

Scandinavians were unexpectedly outpaced in the men's 30 kilometres by an Italian, Franco Nones, but the other cross-country races went to Norwegians. Ole Ellefsaeter was only 16.7 seconds faster than the Russian, Viatches Vedenin, after a killing pace in the 50 kilometres. Harold Grönningen was less than two seconds better than Finland's experienced Eero Maentyranta in the 15 kilo-metres. Ellefsaeter and Grönningen were also in the winning Norwe-gian 4 × 10 kilometres relay team.

The individual biathlon too was won by a Norwegian, Magnar Solberg, but his team was second best to the Russians in the biathlon relay. These skiing-and-shooting events attracted increased interest.

Franz Keller underlined a rising West German talent in nordic skiing when he took the 15 kilometres and jumping combination prize. Scandinavian pride was hurt further in the special jumping. On the 70 metres hill at Autrans, Jiri Raska leapt to a surprise victory for Czechoslovakia, followed by two Austrians, Reinhold Bachler and Baldur Preiml, while Björn Wirkola, the great Norwegian world champion of 1966 and oft-times record-holder, trailed an unaccus-tomed fourth.

More than 58,000 assembled to watch the spectacular jumping climax from the 90 metres tower at St Nizier, where once more Norwegians hid their heads in shame. With the two best jumps of the event, Vladimir Beloussov put Russia ahead of runner-up Raska, who thus proved his earlier 70 metres success to be no flash in the pan. So the nordic events concluded with a wider medals share-out than ever before, with Austria, Czechoslovakia and Italy gaining their first Olympic medals in this branch of skiing.

Both the bobsleigh contests at Alpe d'Huez provided a fitting end to the career of the veteran Italian driver, Eugenio Monti, the sport's outstanding exponent who had previously clinched nine world titles but never an Olympic victory. This time he made no mistake and, in memorable farewell performances at the age of 40, claimed gold medals for both four-man and two-man events.

The latter was a cliff-hanger. The West German boblet piloted by Horst Floth equalled Monti's aggregate time for the four runs and he and Monti thought each would get gold medals for a tie, until attention was drawn to a rule stipulating that the fastest single run would decide such an issue. It was disappointing for Floth but popular sentiment rejoiced over a triumphant finale for Monti. Although the floodlit course had three artificially frozen bends, the sun melted so much of the rest that very early morning starts became inevitable and the four-man result was decided over two runs instead of the normal four.

The luge tobogganing at Villard de Lans was similarly inconvenienced. The women's winner, Erica Lechner of Italy, prevented a medals monopoly by the Austrians and East and West Germans, who overshadowed Poland, the other nation normally strong in this sport. Manfred Schmid, of Austria, narrowly pipped the East German, Thomas Köhler, to win the men's singles but Köhler, partnered by Klaus Bonsack, reversed the order in the two-seaters. The true Olympic spirit was momentarily clouded when three East German women riders were disqualified for heating their metal runners, which is strictly taboo.

A general trend of form upsets extended to one of the figure skating events when Emmerich Danzer, then world men's champion, lapsed in the figures and his fellow Austrian, Wolfgang Schwarz, long accustomed to being Danzer's 'shadow', took the title with dominant free-skating highlighted by well timed triple salchow, double axel and double flip jumps. American Tim Wood was an ominous runner-up above the Frenchman, Patrick Pera, with Danzer humbled in fourth spot.

A feature of the women's freestyle was the contrasting technique of the classical, frail-looking Peggy Fleming, the United States winner, and the robust East German, Gabriele Seyfert, who came second. The outcome was never in doubt because of the American's substantial lead in the figures. Miss Fleming's slender frame belied a remarkable stamina which sustained a widely varied repertoire of smoothly landed double jumps and gracefully fast spins.

The retention of the pairs title by the Soviet husband-and-wife partnership, Oleg Protopopov and Ludmila Belousova, was a commendable achievement at the ages of 35 and 32 respectively. But a long and successful career was obviously nearing its end and many a moist eye breathlessly admired their skilfully timed split lutz lift and characteristic one-handed death spiral.

The speed skating contributed a liberal quantity of thrills, heightened by a cup-tie atmosphere with Dutch and Norwegian supporters armed with rosettes, banners, motor horns and bells. Experts were confounded after predicting that the Grenoble outdoor speed skating oval would not provide such a fast surface as rinks at higher altitudes. A new world time by the Norwegian, Anton Maier, was set in the men's 5,000 metres and, during the eight events, no fewer than 52 improvements were made on existing Olympic records. An important contributory factor may have been the ideally moist ice which had been chemically softened and demineralised to match that formed naturally at mountain rinks.

The Swede, Johnny Höglin, beat Maier by 1.2 seconds to win the 10,000 metres. Kees Verkerk defeated his fellow Dutchman, Ard Schenk, in the 1,500 metres and Erhard Keller, of West Germany, took the 500 metres sprint.

The Netherlands' high reputation in women's ice racing was upheld by Johanna Schut and Carolina Geijssen, who won the 3,000 and 1,000 metres respectively, but their much fancied compatriot, Stien Kaiser, only managed two bronze medals after apparently reaching peak form too early.

Ludmila Titova, who won the 500 metres and came second in the 1,000, was the only successful Russian competitor in a sport for which Soviet racers had been previously renowned. Three silver medals in one event by competitors from the same nation was an unprecedented occurrence, involving a United States trio, Jenny Fish, Dianne Holum and Mary Meyers, in the 500 metres. Although not among the medallists, Patricia Tipper became the first women to represent Britain in Olympic speed skating.

The indoor Olympic Ice Stadium, a spacious and pillarless masterpiece of modern architecture, was designed to seat 11,500 but this figure was appreciably exceeded at all three freestyle skating events and for all the key ice hockey games.

The Russian stickhandlers began the major eight-team ice hockey contest in unbeatable fashion, outclassing Finland 8–0 and East Germany 9–0, but when Sweden only lost 2–3 to them the outcome suddenly appeared less of a foregone conclusion.

In the outstanding match of the series, the Czechs beat U.S.S.R. 5–4 in a tense end-to-end affair which kept the excited spectators on the edge of their seats. Had Czechoslovakia not been held by Sweden to a 2–2 draw in the penultimate match, the Czechs would have won this tournament through being level on points with U.S.S.R., in which case the result of the match between the two, and not goal average, would have decided the issue. So Russia did not win so comfortably as many had at first anticipated. The title was taken with 12 points from seven games, followed by Czechoslovakia with 11 and Canada 10. Anatolii Firsov (U.S.S.R.) topped the final scoring table with 12 goals.

A jury of 50 journalists elected an all-star team from the players on view: Goal: Broderick (Canada). Defence: Suchy (Czechoslovakia) and Scedberg (Sweden). Forwards: Sevcik (Czechoslovakia), Huck (Canada) and Firsov (U.S.S.R.).

As at the Innsbruck Olympics four years previously, the diverse nature of terrain required caused considerable frustration to be suffered by journeys of 20 miles or more between the sites in and around Grenoble. The experience suggested that future applicants to be host would gain the most votes if able to create a more compact, self-contained complex of venues, as at Squaw Valley in 1960.

But, also like Innsbruck, Grenoble had the foresight to build competitors' quarters and press accommodation suitable for later conversion to flats and municipal buildings. These, with the ice stadium, the ski jump and other facilities, have become permanent Olympic legacies to benefit the general public.

SAPPORO, Japan   February 3–13, 1972

Since Squaw Valley in 1960, where everything was so compact and accessible, the Winter Olympics have been frustratingly spread out. Transport tedium was the main criticism at Innsbruck and Grenoble. There was a consequent demand for greater future convenience by concentrating the various sports sites in and around one area.

To this end, Sapporo – venue for the Winter Olympics in February,

THE X WINTER OLYMPIC GAMES 1968

NORDIC SKIING: MEN

	Gold	Silver	Bronze
15 kilometres	Harald Grönningen (Norway)	Eero Maentyranta (Finland)	Gunnar Larsson (Sweden)
30 kilometres	Franco Nones (Italy)	Odd Martinsen (Norway)	Eero Maentyranta (Finland)
50 kilometres	Ole Ellefsaeter (Norway)	Viatches Vedenin (U.S.S.R.)	Josef Haas (Switzerland)
Relay, 4 × 10 kilometres	Norway Odd Martinsen Paal Tyldum Harald Grönningen Ole Ellefsaeter	Sweden Jan Halvarsson Bjarne Andersson Gunnar Larsson Assar Reonnlund	Finland Kalevi Oikarainen Hannu Taipale Kalevi Laurila Eero Maentyranta
70 metres Jumping	Jiri Raska (Czechoslovakia)	Reinhold Bachler (Austria)	Baldur Preiml (Austria)
90 metres Jumping	Vladimir Beloussov (U.S.S.R.)	Jiri Raska (Czechoslovakia)	Lars Grini (Norway)
Combined	Franz Keller (West Germany)	Alois Kaelin (Switzerland)	Andreas Kunz (East Germany)
Biathlon	Magnar Solberg (Norway)	Alexandre Tikhonov (U.S.S.R.)	Vladimir Goundartsev (U.S.S.R.)
Biathlon Relay	U.S.S.R. Alexandre Tikhonov Nikolai Pousanov Victor Mamatov Vladimir Goundartsev	Norway Ola Waerhavg Olav Jordet Magnar Solberg Jon Istad	Sweden Goeran Arwidson Tore Eriksson Olle Petrusson Holmfrid Olsson

NORDIC SKIING: WOMEN

	Gold	Silver	Bronze
5 kilometres	Toini Gustafsson (Sweden)	Galina Koulakova (U.S.S.R.)	Alevtina Koltchina (U.S.S.R.)
10 kilometres	Toini Gustafsson (Sweden)	Berit Moerdre (Norway)	Inger Aufles (Norway)

	Gold	Silver	Bronze
NORDIC SKIING: WOMEN			
Relay, 3 × 5 kilometres	Norway Inger Aufles Babben Enger-Damon Berit Moerdre	Sweden Britt Strandberg Toini Gustafsson Barbro Martinsson	U.S.S.R. Alevtina Koltchina Rita Achkina Galina Koulakova
ALPINE SKIING: MEN			
Downhill	Jean-Claude Killy (France)	Guy Périllat (France)	Daniel Daetwyler (Switzerland)
Slalom	Jean-Claude Killy (France)	Herbert Huber (Austria)	Alfred Matt (Austria)
Giant Slalom	Jean-Claude Killy (France)	Willy Favre (Switzerland)	Heinrich Messner (Austria)
ALPINE SKIING: WOMEN			
Downhill	Olga Pall (Austria)	Isabelle Mir (France)	Christl Haas (Austria)
Slalom	Marielle Goitschel (France)	Nancy Greene (Canada)	Annie Famose (France)
Giant Slalom	Nancy Greene (Canada)	Annie Famose (France)	Fernande Bochatay (Switzerland)
FIGURE SKATING			
Men	Wolfgang Schwarz (Austria)	Tim Wood (U.S.A.)	Patrick Pera (France)
Women	Peggy Fleming (U.S.A.)	Gabriele Seyfert (East Germany)	Hana Maskova (Czechoslovakia)
Pairs	Oleg Protopopov Ludmila Belousova (U.S.S.R.)	Alexandre Gorelik Tatiana Zhuk (U.S.S.R.)	Wolfgang Danne Margot Glockshuber (West Germany)
SPEED SKATING: MEN			
500 metres	Erhard Keller (West Germany)	Magne Thomassen (Norway) Richard McDermott (U.S.A.)	

	Gold	Silver	Bronze
SPEED SKATING: MEN			
1,500 metres	Kees Verkerk (Netherlands)	Ivar Eriksen (Norway) Ard Schenk (Netherlands)	Petrus Nottet (Netherlands)
5,000 metres	Anton Maier (Norway)	Kees Verkerk (Netherlands)	Oerjan Sandler (Sweden)
10,000 metres	Johnny Höglin (Sweden)	Anton Maier (Norway)	
SPEED SKATING: WOMEN			
500 metres	Ludmila Titova (U.S.S.R.)	Mary Meyers (U.S.A.) Dianne Holum (U.S.A.) Jennifer Fish (U.S.A.)	Dianne Holum (U.S.A.)
1,000 metres	Carolina Geijssen (Netherlands)	Ludmila Titova (U.S.S.R.)	Stien Kaiser (Netherlands)
1,500 metres	Kaija Mustonen (Finland)	Carolina Geijssen (Netherlands)	Stien Kaiser (Netherlands)
3,000 metres	Johanna Schut (Netherlands)	Kaija Mustonen (Finland)	
BOBSLEDDING			
2-man bobs	Italy Eugenio Monti Luciano De Paolis	West Germany Horst Floth Pepi Bader	Rumania Ion Panturu Nicolae Neagoe
4-man bobs	Italy Eugenio Monti Luciano De Paolis Roberto Zandonella Mario Armano	Austria Erwin Thaler Reinhold Durnthaler Herbert Gruber Josef Eder	Switzerland Jean Wicki Hans Candrian Willy Hofmann Walter Graf

221

	Gold	Silver	Bronze
LUGE TOBOGGANING: MEN			
Single	Manfred Schmid (Austria)	Thomas Köhler (East Germany)	Klaus Bonsack (East Germany)
2-seater	East Germany Klaus Bonsack Thomas Köhler	Austria Manfred Schmid Ewald Walch	West Germany Wolfgang Winkler Fritz Nachmann
LUGE TOBOGGANING: WOMEN			
Single	Erica Lechner (Italy)	Christa Schmuck (West Germany)	Angelika Dünhaupt (West Germany)
ICE HOCKEY	U.S.S.R.	Czechoslovakia	Canada
	Vienamine Aleksandrov	Josef Cerny	Roger Bourbonnais
	Victor Blinov	Vlado Dzurila	Ken Broderick
	Vitalii Davidov	Josef Golonka	Raymand Cadieux
	Anatolii Firsov	Jan Havel	Paul Conlin
	Anatolii Ionov	Pejr Hejma	Gary Dineen
	Victor Konovalenko	Jiri Holik	Brian Glennie
	Victor Kuzkin	Josef Horesovsky	Ted Hargreaves
	Boris Maiorov	Jan Hrbaty	Francis Huck
	Eugenii Michakov	Jan Klapac	Marshall Johnston
	Jurii Moiseyev	Jiri Kochta	Barry McKenzie
	Victor Polupanov	Jaroslav Jirik	Bill McMillan
	Alexandre Ragulin	Oldrich Machac	Stephen Monteith
	Igor Romishevski	Karel Masopust	Morris Mott
	Viatches Starchinov	Vladimir Nadrchal	Terry O'Malley
	Vladimir Vikulov	Vaclav Nedomansky	Danny O'Shea
	Oleg Zaitzev	Frantisek Pospisil	G. Pinder
	Eugenii Zimin	Frantisek Sevcik	Herbert Pinder
	Victor Zinger	Jan Suchy	Wayne Stephenson

1972 – was a happy choice, the resort being blessed with better geographical conditions. Built on the remains of a delta, Sapporo's surrounding landscape is agreeably attractive, not far from the sea and ringed by mountains which, if not high by Alpine standards, afford much scenic charm and a healthfully beneficial climate.

The second largest city in Japan, Sapporo has a population of nearly a million and is the capital of Hokkaido, the northernmost island of the Japanese archipelago. Its February climate and temperature is comparable to that of Davos, Switzerland. There are ample suitable slopes for the skiing and the snow comes over the Japan Sea from Siberia in reliable amounts of the right, light powdery kind.

Exhaustive research preceded the final selection of each site. Wind velocity was painstakingly measured and weather data for many years past was minutely examined. Close consultation with the relevant international sports federations ensured that no significant factor was overlooked. With a nationally characteristic will to learn in detail, the federations were bombarded particularly with questions concerning those sports of which the Japanese had the least experience.

In all, some 13 sites for the various sports were prepared, at an estimated cost of U.S. $22.5 million. As at most Olympic venues, many of the buildings were destined afterwards to become permanent legacies of longterm use for the local population. This adds to the immeasurable value of worldwide publicity which continues to prompt keen international competition for selection as Olympic host.

Sapporo's Olympic Village was designed to house 2,000 competitors and officials. All the sports sites were completed a whole year prior to the 1972 Games. The Makomanai area, only three miles (4.8 kilometres) south of the city centre and incorporating the competitors' village, was chosen to stage the figure skating, speed skating, final ice hockey matches and all the cross-country skiing and biathlon events.

The slopes of Mount Teine, seven miles (11.2 kilometres) west of the city centre, contained the alpine slalom and giant slalom ski courses and both the bobsleigh and luge toboggan runs. The ski jumping sites were erected even closer at Okurayama, a mountain overlooking the city from the west. Only the downhill ski terrain on Mount Eniwa required much of a journey, some 15 miles (24 kilometres) to the south. The spectacular 90 metres jump site at Okura-

223

yama, a beautiful setting, incorporates seating accommodation for 50,000, with the smaller 70 metres jump hill half a mile away.

For the nordic ski races, including the biathlon skiing and shooting, arrangements were made for the start and finish only a few hundred yards from the Olympic Village at the Makomanai Park, formerly a golf course, the chosen nerve-centre hub also holding both the Olympic Ice Stadium and the speed skating oval.

The latter could seat 50,000 for the opening ceremony. A further 12,000 seats were installed in the covered figure skating and hockey stadium, with the main press and television centres conveniently adjacent. Two other indoor ice rinks in the city suburbs were allocated for the preliminary hockey matches and figure skating practice. The enthusiastic Japanese asked the I.O.C. to allow 16 hockey teams to compete, at least four more than the I.I.H.F. envisaged. The organisers also paid the considerable transportation costs of visiting specialists at the International Sports Week during the preceding winter's dress rehearsal to test the courses.

Those who attended the 1964 summer Olympics in Tokyo needed no reassurance of the Japanese efficiency and attention to detail of organisation – factors which undoubtedly influenced the I.O.C. decision to entrust Sapporo with the XIth Winter Olympic Games.